Under
the Eye
of
Power

Under the Eye

of

Power

HOW FEAR OF SECRET SOCIETIES
SHAPES AMERICAN DEMOCRACY

Colin Dickey

VIKING

VIKING
An imprint of Penguin Random House LLC
penguinrandomhouse.com

LIBRARY OF CONGRESS CATALOGING IN PUBLICATION DATA
Names: Dickey, Colin, author.
Title: Under the eye of power / Colin Dickey.
Description: New York, NY : Viking, [2023] | Includes bibliographical references.
Identifiers: LCCN 2022035654 (print) | LCCN 2022035655 (ebook) |
ISBN 9780593299456 (hardcover) | ISBN 9780593299463 (ebook)
Subjects: LCSH: Secret societies—United States—History. |
Conspiracy theories—United States—History. | United States—History.
Classification: LCC HS204 .D53 2023 (print) | LCC HS204 (ebook) |
DDC 366.0973—dc23/eng/20230321
LC record available at https://lccn.loc.gov/2022035654
LC ebook record available at https://lccn.loc.gov/2022035655

Printed in the United States of America
1st Printing

DESIGNED BY LUCIA BERNARD

for Sova

If we are on the outside, we assume a conspiracy is the perfect working of a scheme. Silent nameless men with unadorned hearts. A conspiracy is everything that ordinary life is not. It's the inside game, cold, sure, undistracted, forever closed off to us. We are the flawed ones, the innocents, trying to make some rough sense of the daily jostle. Conspirators have a logic and a daring beyond our reach. All conspiracies are the same taut story of men who find coherence in some criminal act.

—DON DELILLO, *Libra*

The conspiracy theory of society . . . comes from abandoning God and then asking: Who is in his place?

—KARL POPPER, *Conjectures and Refutations*

CONTENTS

Under
the Eye
of
Power

The Paranoid Republic

T he United States was born in paranoia.

It has been with this country from the very beginning, shadowing it ever since. From the earliest European settlers to reach this land to the present day, we have mused about secret plots, hidden conspirators, invisible groups that threaten to control us. Puritan theologian Cotton Mather, in his defense of his behavior at the Salem witch trials, warned of a "PLOT of the Devil, against New-England, in every branch of it." Never, Mather proclaimed, "were more Satanical Devices used for the Unsetling of any People under the Sun" than the Devil's work against his chosen flock. In 1775, president of Yale Ezra Stiles reported a story that the American Revolution was part of an elaborate plan by a French pretender to the English throne to draw British troops away from their homeland, so as to "leave Engld so defenceless that the Pretender with 20 Thousd Troops might land & march all over Engld &c &c &c." Stiles was skeptical of the theory, but he was not the only one who heard rumors of a conspiracy behind America's independence: Roger Lamb, a sergeant in the British Army, also reported that the American Revolution was organized by the French. "The first step taken by France to secure this object was to employ her secret emissaries in spreading dissatisfaction among the British colonists," Lamb wrote in his memoirs after the war's end, "and the effects produced by her machinations were precisely such as she had intended and expected. The disposition of the inhabitants of North America began gradually to alter from that warmth of attachment to the mother country which had so particularly characterized them." George Washington, in his Farewell Address at the end of his presidency, described unity of government as the central pillar of democracy and "that very liberty which you so highly prize," then immediately warned that unnamed foreign and subversive forces would employ "many artifices" to weaken it, "often covertly and insidiously."

One of the most enduring narratives that defines the United States is simply this: secret groups are conspiring to pervert the will of the people and the rule of law. The specifics change, but the core narrative remains stubbornly the same. This book is a history of that narrative: where it comes from, how it's evolved through successive generations, and why it remains so powerfully evocative.

For many in America, the failed 1964 presidential campaign of Barry Goldwater was their first experience with conspiracy theories bleeding over from the fringes of culture into the mainstream. Goldwater's embrace of far-right anti-Communist paranoia, and his refusal to distance himself from his most paranoid supporters ("Instead of just laughing these people off," he told Steve Allen in May 1964, "I recognize them as people who are concerned, people who recognize that some things in this government are not going the way they like.") shocked journalists and the intelligentsia. That someone with a real shot at the highest office in the land could make common cause with conspiracy theorists was a sobering wake-up call, and it led, most famously, to historian Richard Hofstadter casting a long view over the history of American democracy, trying to understand where its fringe conspiracists come from. Taking in its anti-Catholics, its anti-Illuminati, its anti-Masons, and grouping them together with the John Birch Society and other 1960s nativist campaigns, Hofstadter's late 1964 essay "The Paranoid Style in American Politics" argued that a certain kind of nativist paranoia is a fundamental component of American democracy.

Hofstadter saw this element of America as a perpetual fringe movement. Every so often, as with Goldwater's presidential campaign, the paranoid nativists got perilously close to power, but that didn't change the fact that they existed primarily on the margins, and were best constrained by a healthy, sensible middle ground. Hofstadter fretted that in a "populistic culture like ours, which seems to lack a responsible elite with political and moral autonomy," democracy was open to being co-opted by "the wildest currents of public sentiment for private purposes," where "a highly organized, vocal, active, and well-financed minority could create a political climate in which the rational pursuit of our well-being and safety would become impossible." The solution, he argued, was a rational, civic-minded centrism that could moderate and restrain these dangerous excesses.

The 2016 election seemed to many a confirmation of Hofstadter's warning of what happens without a sensible middle: a fringe candidate espousing obvious lies and conspiracy theories swept into power while the sensible moderators of American politics were asleep. Donald Trump's embrace of an endless string of conspiracy theories—that Barack Obama was not born in America, that the father of his Republican primary opponent Ted Cruz was involved in the assassination of John F. Kennedy, that Bill Clinton had a hand in the death of deputy White House counsel Vince Foster, to name just a few he had espoused before taking office—would have seemed to utterly disqualify him as a serious candidate for the highest office in the land. In the wake of his election, many concluded that his win was a fluke, the result of a series of democratic safeguards breaking down that allowed for the American fringe to erupt into the mainstream, echoing Hofstadter's thesis of American democracy. It was a dispiriting event for many who believed in rational arguments and the truth; as political scientist Paul Musgrave wrote in the *Washington*

Post in the days before Trump's inauguration, "Conspiracy thinking has been normalized in American politics in a way that almost nobody could have expected a year ago." Months into his tenure, those who'd long assumed that Trump's paranoia was anathema to the office of the presidency were horrified to discover that, in the words of columnist Maureen Dowd, the "office has not changed Trump. Trump has changed the office."

But Donald Trump was not the first American president to embrace conspiracy theories. Throughout 1774 and 1775, George Washington believed that England was controlled not by George III but by a secret cabal of ministers fomenting dissent in the colonies. Abraham Lincoln argued that political developments in the 1860s were the work of a "slaveocracy": a combine of wealthy enslavers who were perverting the will of the American people from behind closed doors. In 1971, Richard Nixon told his aide Bob Haldeman that "Jews are all over the government," further arguing that they were, by nature, "disloyal." Even Trump's 2016 rival, Hillary Clinton, seemed to give serious consideration to the theory that the American government is covering up evidence of extraterrestrials.

It's not just the presidents. A 2019 survey revealed that 21 percent of Americans believe that the Illuminati secretly control the world and 23 percent believe that the attacks on September 11 were an inside job. In 2021, there were 15 percent of Americans willing to agree with the statement that the US government, its media, and the financial markets "are controlled by a group of Satan-worshipping pedophiles who run a global child sex trafficking operation." That translates to tens of millions of Americans who believe that secret actors are pulling the strings behind world events. If Hofstadter is right that conspiratorial thinking mainly exists along the edges of democracy, why do so many people—including some of the most powerful people in the country—continue to subscribe to it? What if paranoia, particularly a paranoia of secret, subversive societies, is not just peripheral to the functioning of democracy, but at its very heart?

Viewing conspiracy theories as perpetually fringe ideas depends on a dramatic distortion of American history. In the eighteenth and nineteenth centuries, conspiracy theories were not only tolerated, they were understood to be the factual explanation of the way the world worked. The events of history were the product of human actions, and if such actors were not immediately visible, that didn't mean that they weren't out there somewhere. It may be difficult, from a twenty-first century vantage, to immediately recognize them as such, because they often lacked the paranoid affect of modern conspiracists. These theories were not ranted about by men on the street corner; instead, they were calmly discussed by ministers and presidents.

Another reason the conspiracy theories of early America seem unfamiliar to us now has to do with their target: originally, nearly all such theories hypothesized an attack on the government from external forces, conspirators either foreign or otherwise diabolical. Conspiracists believed that the country's democratic government, its shining innovation and proof of America's supremacy, was under constant attack. The sole exception to this belief was the Slave Power conspiracy theory advocated by abolitionists and Republicans in the 1850s, which argued that the government had already been infiltrated by a cabal of enslavers and their minions, who'd perverted the national will. But this was an outlier; for the most part, the government was seen as the target of conspirators, not its home.

Only in the twentieth century did this gradually change. By 1960, when Eisenhower warned of a "military-industrial complex" in his farewell speech, he echoed a prevailing belief (one that has only become stronger since) that the American government has been overrun by conspirators who control it through shadowy means and prevent the flourishing of representative democracy. Since then, the distrust has become more firmly entrenched: a survey of American fears in 2021 found that more Americans (79.6 percent) reported being afraid of corrupt elements in their own government than they did of loved ones dying (58.5

percent). We have gone from a nation paranoid that conspirators are out to attack our government to one that believes that the government itself is the conspiracy.

Of course, there are conspiracy theories and then there are actual conspiracies. On the surface, it may sound to someone unfamiliar with American history that there is little difference between alleging the Ku Klux Klan was behind JFK's assassination and arguing that the most powerful man in the United States was behind a bumbling, idiotic break-in at the Watergate Hotel. The difference is that over time, one of these theories was repeatedly and thoroughly confirmed while the other was not. Accordingly, while nearly all conspiracy theories have a degree of plausibility, and many contain at least some small kernel of truth, history suggests that genuine conspiracies have a tendency to unravel almost as soon as someone goes looking into them. Whistleblowers, deathbed confessions, sworn depositions, petty vengeance—any number of basic human motivations will undermine an active conspiracy. And the larger a conspiracy supposedly is, the more actors it will require to be successful, which in turn demands a larger and larger sphere of absolute secrecy for the conspirators to remain undetected. Bob Woodward and Carl Bernstein learned a great deal about Watergate from secretaries and other low-level office workers—people integral to the implementation of Nixon's schemes but who lacked the ideological dedication of his higher-ups.

Thus, while many conspiracy theories may seem plausible in the immediate wake of whatever event they respond to, the more time that elapses between the positing of a theory and the appearance of any kind of objective evidence that supports it, the less likely it is that it is valid. The conspiracy theory posits at its core an unshakable tenet: the Jews are behind everything, the government has evidence of UFOs, etc. That tenet must be absolutely impervious to any counter-indicative evidence; everything and anything must be made to "prove" the central tenet. But this is a difficult rhetorical and logical position to maintain, and thus it requires the constant shifting and reinterpretation of the past, present, and future. To maintain a conspiracy theory in the absence of evidence, particularly as more time elapses, requires an increasingly extreme contortion of reality and the past. And as such, the most vital step in thinking past conspiracy theories is to start by engaging with them historically.

There are a myriad of conspiracy theories out there, but beliefs in secret groups of malevolent actors have not only been among the most durable in American history, they have also had the most concrete effect on the shaping of this country. Various secret societies have fascinated Americans through the years, but the fear has remained much the same, with only the names and details changing. We have distrusted actual secret societies—most notably, Freemasonry, whose roots predate the United States but which has become intertwined with the country's founding and its subsequent story. (Furthermore, various other secret and not-so-secret groups, from the Ku Klux Klan of the 1920s to the John Birch Society, have implicitly or explicitly adopted Masonic structures and ritual.)

Alongside these actual organizations is a long tradition of mythic secret societies—groups that exist only in the fevered imagination of Americans. The Illuminati, for example, which appears early on in the American story and gradually becomes a bedrock feature of myriad American conspiracy theories. And then there are groups that exist in a sort of strange gray area. To what extent, for example, was there a secret plot by enslaved Americans to set all of New York City on fire in 1741? How organized and networked—and violent—were the Molly Maguires? In some cases, there are simply no easy answers. What becomes clear in a history of secret societies is how the very idea of such groups is often enough to trigger a strange and legally nebulous zone, where we end up unable to rescue enough basic factual history to understand what really happened.

At nearly every crucial juncture of American history—from the founding of the nascent democracy to the question of slavery to the country's post–World War II assumption of itself as a world power—conspiracy theories about secret groups were deployed out of anxiety about those transitions and developments. At key moments when we have undergone major cultural or political shifts, fears of secret groups with hidden agendas are stoked to stymie and blunt the effects of those shifts. Conspiracy theories have also been a regular tool in maintaining and regulating how America will accept and integrate new populations, from religious to ethnic groups. Every time a traditionally marginalized segment of America has attempted to fight for equity, conspiracy theories have been used to suppress or curtail that fight.

While many of these conspiracy theories originate on the right of the political spectrum—and are used to sabotage progressive change in favor of conservative, reactionary, and often outright racist, sexist, and homophobic ideals—conspiracy theories of course exist on the left as well. In the nineteenth century, the Slave Power conspiracy theory formed a bridge between abolitionists and other Northerners who were otherwise more ambivalent about slavery, ultimately helping to drive Lincoln's election and the Civil War. While conservative conspiracy theories often invent mythical power structures or demonize marginalized groups, conspiracy theories on the left tend to exaggerate existing power structures rather than inventing new ones. Government agencies abusing civil liberties, corporations wielding outsized power, well-connected politicians with occult connections—such narratives work to make sense of and simplify existing power imbalances, and they focus less on wholly invented groups.

Conspiracy theories regarding secret societies are effective because they foster and encourage moral panics, which create a climate whereby reactionary forces can control and regulate public discourse. Any hope of forming a more perfect union involves first reckoning how central such conspiracy theories are—they are not merely the province of the distant fringe, best ridiculed or ignored.

After all, we ignore such threats at our peril. And almost always, these moral panics are forgotten almost as soon as they subside. The Salem witch trials remain the most famous American moral panic about a secret group of infiltrators and saboteurs, and one of the few that still gets talked about, always treated as a singular and unique event. The other major American social panic that's familiar to most of us is the Red Scare of the early 1950s, exemplified by Joseph McCarthy's allegations of secret Communists in the government and military. Often referred to as a "witch hunt," and allegorized by Arthur Miller in his 1953 play about Salem, *The Crucible*, it's held up as the modern-day equivalent of Salem.

These two moral panics became metaphorically linked to each other in popular consciousness, and now stand as cautionary tales of aberrant distrust and paranoia. The way both stories get taught is similar: during these two brief, horrible periods, Americans went too far, things got out of hand, and innocent people suffered. We must never again let such things happen.

But these things happen all the time. In terms of sheer lives lost, the New York slave conspiracy panic of 1741 resulted in more (almost certainly) innocent people executed—even though it's not generally known by the public or taught in schools today. (That the lives lost were overwhelmingly Black may have something to do with it.) The show trials of the Molly Maguires and the Haymarket martyrs involved the same hysteria and egregious miscarriages of justice, and yet outside of labor history they are rarely mentioned. The Satanic ritual abuse panic of the 1980s ruined dozens of lives and was almost immediately brushed under the rug afterward (one prosecutor who made a name for herself pursuing Satanists, Janet Reno, went on to be Bill Clinton's attorney general). And this represents only moral panics where the convictions and executions were attributable to official, legal means—more people were killed at an El Paso Walmart in August 3, 2019, than at Salem, victims of a murderer who subscribed to the Great Replacement conspiracy theory alleging

that whites are being systematically bred out of America. The belief that
Salem or the McCarthy hearings were singular outliers is a fundamental
distortion of our understanding of the American justice system and its
relationship to popular imagination.

Thus this attempt to maintain Salem as a singular and unrepeatable
incident in America's history—a specific event of disgrace from which
we have learned and which we resolve never to repeat—is a deeply mis-
guided understanding of how American history and American democracy works. To assume that conspiracy theories have mostly lingered in
the margins of American political thought, policed by a sensible middle,
only occasionally erupting into the mainstream, is to misunderstand
the story entirely. These panics have been with us all along. Their prevalence and success depends on our willingness to treat each moral panic
as an isolated, exceptional incident, an embarrassing bit of xenophobic
exuberance that flares up briefly and then fades away, best forgotten
entirely.

Moral panics arise regularly, almost like clockwork, as a means to
place certain elements of behavior and thought outside the bounds of
acceptable American discourse. Hysterias about Satanists or Freemasons
or the Jews are not spontaneous, irrational bursts of fear from an irrational and ignorant populist—they are almost always a carefully controlled and nurtured rhetorical tool to shift and shape what will and
won't be considered "American." What happened in Salem in 1692 is
not a singular outlier; it was as American as apple pie.

When faced with moral panics like the Salem witch trials, we often
seem receptive to explanations that cast the accusers as outliers—that
what drove them was hysteria borne of religious mania, or even (as some
have suggested) ergot poisoning. The actual explanations behind Salem—
rising complications surrounding money and real estate, and internal
tensions over how to deal with the neighboring Indigenous populations
pushing back against these colonizers—are so prosaic, so commonplace,
that they seem unable to account for such wild spectacles. But once we

recognize that moral panics and conspiracy theories around secret societies such as those that gripped the people of Salem are commonplace, woven into the fabric of American life and expressed repeatedly nearly every generation, everything begins to fall into place. Moral panics are common because their causes—unresolved tensions surrounding America's long history of racism, slavery, xenophobia directed toward immigrants, and Native genocide; class and money in American capitalism; or democracy itself—are also common. The Salem witch trials of 1692 and the Red Scare of the 1950s were not outliers in an otherwise mostly healthy democratic system; they are two more or less unremarkable panics from a long list of similar tragedies that make up American history, the rest of which are neglected, forgotten about, or actively erased from view so as to make these two events seem the exceptions rather than the rule.

To admit instead that they are a constant facet of American culture, that they never go away, even if they sometimes shift guise and focus, is to rethink how we see America's constant, if sometimes difficult, forward progress. To believe in America is to believe, for many of us, in a nation that is always in a state of improving, that has its shortcomings and injustices but seeks to build on the mistakes of the past and make a better world for future generations. We believe, in defiance of all available evidence, that the arc of history bends not only toward justice, but toward wisdom and clarity. Sometimes paranoia grips our nation, such thinking goes, but we not only think that such things are momentary blips but also that once we've learned better, such beliefs will not appear again.

American history suggests the exact opposite. It suggests that on a fundamental level, conspiracy theories involving secret groups and subversive forces have become inextricable from how we participate in democracy. It is my hope that by better understanding this process, we might better begin to imagine more lasting solutions to the problems spread by such paranoias.

T here is always a fundamental contradiction in writing about secret societies. Take the Freemasons, an organization around which conspiracy theories swell constantly. Not being a Freemason myself, I can't definitively assert what happens in their secret rituals one way or another. Had I joined the Freemasons for research purposes, getting myself initiated into their secret rites and rising through the ranks until I had reached the highest echelons and visited the inner sanctums, I would be no better off—for if I were to write an exposé on what I had witnessed, revealing that there were no deep secrets, that it was largely a social club of middle-aged men, who would believe me? Clearly, one could argue, by that point I was myself just a Freemason trying to throw everyone off the trail.

In other words, the mechanism of secret societies is such that one can never definitively debunk or disprove a conspiracy theory about them, because they are untouchable by the normal laws of open scrutiny. And whether or not such societies exist, it is far more important that there be the *idea* of a group beyond normal scrutiny, whose activities cannot be proven or disproven one way or another.

While this book offers a fair amount of historical background about what we do know for sure about these groups, for the reasons outlined above, I cannot hope to reveal once and for all what happens behind closed doors. Nor is that the particular aim of this book. Rather, I'm more interested in this idea of the secret society, which exists not in closed-off rooms but in the minds of the general public. This idea can be far better tracked and outlined, and its impact, I would argue, is far more consequential than whatever Freemasons or whomever may really be doing behind closed doors.

It is the idea of the secret society—the fiction and suspicions, the paranoia and speculation—that has time and time again driven events in American history, far more so than the groups themselves (many of which never existed anyway). It is a necessary fiction that drives America, and it's time to stop treating it as an aberrant and fringe obsession. If we hope to stop the rising tide of conspiracy theories that increasingly are dominating twenty-first century politics, it would be helpful to first recognize the long, quite mainstream history of such beliefs, then admit that they did not spring out of nowhere in the past decade. Donald Trump, Facebook, Alex Jones, Covid denialists, anti-vaxxers—all these actors have fanned the flames of paranoia and furthered their spread. But the fire has been with us from the start.

No imagery is more immediately associated with secret societies— and more publicly prominent—than the symbols of Freemasonry: the square and the level and the compass—and, most of all, the mysterious eye that radiates down from above. What do they mean and why are they everywhere? Why is this supposedly secret society so plainly visible, its symbols here for all to see?

PART ONE

As Above,
So Below

~

Americans prefer to isolate villains who despoil a preexisting
innocence, rather than admit that there might not have
been any innocence there in the first place.

—Rick Perlstein, *Before the Storm: Barry Goldwater
and the Unmaking of the American Consesus*

ONE

The Arch and the Cenotaph

T he landscape seems to swell up toward it, this massive stone arch. The way it stands on this gentle hill, projecting dominion over the rolling fields that stretch out in every direction. All around is the natural splendor of rural Pennsylvania, and strolling through the bucolic landscape, you can almost forget that the purpose of such a place is to commemorate a savage war waged here several hundred years ago.

The heat is oppressive on the late June day when I arrive at Valley Forge National Historical Park to see the United States National Memorial Arch. It's the summer of 2021, when many are still preferring parks to indoor spaces, and yet the blistering humidity—like a suffocating hand of God pressing down from above—has driven nearly everyone away; only a few scattered people are out here. Designed by Paul Philippe Cret in imitation of Rome's Arch of Titus, the sixty-foot-tall arch is not as large as a similar one in New York City's Washington Square Park, but standing here alone, it feels much more significant, looming over everything.

Beyond the arch and across the road is a marker resembling a large gravestone, embedded with a series of architectural tools and other strange symbols: a trowel, a hammer, a level, two hands in prayer. The granite marker details both the construction and the renovation of the arch. Originally completed in 1917, it was badly in need of repair by the 1990s. The National Park Service was strapped for cash and couldn't afford to save the arch.

The Freemasons stepped in. The fraternal organization raised $1.5 million for the renovation of the arch, and at its rededication, they added this granite marker. One side of the granite tablet states that the renovation project "was funded entirely by the Freemasons of Philadelphia"; the other side notes George Washington's connection to Freemasonry and states that "the Freemasons of Pennsylvania place this monument so that future generations will know that freedom was as important in 1997 as it was in 1777–1778." The arch may be there to remind visitors that this is a place of war and sacrifice, but the granite marker is there, curiously, to remind visitors of the power of the Freemasons.

Walking back to the arch itself, I notice something I'd missed before: the plaque on the interior arch is a dull bronze, already weathered with age, and under the unyielding summer sun the relief is difficult to make out. But it's there: the Eye of Providence.

The same eye that figures on the dollar bill: a symbol of divine providence or a symbol of a secret New World Order. Perhaps it is merely meant to suggest the approving eye of God looking down on us, or perhaps it is an insignia of a hidden group of conspirators, signaling globe their plans for world domination, hiding in plain sight, taunting us.

Freemasons these days often bristle at the suggestion that they're an all-powerful society pulling the strings behind the scenes. And yet, everywhere you look there are signs that the Masons want you to see to remember how entwined they are with power—specifically, presidential power. In stone and bronze, their symbols dot the landscape, all insinuating a deep and abiding connection between Freemasonry and

America's most powerful figures. This is where the conspiracy theories surrounding the Masons start. Why, some wonder, would a supposedly secret society litter the country with prominent and obvious symbols, seemingly hiding in plain sight?

A 2017 thread on the website 4chan (a site infamous for its racist, pornographic, conspiratorial, and anarchic content) devoted to Freemasons ran through the various accusations that float around concerning the fraternity. While one "anon" (all posts on 4chan are, by default, anonymous) attempted to explain that Freemasons are, in actuality, stunningly boring old men devoted mainly to philanthropy and drinking, another added "every freemason I've know in real life was an ultra conservative evangelical mega christian in their day time persona." Others, though, weren't buying it. One anon claimed that any defense of the Masons is "gonna be filled with b.s. Mockery. They will make themselves look like the average Joe." This person then added, presumably referencing the Masonic apron, "Won't even tell u their dumb outfits to cover the private parts is a mockery of adam and eve. When they knew they were naked and wanted to cover up." Another pointed out that if the Masons are involved in nefarious dealings, "they aren't gonna talk about it openly if they do. It's a load of shit It's obvious that the triangle and eye are Lucifer."

There is a lot of talk about the number 33: referencing not just the thirty-third degree of the Scottish Rite (one of the main branches of Masonry practiced in the United States) but the number of years the Twin Towers stood before being destroyed on September 11, 2001 (they actually stood for twenty-nine years, but who's counting), and suggesting that 33 is a reference to the number of the beast, 666. The translation of the number 33 into the number of the beast is so obvious, so self-evident, that there can be no other explanation. As one user exclaims, "They're totally just rubbing our noses in it and expecting us not to notice!"

Few sentiments capture the perspective of the conspiracist like this one: not only are these evil groups acting in secret, they're also being very public about it. Conspiracy theorists will decode symbols and translate public statements by politicians and celebrities using incredibly obtuse and byzantine methods, and then proclaim that not only are such statements evident to all, they're purposefully designed to be, to taunt us.

It's not just on the dark corners of the Internet. In 2016, the FBI arrested a man who had bought several machine guns and silencers, and who, they alleged, was planning an attack on the Freemason temple in Milwaukee, and was claiming, "They are all Masonic; they are playing with the world like a game, man . . . these are the ones that need to be killed." This was after a 2004 attack on a Masonic lodge in Istanbul that wounded six and killed two, including one of the attackers. And 2021 alone saw arson attacks on Masonic lodges in Dublin, Ireland, and in Vancouver, Canada, where the perpetrator claimed that lodges were used by "dark souls and evil" to perpetrate mind control. (Another attack by neo-Nazis in France was foiled before it could be carried out.)

It's hard to quantify exactly the public attitude toward Freemasons, but they are—as we shall see—often used synonymously with two other conspiracy theory groups: the Illuminati and the New World Order. A 2021 survey reported that over 47 percent of Americans agree or strongly agree with the statement that the government "is hiding something" about the Illuminati and/or the New World Order (up from 42 percent in 2018, suggesting the influence of the Covid-19 pandemic on such beliefs). While the Illuminati are alleged to be a shadowy organization behind the scenes, the Freemasons are often singled out as a public-facing version, which is why their lodges are so frequently the targets for attacks.

The conspiracist sees the world as not just inherently fraught with peril but loaded with symbolism everywhere. No image is innocent. To believe in a secret society is not just to believe that an invisible malevolent hand controls everything—it is to believe that the world is alive with symbols ready to deciphered, and that there is no noise, just signal. It's partly why we're so fascinated by these societies and the cranks who obsess over them: they invite us to see the world as pregnant with meaning and direction. Even for those of us not given to paranoia, there's something perpetually fascinating about these symbols: Who hasn't spent at least some time wondering about the eye on the pyramid on the one-dollar bill? It's the same fascination that's driven our love of mega-bestseller Dan Brown's *The Lost Symbol* (a novel about a secret Masonic pyramid hidden somewhere in Washington, D.C.) and the 2004 Nicolas Cage blockbuster *National Treasure*, which also revolves around decoding Masonic symbols to unearth the titular treasure.

The Freemasons may be a secret society, but their symbols are everywhere. If any secret group seems to be rubbing our faces in . . . well, something . . . it's these guys.

Several hundred miles to the north of Valley Forge in a small cemetery in Batavia, New York (about a thirty-minute drive east from Buffalo), there is a very different monument to the Freemasons. The graves here are old, the marble starting to wear smooth, but the Masonic symbols are on numerous headstones: the compass, the square, the all-seeing eye. But these are commonplace; you can find such symbols everywhere. What sets apart the Batavia graveyard is technically not a grave at all: it's a cenotaph, a memorial without a body.

In the southwest corner of the cemetery, a solid, square plinth, a few feet long on each side and higher than my head, dwarfs the neighboring headstones. Out of its top rises a simple column some forty feet high, topped with a statue of a man named William Morgan. Because it's so tall, you can't really see the statue well from the cenotaph's base; it's best appreciated from across the street, where you take the full height of it in and get the best view of Morgan's distant gaze. Then you can walk closer to read the inscriptions on the plinth that detail how, in 1826, Morgan was abducted and murdered by the Freemasons.

"Sacred to the memory of Wm. Morgan," one side reads, along with a short biography that calls Morgan "a martyr to the freedom of writing, printing, and speaking the truth." On another face is a quote from Morgan himself: "The bane of our civil institutions is to be found in Masonry, already powerful and daily becoming more so. I owe to my country an exposure of its dangers." Located on the edge of the cemetery, what seems most striking is that Morgan faces outward, away from the other graves. Even in death, it seems, he's turned his back on the community that betrayed him.

Morgan had himself been a Mason until he grew disillusioned with the organization and threatened to publish a book detailing the rites and secrets of his lodge. The Masons first harassed and threatened him and his publisher, David Miller, including attempting to burn down Miller's printing press. Then, on September 11, 1826, the Masons (whose numbers included many in local law enforcement) had Morgan arrested on false pretenses. The next morning, a man unknown to Morgan arrived to pay his bail; as he was being roughly escorted out to a waiting carriage, Morgan cried out to horrified onlookers that he was about to be murdered, and then he was taken away into the night.

William Morgan was never seen again. His body was never recovered.

The riddle of American Freemasonry can first be sensed in these two very different monuments: one bursting with civic pride, a philanthropic organization with nothing to hide that sees itself as a vital part of the American story, the fraternal organization of presidents and Founding Fathers. The other monument speaks to a dark, conspiratorial organization that murders to keep its secrets.

It is impossible to fully understand America without reckoning with the Freemasons and this duality. Not because so many founders (Washington and Franklin foremost among them) were themselves Masons, though that's an important element to the story. Rather, as the founders, in the early days of the republic, were attempting to figure out just how to construct civil society in this new democracy, they turned to the structure of the Masons for inspiration. But Masonry would also lead to the earliest populist backlashes in America (spurred by the national outcry over Morgan's disappearance), and this, too, is vital to understanding how America came to be what it is today. As the country's foremost elite society, one composed of men who saw their roles as first among equals, whose duty it was to shepherd the country to its destiny, it was only a matter of time before it became a target of populist conspiracy theories.

The way that large segments of American culture lionize billionaires like Bill Gates and Beyoncé, while other segments simultaneously accuse them of belonging to dangerous secret societies (and some hold both attitudes at once), is all just the latest articulation of a long-standing confusion in American culture. And it is one that began with the Freemasons.

TWO

The Craft

T he National Memorial Arch is not the only public monument in the region paid for or conserved by the Masons. Adjacent to the national park is Freedoms Foundation, a nonprofit civic group, and overlooking the Foundation's Medal of Honor Grove is a massive statue of Washington kneeling in prayer, donated by Freemasons in 1967. They also maintain several statues in Philadelphia itself, including one of a young Benjamin Franklin working his printing press and James A. West's statue, *The Bond*, which depicts Franklin handing a Mason's apron to Washington. This last stands outside of the Masonic Temple: a medieval stone castle in the heart of downtown, the building contains a library, banquet hall, and seven different lodge meeting rooms, each decorated in a distinctive style. It stands across the street from Philadelphia's city hall, in case there's any confusion about how close to the seat of power the Masons are in this city.

The Temple is open to the public, and the tour will take you through the nine beautiful and ornate meeting halls, including the Egyptian, Ionic, and Norman rooms. Throughout the tour, I see the Eye of Providence, which appears in the intricate ceremonial aprons on display in the museum and is worked into the motifs of various decorative elements throughout the building.

The Eye of Providence is proof, depending on which conspiracist you talk to, that the government is secretly controlled by shadowy cabals, and the ubiquity of the eye is proof they're doing it out in the open for all to see. For Fritz Springmeier, author, conspiracy theorist, and convicted armed robber, the eye represents the Egyptian god Osiris, who had "debauched revelries (saturualias) celebrated in his honour," and the image "pops up everywhere the Illuminati has been," from St. Petersburg's Palace Square to the Mexican senate building, and, of course, Washington, D.C. Milton William Cooper, in his perennially selling conspiracy bible *Behold a Pale Horse*, explained that the "One Dollar bill has an unfinished top, with the Eye of Horus hovering over it," and the reason the pyramid "on Our One Dollar Bill is unfinished [is] because the New World Order—Kingdom of Antichrist—is an unfinished work." Increasingly, the distinctions between the Illuminati, Satanists, or Masons have all collapsed for conspiracists, who treat them as interchangeable synonyms for the same secret group.

Ubiquitous now, the image of the eye contained in a triangle, floating above everything, has a more recent provenance than one might think. It dates back to the Renaissance, when it was definitively a Christian symbol representing God's watchful, benevolent gaze (the three sides of the triangle would have stood for the Holy Trinity—Father, Son, and Holy Ghost). By the eighteenth century, it had lost some of its direct religious connotation, but it still suggested a kind of benevolent watchfulness. In post-revolutionary France, for example, it had come to stand in for an abstract symbol of Enlightenment thinking and a reasoning free of theology, which is how it appears in Jean-Jacques-François Le Barbier's 1789 painting *Declaration of the Rights of Man and of the Citizen*: an eye in a triangle radiating light above a new declaration of rights free of religion or corruption.

The founders of the United States, God-fearing men who were none-theless attempting to forge a new democracy free from religious autoc-racy, found in this multivalent image the perfect symbol. Charles Thomson, secretary of the Continental Congress, was tasked with com-ing up with a seal for the new United States, and with help from lawyer and artist William Barton, he proposed the eye atop the unfinished pyramid design. The pyramid was to suggest both "strength and dur-ation" as well as the potential for future growth (hence unfinished), and the eye represented God's benevolent (if detached) oversight over the new project of democracy (hence the Latin motto Thomson suggested, Annuit coeptis: "He favors our undertakings").

For the Freemasons, who adopted the Eye of Providence as an image a few years later, it has two different meanings. Per Thomas Smith Webb's 1797 Masonic handbook, *The Freemason's Monitor; Or, Illustrations of Masonry: in Two Parts*, it is a reminder of God's all-seeing eye, "Whom the Sun, Moon, and Stars obey, and under whose watchful care even Comets perform their stupendous revolutions, pervades the inmost re-cesses of the human heart, and will reward us according to our merits." But it is also a reminder of the need for secrecy: "The eye upon your apron," Webb cautions, "is to remind you to have a careful watch over the conduct of the craft in general."

The tour of the Masonic Temple ends with the Grand Banquet Hall on the first floor: there, a massive, dead-eyed bronze statue of Benjamin Franklin holds court (he's intimidating enough that the Masons had to subsequently install a curtain for the weddings and other rental parties that didn't want his ominous eyes watching them), and, along the north wall, are four stained-glass windows, each depicting a former president (Washington, Andrew Jackson, Teddy Roosevelt, and Harry S. Truman, that same Eye of Providence floating above his head). The message here is unmistakable: a powerful organization, connected to powerful men.

The origin of Freemasonry, historian Frances A. Yates wrote in 1986, "is one of the most debated, and debatable, subjects in the whole realm of historical enquiry"—a statement whose resonance has only grown since then. As Yates notes, "One has to distinguish between the legendary history of Freemasonry and the problem of when it actually began as an organized institution," and yet, doing so is difficult despite the quantity of great scholarship devoted to the question.

The problem is that both proponents and its detractors of the organization have sought to mystify and dramatize its history. For those who embrace Freemasonry, there is an attempt to connect it to a grand, mystical tradition that nearly transcends time, stretching unbroken all the way back to the Solomon's Temple. Those who seek to stoke fears about Freemasonry likewise gain currency by exaggerating and elaborating its mysteries and purposes. The result is that getting a clear, factual history of the organization has become more or less impossible.

But some facts can be sketched. The masons were once a guild like any other craftsmen's guild: they worked in stone, and they made a distinction between the laborers who dealt with heavy, thick stone that was shaped into blocks, and stones like limestone that could be carved into sculptures—"free" stone, hence "freemasons." In the wake of the Black Death, labor shortages meant that workers could charge higher rates. This, in turn, led to a crackdown by the state to cap wages. Masons, who were in particular demand by the wealthy because of their ability to build great symbolic edifices like cathedrals and palaces, recognized that their skills were in such high demand that they could circumvent these restrictions and set their rates higher. But to do so, they had to meet in secret, forming what were essentially illegal trade unions.

It's worth lingering on this fact for a moment. The true origin of the secrecy of the Freemasons originated from an attempt to secure better paying wages among the working class. The outlawing and vilification of such meetings came from the government acting on behalf of the church and the aristocracy. The foundation, then, is set here: when the public world is controlled by the elite, working openly to ensure an unjust world, those who want a more equitably distributed world meet in secret. And they are often demonized for this reason.

As the demand for gothic architecture fell, so, too, did the fortunes of stonemason guilds. But then something strange happened: the craftsmen began allowing non-craftsmen into the guild. In 1646, Elias Ashmole recorded in his diary that he had been inducted into the freemasons. Ashmole was many things: a lawyer and a politician, an occultist and an alchemist, an astrologer and an antiquarian. What he was not, by any means, was someone who worked in stone.

The turn from "operative" masonry (the elements of Freemasonry that dealt with those who actually worked in stone, involving the tools and tactics of plying their trade) to "speculative" masonry (a new version of the fraternity in which the masonic elements became symbolic, and the organization began to take on mystical, alchemical, and political elements) is difficult to trace for certain. We have, at best, conjectures. It may have been as simple as the fact that, by the seventeenth century, demand for stonework had fallen to the point that guilds began accepting non-stonemasons (in particular, wealthy aristocrats) as members simply to survive. It may have also been the case that an organization of builders was attractive to those who studied alchemy and the occult, which often used architectural metaphors in their writings. That these lodges were closed to the public and insular offered an incentive in that ideas could be discussed freely without worry of public scrutiny.

By the eighteenth century, Freemasonry had completed its transition from being a guild of laborers and artisans to a fraternal organization defined primarily by its secrecy and a love of esoteric symbolism and rituals. Rather than sharing techniques for shaping stone or networking for lucrative work, Freemasons bound themselves together through bizarre rites.

An initiate seeking admission to the brotherhood would be blindfolded, the left leg of his pants rolled up past his knee, and the right sleeve of his shirt rolled up as well. His left arm would be taken from his shirt, exposing his left breast, and a loose slipknot of rope would be placed over his neck. Entering the lodge this way, he is led around the room three times, and then certifies that he is at least twenty-one, "of good report," and "free-born." He pledges a belief in some kind of supernatural God (it need not be a Christian one), inscribes on the floor a Mason's square (the right-angle tool that appears as part of the brotherhood's insignia), and then places his hand on the sacred book of his faith and pledges never to reveal any of the secrets he is about to learn. His blindfold removed, he is thus initiated into the lodge and is taught the secret handshake and symbols of the Masons.

This was only the first degree; there were two more to come, the third of which—the rite to become a Master Mason—involves a ritual reenactment of the murder of Hiram Abiff, the mythical architect who supposedly built Solomon's Temple and the spiritual ancestor of the Masons. For each degree, the Mason would receive a different apron with a specific set of symbols that communicated sacred truths to the brother. He would learn the importance of moral uprightness, fidelity, and charitable works, all of which would be represented by various architectural symbols and secret words.

While the first two aprons feature mainly architectural motifs, the Master Mason aprons are distinguished by their inclusion of a skull and crossbones, a reflection of the final lesson imparted by Masonic teaching and echoing a long-standing religious tradition, the memento mori. Freemasons reminded their brethren through these rituals that death was inescapable and that the way to master it was through facing it rather than denying it. Melding occult traditions, Masonic symbolism was notably heterodox, incorporating Greek mysteries and Egyptian symbolism, alchemy and astrology alongside Christianity. It was this curious assemblage that helped give Freemasonry its allure and its impenetrability.

And even if the Freemasons have long since moved away from their original stonecutting guild, they continue to see architecture as a vital and central metaphor for understanding their work. It was in the construction and contemplation of great monuments and buildings that the symbolic teachings were preserved and deciphered. If mastery of death was the ends to Masonic teaching, architecture was the means.

What we have of Freemasonry, then, is a series of fairly straightforward moral codes dressed up in a byzantine set of rituals and symbols. The origins of the rites themselves remain murky, but over time their primary purpose seems to have been merely to build a sense of community and shared purpose.

Additionally, though, the secrecy that the Masons offered created a safe space for discussing liberal ideas in the uncertain political climate of the Enlightenment. The brothers could discuss secular philosophy and new scientific developments, and could exchange ideas about governmental reform, becoming an incubator for radical ideas (particularly amidst hostile or repressive regimes, as in pre-revolutionary France)—all so long as members agreed that what happened in the lodge stayed in the lodge. In England, a large number of Fellows of the Royal Society joined Masonic lodges in the late seventeenth century, meeting privately with radicals and agitators at the same time they were maintaining their public reputation.

Places where such a cross section of individuals could meet and exchange ideas soon became a threat to established power structures. Rumors circulated, such as in France, that the Masons' love of secrecy was cover for homosexual activity. And in April 1738, Pope Clement XII published an encyclical banning Catholics from joining Freemasonry altogether. It is, he argued, "in the nature of crime to betray itself and to show itself by its attendant clamor. Thus these aforesaid Societies or Conventicles have caused in the minds of the faithful the greatest suspicion, and all prudent and upright men have passed the same judgment on them as being depraved and perverted." In an argument that would become a hallmark of denunciations of secret societies, the pope concluded: "For if they were not doing evil they would not have so great a hatred of the light."

In two hundred years, Freemasonry had transformed from a trade union, to a fashionable private club for the European elite, to a dangerous and subversive threat to Church and State, its reputation augmented at every point by its vaunted secrecy. What could they possibly be hiding? John Coustos, an English Freemason captured by the Portuguese Inquisition in Lisbon in 1743, was tortured repeatedly over a matter of months, his bones broken, then reset, then broken again, as authorities demanded to know what the secret of Freemasonry was and what the purpose of their secrecy was. Coustos told his captors that the only purpose of the rituals was "to maintain the secrecy which all the members are to keep. . . . The final purpose of such procedure was such secrecy." He further explained that over time, the secrecy had itself become a recruiting tool: "as Secrecy naturally excited Curiosity, this prompted great Numbers of Persons to enter into this Society."

Or, as Benjamin Franklin famously wrote, "THEIR GRAND Secret is *That they have no Secret at all.*"

Like smallpox and Christianity, Freemasonry had traveled across the Atlantic with the early colonists and changed the landscape of North America forever. The first lodges on American soil appeared in the early 1730s, and the organization spread quickly through the colonies. The flowering of an organization sworn to secrecy during this period is curious, since this was an era when colonial settlers were riven with fears of conspiracy and secret groups. As the historian Gordon S.

Wood put it, "Everywhere people sensed designs within designs, cabals within cabals." These conspiracy theories took any number of forms, but the overwhelming mood of the colonies was one of pervasive suspicion.

Colonists were, for one, fervently anti-Catholic, believing the pope to be regularly fomenting plots against Protestant settlers. Anti-papal pamphlets and tracts echoed these accusations, such as Benjamin Keach's 1681 diatribe, *Sion in Distress or the Groans of the Protestant Church*, which warned of a sexually depraved Church that "not only countenanced the Stews and Brothel-Houses, where abominable Sodomy and Adulteries are practiced, but even [the] Nunneries are become Habitations of Whoredome and Filthiness, the bottoms of whose Motes and Ponds have shewed the Murders of New born Babes." During the French–Indian War, Benjamin Franklin accused the Catholics in his midst of giving aid and comfort to the enemy, wondering aloud in "Plain Truth," his 1747 political pamphlet, "Are there no Priests among us, think you, that might . . . give an Enemy . . . good Encouragement?" As the descendants of English emigrants, colonists still bore the longstanding religious hatred that stretched back to the Reformation, and they were quick to blame Catholicism for all manner of ills they had to endure. Catholics not only made easy scapegoats, they also provided a way to off-load troubles in the colonies to the distant power structure of the Vatican, nebulous and abstract and (surely, Franklin and others believed) capable of anything.

Politically, the colonists also saw conspiracy wherever they looked. As tensions between Britain and her American citizens increased, many blamed a cabal of cabinet ministers for undermining the authority of George III. Nor was this simply a perspective from the margins. Colonial America's leading scholars and thinkers—the men who would ultimately help forge the new nation—all subscribed, to varying degrees, to a belief in conspiratorial machinations driving world events. Thomas Jefferson spoke for many white colonists as he tried to make sense of the rapid change coming from England, noting how the sudden increase of oppressive taxes and repressive laws hinted at something beyond arbitrary incompetence. "Single acts of tyranny may be ascribed to the accidental opinion of a day," he wrote in July of 1774, "but a series of oppressions, begun at a distinguished period, and pursued unalterably thro' every change of ministers, too plainly prove a deliberate, systematical plan of reducing us to slavery." Faced with sudden changes that seemed to defy easy logic, conspiracy made the most sense. (That men like Jefferson and others were afraid of being "enslaved" by Britain but were themselves literal enslavers is a tremendous and terrible irony that remained entirely lost on most—but not all—of them. Washington, nearly echoing Jefferson, wrote that same year of "a regular, systematic plan" whose ultimate goal was "to make us tame and abject slaves, as the blacks we rule over with such arbitrary sway." White enslavers knew what a lack of liberty looked like, and they would continue to insist that their "Americanness" was derived from the liberty they explicitly denied others.)

This was partly a function of distance: colonists, separated from their government by the Atlantic Ocean, often struggled to understand what was happening in Britain. Left to make sense of the increasing hardship enforced on the colonists by the British government, conspiracy often seemed the only explanation. Joseph Warren, a Massachusetts doctor and politician, argued that the Stamp Act of 1765 was designed to foment rebellion: "If the real and only motive of the minister was to raise money from the colonies," he stated in 1772, "that method should undoubtedly have been adopted which was least grievous to people." The Stamp Act, thus, "has induced some to imagine that the minister designed by this act to force the colonies into a rebellion, and from thence to take occasion to treat them with severity, and, by military power, to reduce them to servitude."

Political conspiracies, of course, were nothing new. But in classical and medieval periods, they mostly referred to the machinations of a select group of people in power: palace intrigues, coup attempts, Machiavellian maneuvering. But something was changing in the eighteenth century, leading to a new tendency to see conspiracies everywhere—no longer just the work of the powerful against the powerless but part of the social fabric of society itself. There was a new sense that all historical events were the work of hidden hands, that conspiracies pervaded the work of humanity at nearly all levels and could explain any number of otherwise inexplicable phenomena.

The sermons delivered in this period (many of which were subsequently published for further distribution) echoed this belief. Prominent pastor Ebenezer Baldwin stated plainly that if one viewed "the whole conduct of the ministry and parliament, I do not see how any one can doubt but that there is a settled fix'd plan for enslaving the colonies, or bringing them under arbitrary government, and indeed the nation too." This feeling only grew in the run-up to the events of 1776. In a popular and oft-cited sermon from that January, Aaron Burr's nephew Samuel Sherwood, an outspoken proponent of independence, warned of "intrigues and dark plots that were contriving against us." These were not lone fringe voices in the wilderness; these were important and respected leaders. And this belief came not from the fringes of American culture; it came from the defining philosophical movement of the day, the Enlightenment.

With the Scientific Revolution and a rise in the humanist belief that (to quote Greek philosopher Protagoras) "man is the measure of all things," it had become increasingly unfashionable to blame the confusing and inexplicable on "God's mysterious ways." Instead, the ideas and actions of humans defined the world and the contours of history. But seeing human agency at the center of the world does not, by itself, eliminate the confounding or the random. The world was still just as marked by the strange, but now it was thought that anything that happened, no matter how seemingly chaotic or bizarre, could be traced to the workings of someone. Which could only mean that any strange happenings had to be the work of hidden actors whose motives and purposes were not immediately knowable. As Princeton University president Samuel Stanhope Smith argued at the time, "chance" was nothing but "a name to cover our ignorance of the cause of any event."

For the leading intellectuals of the era, in other words, there was nothing paranoid about seeing plots and conspiracies everywhere; to the contrary, such suspicions were themselves proof of an enlightened vision that saw human agency as the motor of history. Such thinking was by no means strictly limited to American colonists. Constantin-François de Chasseboeuf, Comte de Volney, argued in 1791 that the source of humanity's tribulations was not to be found in "the distant heavens"; rather, "it resides in man himself, he carries it with him in the inward recesses of his own heart." And the famous Scottish philosopher David Hume (whose work would heavily influence James Madison and Alexander Hamilton as they helped draft the Constitution) argued that only the ignorant "take things according to their first appearance, and attribute the uncertainty of events to such an uncertainty in the causes." Enlightened thinkers, by contrast, recognize that causes in nature are not always immediately evident, and know that a "contrariety of events may not proceed from any contingency in the cause, but from the secret operation of contrary causes."

American's leading thinkers embraced this conspiratorial outlook, and it filtered through to everyday sentiment. If surface events didn't have an immediately visible cause, that didn't mean they were random; rather it meant that, more likely, a secret hand was at work. The rapid succession of taxes (including the Sugar Act of 1764, the Stamp Act of 1765, the Tea Act of 1773, and the Coercive Acts of 1774) imposed on the colonies could not simply be the work of an inept or greedy Parliament; it was far more easy—far more enlightened—to assume a secret and deliberate plot behind it all. Thus, in 1774, the Continental Congress approved a draft of a message for "the people of Great Britain," authored by (among others) future Supreme Court chief justice John Jay, in which he concluded that these new laws discussed "the progression of the ministerial plan for enslaving us" and called on those across the Atlantic to "Admit that the Ministry, by the powers of Britain, and the aid of our Roman Catholic neighbors, should be able to carry the point of taxation, and reduce us to a state of perfect humiliation and slavery." In a real sense, during the Enlightenment, conspiracy theories took the place of God. The world's first exercise in democracy was also, then, an exercise in paranoia.

And yet, somehow Freemasonry escaped this taint of secret conspiracy, at least at first. In 1739, Masons marched proudly through Boston, celebrating the feast day of their patron, St. John the Baptist. The brothers wore their masonic aprons, as well as jewels to signify both their status and their association with Freemasonry. As they paraded through the town, spectators lined the streets and crowded balconies to see the men go by in their finery. Their procession led them to the house of the governor of Massachusetts, who treated them to a grand banquet; meanwhile, in the harbor, a sloop flying a Masonic flag fired its guns to mark the day.

Masonic parades were a normal part of colonial society: in Philadelphia in 1755, a grand parade of over a hundred Masons processed through the streets, complete with sword-bearers, musicians, and local dignitaries—including the mayor, Benjamin Franklin, and Franklin's son William (who carried with him a crimson cushion bearing a Masonic bible). These were not, in other words, men eager to keep hidden their membership in a society secret. Rather than a shadowy organization pulling strings behind the scenes, the Freemasons of the eighteenth century were a prominent, public group who sought to display their power and clout in the open streets.

Freemasonry was not the only fraternal organization formed by the colonists; there was the Society of Cincinnati, a rival fraternity for members of the military and their sons; and the Independent Order of Odd Fellows, an import of an eighteenth-century British fraternity whose

American branch was founded in Baltimore in 1806. As Alexis de Tocqueville would later marvel, "Americans of all ages, all stations in life, and all types of dispositions are forever forming associations. There are not only commercial and industrial associations in which all take part, but others of a thousand types—religious, moral, serious, futile, very general and very limited, immensely large and very minute." Many of these were modeled on mutual aid societies once championed by Benjamin Franklin, such as the Union Fire Company and the Library Company of Philadelphia (institutions whose successes would ultimately lead to their widespread adoption for the public good).

But Freemasonry offered something very specific and useful: it was open to (nearly) all comers. And through its rituals, meetings, and associations, it offered young men an introduction to civic participation in the public sphere. As such, Freemasonry became how a young, ambitious man rose in the world of the colonies. George Washington, who lacked a college education or the aristocratic pedigree of his peers, became one of the first inductees of a new Fredericksburg lodge in 1752 when he was twenty years old, in keeping with what Ron Chernow has called the "naked, sometimes clumsy ambition" of his youth.

Washington would remain a lifelong supporter of Freemasonry; during the Revolutionary War, he would speak of the conflict in Masonic terms, telling his troops that the "Grand Architect of the Universe" did not "see fit to suffer his superstructures and Justice, to be subjected to the Ambition of the Princes of this World, or to the rod of oppression, in the hands of any power upon Earth." Washington's journey from an uneducated plantation owner to the head of a new nation cannot be entirely disentangled from his involvement in Masonry, which allowed the young man connections and prestige that would serve him in his meteoric rise. Alongside Benjamin Franklin's similar story, Washington's relationship with Freemasonry offers one of the clearest lessons of its utility for a generation of young men eager to establish themselves as a new elite independent of hereditary titles.

Other Americans attempted to make use of Masonry's resources in a similar manner with less success. In 1784, a lodge was founded by a group of free Black men; Prince Hall and fourteen other men had originally petitioned to join Boston's St. John's Lodge, but when they were denied, they petitioned for—and received—an independent charter from the Grand Lodge of England. Through the years, Prince Hall Lodges (as they became known) would develop an almost parallel organization structure to a still almost entirely white-dominated Freemasonry. At various points in Freemasonry's history, Prince Hall members have been both welcomed as fellow Masons and brothers and excluded due to long-standing racist attitudes of American Masons.

The confused attitude mainstream Masonry had toward the Prince Hall Lodge is just one of many illustrations of both the allure and complications of Freemasonry. America was built not on the promise of equality but rather on the promise of equal access to privilege. As political philosophers of the Enlightenment era struggled to imagine a form of government that depended neither on a sovereign or the church, many were nonetheless hesitant to embrace full, participatory democracy. Even if all men had been made equal by the Creator, it did not follow, America's founders concluded, that all men should have an equal stake in governance. The form they eventually sought—a republicanism that relied on mechanisms like the Electoral College, the Senate, and the court system to moderate the unbridled will of the populace—required a cultured elite: an elite that could be both respected by the general public and trusted to act philanthropically in the best interests of the nation.

The Masons emerged as a model for what this might look like. Rather than being a shadowy organization committed to secrecy or a persecuted group of free thinkers, early American Masons were self-consciously public and proud, eager to prove to their neighbors that they had both the status and predisposition to lead the country. It would be a while yet before the Freemasons were associated with hidden attempts to subvert the will of the public; in the eighteenth century, they were instead seen as embodying that very will.

In Europe, such men were seen as enemies of both royalty and the Catholic Church, and so in North America, they were received not as subversives but as the future of the colonies. And so as Franklin and his Masonic brothers marched proudly through the streets of Philadelphia that June day in 1755, the public thronged to witness such an awesome display of esteemed men in their finery. It was, according to one witness, "the Greatest Procession of Free Masons . . . that was ever seen in America."

THREE

The Dreadful Fire

I n the summer of 1798, a Lutheran minister named G. W. Snyder wrote to the former president George Washington, worried about the rising threat of a secret group of saboteurs that had successfully brought down France: the Illuminati. Washington wrote back that September, relating to Snyder that he had already heard "much about the nefarious and dangerous plan and doctrines of the Illuminati." Perhaps realizing that such a response was dismissive, Washington felt compelled to later clarify: "It was not my intention to doubt that the doctrines of the Illuminati and the principles of Jacobinism had not spread in the United States," he wrote to Snyder a month later. "On the contrary, no one is more satisfied of this fact than I am."

In 1798 , the Illuminati panic hit the United States, as religious leaders and politicians of all persuasion began to openly worry about a secret group bent on undermining the new project of democracy in the United States. The Revolutionary War's "shot heard around the world" had quickly set off another successful revolution against monarchism in France, but almost immediately things had gone sour, the Revolution sliding into the Terror with its thousands of politically motivated executions. Americans were aghast at what they saw, and nervous that something similar could yet befall the United States. And because they believed that such events do not happen by chance or accident, they were open to arguments that the Terror had been engineered behind the scenes, though at first it was not clear who could be behind such madness or why. Eventually, a Scottish physicist and a French priest would provide an answer.

The Scot was a man named John Robison, who'd been stoking fears of a secret organization in a pamphlet he'd published in 1797, entitled *Proofs of a Conspiracy against All the Religions and Governments of Europe, Carried on in the Secret Meetings of the Free Masons, Illuminati, and Reading Societies.* In it, Robison alleged that the French Revolution had been secretly engineered by a cabal that had infiltrated the Freemasons and had worked behind the scenes to bring about the Jacobins' Reign of Terror. The pamphlet was an immediate, incendiary success, going through at least four printings in its first year: Robison's words struck a deep chord of fear among the clergy and the elite of New England, who feared that these subversive atheists were bent on sabotaging America.

Among those who read Robison's work in horror was Jedidiah Morse, a Federalist and pastor most known as a talented cartographer (as well as the father of the inventor of the telegraph, Samuel Morse). Morse had risen through the ranks of power in New England and commanded a spiritual authority throughout the region. On May 9, 1798, Morse delivered a sermon in which he warned that the nation was passing through "a day of trouble, of reviling and blasphemy." He accused the Jacobins of France of plotting to overthrow the US government, lamenting "the astonishing increase of irreligion," and despairing of attacks against politicians and clergy members in the local press. Who was behind this degeneracy? There was reason to suspect, he argued, "that there is some secret plan in operation, hostile to true liberty and religion, which requires to be aided by these vile slanders."

Morse didn't believe that irreligion could spread without help; the only reason for the rising secularism he perceived in France (that he now feared was spreading to North America) had to be human agents working behind the scenes to corrupt the minds of God-fearing citizens, and, behind them, the Devil himself. Citing Robison's book, he went on to unmask this secret plan as being the work of the Illuminati, concluding that God was at work teeing up a final, apocalyptic battle between good and evil, and, for this reason, "dreadful fire of Illuminatism may be permitted to rage and spread for this purpose."

Morse was not some fringe prophet of doom; he was a well-connected and well-respected member of New England's elite. Not everyone believed his theories outright, but Morse was not a man who could be ignored, so they received extensive discussion in the local press. A member of the American Academy of Arts and Sciences, he counted as his friends other luminaries such as Daniel Webster and Yale University president Timothy Dwight, who would soon add his own voice to the chorus of anti-Illuminati fearmongering.

On July 4, 1798, Dwight gave a sermon warning that the "ultimate objects" of the Illuminati were "the overthrow of religion, government, and human society civil and domestic. These they pronounce to be so good, that murder, butchery, and war, however extended and dreadful, are declared by them to be completely justifiable, if necessary for these great purposes." For all our contemporary problems resulting from demagogues pushing apocalyptic conspiracies in the political sphere, it's important to remember that these wild accusations have been with us since the start.

Unlike the origins of Freemasonry, the origins of the Illuminati, remarkably, are largely well known and uncontroversial. By 1776, Adam Weishaupt, a Bavarian Jesuit and professor of canon law at the famous University of Ingolstadt, had become increasingly disillusioned with the Catholic Church—while at the same time increasingly intrigued by the potential of the Freemasons for creating a more just world. In time, Weishaupt came to believe that only a secret society could spread secular, rationalist ideas in a repressive, religious environment. He founded a small group modeled on the Freemasons through which he hoped to someday found a new society altogether, based on a rational government free from religious influence.

He called it the Illuminati. With just five members initially, he sought to build out a network of "schools of wisdom," wherein new and progressive ideas could be explored. He recruited young noblemen for his new group, seeking acolytes both rich and impressionable; as with Freemasonry, there were "grades" that initiates could work their way up through: Novice, Minerval, and Illuminated Minerval. Gradually, the group expanded from a few dozen to several thousands, until finally attracting the attention of the authorities. In 1784, the Duke of Bavaria, Karl Theodor, banned all secret societies, hoping specifically to suppress the Illuminati. Two years after that, his police conducted raids on the houses of several high-profile Illuminati, and at the house of Franz Xaver von Zwack, authorities confiscated a trove of heretical documents, including essays that defended atheism and suicide, promoted counterfeiting and abortion, claimed the Illuminati had the power over life and death, and sketched out plans to include women. Sunlight proved a powerful disinfectant, and, once illuminated, the Illuminati dissolved.

Weishaupt's organization might have been entirely lost to history as a minor footnote if not for the French Revolution. In a few short years, the country had gone from a seemingly stable monarchy wedded to the Catholic Church to a violent and bloody regime of atheists. For many, both then and now, it was difficult to make sense of what drove such a rapid and stark change. In 1793, a writer in Vienna, Leopold Hoffmann, first suggested that there might be a hidden hand behind this shift; collaborating with another writer, one Dr. Zimmerman, the two suggested that Weishaupt's Bavarian Illuminati may have somehow not only survived but seeded the discontent that exploded into the French Revolution.

The fantasy of the Illuminati was difficult to kill because the very idea of such a group was liberating: it opened up all sorts of possibilities for how to understand the world. And in the same way a public denial of a conspiracy often is treated as further proof of that conspiracy, the fear of the Illuminati seemed to only be strengthened by how short lived it was and how easily it was suppressed.

In 1797, the French Jesuit Augustin Barruel was taking stock of what had happened to his country; surveying the political wreckage, he could only see conspiracy. And he took Hoffman and Zimmerman's hypothesis and ran with it. It wasn't necessarily that Barruel was uniquely paranoid; after all, the Jacobins had themselves repeatedly used the specter of conspiracy as a rhetorical tool to enable their own rise. Conspiracy had become the most natural way to explain why things had turned out the way they had. Barruel saw in the Revolution and ensuing Terror the handiwork of philosophers like Voltaire and Rousseau, who had long railed against the excesses of the monarchy and the church. But how had they been so successful at carrying out such a complete overthrow of the old order? They'd used a secret network of Freemasons, Barruel reasoned, at the apex of which sat the Illuminati. Barruel's conspiracy theory posited that the entire French Revolution was not a story of exuberant democracy descending into unpredictable chaos, but rather a carefully orchestrated plan by philosophers who'd long seeded the French landscape with subversive agents.

Philosophers, Barruel alleged, had laid the groundwork for seditious thought, distributing free pamphlets and keeping the public in a state of constant agitation. From there, Freemasonry provided the network of dozens of secret lodges where these dangerous ideas could travel. It was within this network spread throughout the continent that they provided an efficient means of communication between various subversive elements who could operate in local and state government. Because the Freemasons maintained a strict hierarchy, they could shield the foot soldiers from the true workings of the conspiracy—those at the lower echelons of the Freemasons' organization were unwitting conspirators, Barruel surmised, acting on orders they did not question, the true meaning of which was known only to a select few at the top—what Barruel termed "the Illuminization of Freemasonry."

As with Robison's pamphlet, Barruel's memoirs were rushed into multiple languages and sold out rapidly, leading to subsequent editions that allowed him to elaborate more on what was to come. The philosopher Edmund Burke wrote to Barruel to gush praise ("I cannot easily express to you, how much I am instructed and delighted by the first volume of your History of Jacobinism"). Mary Shelley and her husband, Percy Bysshe Shelley, poured over the volumes together, and the English essayist Thomas De Quincey would later record his own youthful fascination with Barruel's accusations. America's own Charles Brockden Brown incorporated Barruel's conspiracies into his gothic fiction, *Wieland; or, the Transformation*, and its unfinished sequel, *Memoirs of Carwin, the Biloquist*. Whether or not one entirely believed Barruel's allegations, one had no choice but to reckon with them.

More than anyone else, Barruel laid the groundwork for how we've come to think of secret societies within nations—the wide sweep of political change is complex, given to chance and chaos as much as order and planning, and in the face of so much ambiguity, many choose to see conspiracy above all else. Barruel also helped establish the belief that political change happens as a result of foreign invaders hidden among us. The Illuminati or the Masons are a kind of virus, an intruder; foreign bodies that have infiltrated the healthy body of the nation and are undermining it from within.

Such subversive groups terrify us differently than, say, warring armies from other countries at our gates. Americans may have been used to thinking of George III's ministers as a secret cabal pulling the strings, but this was something new. This was a more or less wholly fictitious group, conjured up out of thin air, being used as a causal mechanism to make sense of world affairs. Unseen yet diseased, the very idea foments paranoia. If the nation is often analogized as a human body, then conspiracists see secret societies as the viral infection that must be eliminated.

Above all, the Illuminati panic arose out of a sense that the established centers of power were losing their grip on society. Barruel was looking for some kind of explanation as to why the French public might have turned on their king and church, and he refused to accept public sentiment as a sufficient rationale.

At the same time that Barruel was bringing out his elaborate theory of conspiracy, John Robison was coming to much the same conclusion in Scotland. In his 1797 pamphlet, Robison argued that the Jacobins in France were the open manifestation of the hidden system of the Illuminati and that, having crushed religion in France, they were now spreading. "An association has been formed," Robison asserted, "for the express purpose of rooting out all the religious establishments, and overturning all the existing governments of Europe." Like Barruel, he argued that the French Jacobins were the public face of something much darker: "The intelligent saw in the open system of the Jacobins the complete hidden system of the Illuminati," he explained. "We knew that this system included the whole world in its aims, and France was only the place of its first explosion." Also like Barruel, Robison saw Masonic lodges as the main venue for this sedition. Himself a Mason, Robison asserted that the irreligious Illuminati had gained control of the structure of the Freemasons and perverted it, bending the Masonic structure to their atheistic aims.

The reactionary nature of these early conspiracists cannot be understated. If the ideas of the Illuminati seemed initially seductive, promising egalitarianism, human rights, and equality, they were all just a front, since the true goal was to seduce the public away from religion: "The aim of the Order is not to enlighten the mind of man," Robison wrote, but rather "to get rid of the coercion which must be employed in place of Morality, that the innocent rich may be robbed with impunity by the idle and profligate poor." Replacing religious authority with secular law had been one of the great innovations of American democracy, but to Robison this swapping of "unjust casuistry" in place of "just Morality" was the beginning of the End.

B arruel's memoirs had yet to be translated into English by the time Robison's pamphlet reached the United States, whose citizens were already turning on each other in a bitter ideological divide so soon after their independence—a feud that helps explain why fears of the Illuminati found such a receptive audience in the early days of the republic. Like the Freemasons, the Illuminati were perceived to be an international organization—their bounds of fraternity or conspiracy exceeded any one nation. And here was the United States, desperately trying to constitute itself as a new nation, a nation that had distinct, identifiable, and nonpermeable borders.

A belief in an international secret cabal pulling the strings behind the scenes not only indicates a lack of faith in one's government and its ability to exert power, it also indicates a lack of faith, on a fundamental level, in a national identity, a sense that all Americans share some inalienable "Americanness" that binds us despite superficial differences. What the Illuminati scare suggests is that this anxiety was with us from the start. No sooner had Americans gone through the Revolution together and forged from their bloody victory the idea of a more perfect union than they had begun immediately to suspect their peers of being subversives, and in doing so revealed that they had no faith in the concept of an indivisible American identity.

As the election of 1800 approached, the New England Federalists (who supported their man John Adams for reelection) denounced Thomas Jefferson and his supporters, whom they believed to be responsible for a rising atheism in the United States, and whom they intimated might be in league with the Illuminati. On July 4, 1798, after Yale president

Timothy Dwight warned that the ultimate object of the group was the overthrow of American government and culture itself, his brother Theodore proclaimed that while he didn't know any actual Illuminati, if he were to hazard guesses, he'd name Representative (and future treasury secretary) Albert Gallatin and Thomas Jefferson.

The New England Federalist's call to arms over the Illuminati echoed up and down the country. Morse's sermons were reprinted as far as Philadelphia and South Carolina, and William Cobbett, a partisan newspaper editor and foe of Jefferson, rushed out a publication of Robison's book in America. Theodore Dwight gave speeches and published articles far and wide accusing Jefferson of being "the very child of modern illumination, the foe of man, and the enemy of his country." While President Adams himself was somewhat skeptical of Morse's paranoia, he nonetheless signed into law that summer a series of bills, the Alien and Sedition Acts. The Sedition Act of that July made clear what was on everyone's mind, making it a crime for any person to "unlawfully combine or conspire together, with intent to oppose any measure or measures of the government of the United States."

Not all of this was received entirely uncritically; anonymous respondents in various newspapers pushed back, demanding proof. In the July 27 edition of the *Massachusetts Mercury*, someone writing under the name "Censor" demanded some evidence for Robison's sources, commenting that, "At this distance, it is impossible to decide on the truth of his assertions, or the respectability of his testimonies." Other detractors, often under other colorful noms de plume like "Trepidus," repeatedly chimed in, trying to cool the heat of Morse and the Dwight brothers' conspiratorial musings as they spread throughout New England.

As a skeptic put it in the May 9, 1799, edition of the *Independent Chronicle*, if Morse had proof, why not go to the government and President Adams instead of putting it in "the alarming narrative in a ninepenny sermon"? Why treat it "in so loose a manner as to render it only subservient to a second or third edition of a political fulmination"?

Perhaps, just perhaps, the writer suggested, this was less an actual conspiracy and more a political ploy to agitate resentment and fear toward Thomas Jefferson's Democrats.

Morse shot back, accusing his detractors of abandoning religion and morality, and, in lieu of actual proof, offering an increasing hodgepodge of circumstantial evidence that did little to convert holdouts. In a move that would in time become familiar, though, Morse announced that he had, in his possession, "complete and indubitable proof that such societies do exist, and have for many years existed, in the United States. I have, my brethren, an official, authenticated list of the names, ages, places of nativity, professions, &c. of the officers and members of a Society of Illuminati." Anticipating Joseph McCarthy by over 150 years, Morse understood that you didn't have to actually manifest proof if you loudly and repeatedly stated that you had it in your possession.

It was easy to see why these New England luminaries, whose origins in Puritan culture had long cemented their religious and governmental power, would be both uncomfortable with anyone attempting to take the First Amendment's separation of Church and State seriously and so were susceptible to paranoia about subversive atheists attempting to overthrow the church. But having successfully stoked the public's fear of the Illuminati's infiltration of the United States, they were perhaps not prepared for how quickly this paranoia was turned against them.

Had the Federalists known, they might have been kinder to a man named John C. Ogden. A little-known and long-forgotten preacher, Ogden had tried for years to establish himself in New England but had been constantly driven out by the established power structure of the Congregationalists in Connecticut and Vermont. By 1793, he had been obligated to leave New England for New York and Philadelphia, pursued by bad debts and ostracized for his abrasive personality. Embittered, he began publishing a series of anonymous articles in the anti-Federalist paper the *Philadelphia Aurora* about a conspiracy he had uncovered.

The New England of Morse and the Dwight brothers may have been publicly against Illuminatism, Ogden argued, but this was all a front: they were in fact secret Illuminati, and it was they—not Thomas Jefferson—who were bent on destroying America's young democracy. Through his anonymous writings, Ogden set out to expose a conspiracy of the "New England System," in which the Congregationalist clergy, led by Timothy Dwight at Yale, controlled New England politics and higher education. Calling Dwight "the Pope of Connecticut," and his new home the "papal palace at Yale," Ogden railed against this "Hydra of clerical despotism," and by November 1799 was referring to the Congregationalist clergy in New England as "The Illuminati."

Dwight and his fellow New Englanders had long preached against the Illuminati because of their irreligion, but Ogden understood that the Illuminati could represent something far more terrifying and primal than simply atheism. Secret societies were terrifying because they presupposed a group of foreign invaders whose motives could never be fully known. Through insinuation, gossip, and rumor, it was easy for Ogden to simply project the accusations the New England Congregationalists had made back at themselves. The *Aurora* was already one of the most powerful and influential newspapers in the country, and Ogden's articles were serialized and spread by dozens of local papers as well, furthering the reach of his voice.

The tight-knit structure of control in New England politics was a mostly secret enterprise controlled by a few wealthy, well-connected individuals, and thus was vulnerable to Ogden's counterattacks. As Ogden's editor at the *Aurora* explained in 1800, Connecticut was governed, in the absence of a constitution, by "certain ancient usages and customs." The most important of these, he wrote, was a hierarchy "directed by a sovereign pontiff, twelve cardinals, a civil council of nine, and about four hundred parochial bishops." Depicting the state's power structure as byzantine, foreign-sounding, and impenetrable was more than enough to cast suspicion on it. The *Aurora*, in other words, was able to use the inherent contradiction between early America's reliance on and distrust of religion to suggest that any religious ceremony, any institution that incorporated religious customs, might very well be a front for the Illuminati.

The smear campaign worked; the "Illuminati" term was bandied about in the Federalist press so often, both as a serious accusation and as an object of ridicule and contempt, that the original sting of the Dwight brothers' and Morse's accusations was effectively lost. And while they had once denounced Thomas Jefferson as being an Illuminati stooge, now Federalists were leveling that same accusation at John Adams, claiming he was controlled by his Illuminati handlers back in Connecticut. That November, Adams lost his bid for reelection. Did Ogden's conspiratorial whisper campaign tip the scales? A bitter, close-fought election, there were too many factors at play to say how crucial the *Aurora*'s part was in all of this. But Ogden had revealed an important lesson about democracy: paranoia, once unleashed, is impossible to control and remarkably easy to turn back upon its source.

The American electoral system had undergone one of its earliest tests, and it nearly failed. Moreover, no one was held accountable or forced to publicly admit their part in the panic. And for the time being, the threat of the Illuminati—a seemingly bizarre footnote, nothing more than an excessive outpouring of emotion best left forgotten—faded from view.

FOUR

"There Is Something Earnest in All This, but the Object Is Concealed"

E ven as writers like Barruel and Robison claimed that Free-masonry had been infiltrated by Illuminism, they were careful not to attack the fraternal organization outright (Robison, af-ter all, was himself a Mason). Masonic lodges had continued to grow and flourish through the early decades of the nineteenth century, and they were still seen as a well-respected cornerstone of American society. How, then, did such an illustrious and generally beloved and trusted organization end up entangled in a murder in upstate New York? What led the Masons of Batavia to turn on one of their own, abducting him in broad daylight, his body never to be recovered? What happened be-tween the founding of the country and the 1820s that so drastically changed the nature of the fraternity, and—ultimately—the public per-ception of it?

A secret society—with its own laws and norms, answerable only to its own members—can only exist in a democracy for so long if those norms are not in line with the rest of the country. And the brand of Freemasonry practiced by the men of upstate New York in 1826 was a far cry from the Freemasonry of Benjamin Franklin ninety years ear-lier. A schism had taken place in the late eighteenth century, with a new kind of Masonry emerging. This new version, paradoxically, called themselves the Ancients, distinguishing themselves from the lodges that Franklin and his peers belonged to, which they dubbed "the Moderns." Arising out of a London order that allowed membership for lower-class men (often Irish), the Ancients had quickly developed their own rites and rituals, claiming to be restoring Masonry to an earlier tradition and accusing Moderns (primarily the men of Franklin's generation) of having forgotten the old ways of Masonry.

But there were more important differences: Ancient Masonry opened its doors to a different kind of member. This was not a Masonry for the aristocratic elite; this was one for the solidly middle-class: soldiers, shop-keepers, and laborers replaced lawyers, landowners, and politicians in these lodges. And whereas Moderns were primarily interested in con-solidating their influence in the powerful cities on the Eastern seaboard, Ancients Masons sought out smaller cities and towns. As a result, the number of Ancient lodges exploded throughout the country and mem-bership rolls increased exponentially.

At least on paper, the goal of the fraternity was still the promotion of virtue. But it was also, now as then, a means of networking and devel-oping social and economic ties. Upwardly mobile men, particularly of the lower-middle class, understood that the fastest way to get ahead was through the lodge. If Modern Masonry had relied largely on wedding itself to established networks of power, allowing a few social climbers in while being mostly concerned with preserving influence among the elites, this new brand of Masonry would be a means for the middle class to flex its muscles.

There was a curious side effect of such a massive increase in Masonry throughout the country. No longer were lodges composed primarily of men from the same class, bound together in maintaining their power. Freemasons were now a much more loosely connected, diverse, and dy-namic bunch. Something was needed to keep them together.

Enter Thomas Smith Webb. The son of a mechanic and bookbinder by trade, Webb rose through the ranks of New England society, establishing himself as a self-made "gentleman." But his more lasting impact was his work to help formalize a series of rituals for use in Masonic lodges, which collectively became known as the York or American Rites (as opposed to the Scottish Rite). Webb thought that the most important aspect of Masonry was its rituals, which would bind brothers together in the strongest manner possible. New rites and rituals allowed Masons to ascend to higher ranks, which meant increasing levels of exclusivity and prestige. (With some degrees costing as much as twenty-five dollars, these rituals also meant increased revenue for the lodges.) His *Freemason's Monitor, or, Illustrations of Masonry* offered a standardized set of rites to help bind American Freemasonry into one coherent, cohesive organization. In ten years, the book went through eight editions and sold sixteen thousand copies—not bad for a secret manual that could not be allowed into the hands of the public.

Webb's rituals were far more elaborate, and esoteric, than anything American Masons had seen before. He added more mystical rites, developing increasingly strange and macabre rituals—the more esoteric, the more taboo, and the more difficult these rites were, Webb reasoned, the closer those who'd participated in them would be bound. The Royal Arch ritual that Webb devised would involve members banging on pots and pans while pushing and shoving the initiate. Another ritual he invented, the Knights Templar degree, involved the candidate drinking wine from a human skull. These were tribulations, meant to be difficult and to push the candidate through suffering to a level of bonding and connection with his brothers. They did not call the brother to an exalted, dispassionate rationality, by which he might assume the mantle of a civic leader for a new democracy. Instead, they were meant to stir and excite one's emotions and passions.

In this increasingly diffuse and enlarged fraternity, Webb's innovations helped forge a sense of communion and connection through rituals of hazing and symbolism that bordered on the ludicrous. Many of these new rites contained what was not much more than incoherent babble, but transmuted through the alchemy of the secret ritual, they took on a momentous importance to the members. The Masonry of the 1820s was thus more dependent on its secrets than previous generations had been, which helps explain why the men of Batavia's Lodge 433 had managed to whip themselves into a frenzy over Morgan's threatened revelations.

H iram Hopkins and Samuel Greene each joined Freemason Lodge 433 for different reasons. Hopkins had come out to western New York in the early 1820s, and soon found out the only way to get elected to local office was through the support of the Masons, which meant joining the fraternity. And being a Mason, according to the oath he subsequently took, meant keeping your brothers' secrets, no matter what ("murder and treason excepted," of course). Samuel Greene had come to Batavia to open up a tavern; as he got to know the town, he saw that both his deacon and his doctor were Masons, and soon enough a friend, Ebenezer Mix, invited Greene to join the Masons. "Little did I dream," he would later recall, that only months after joining up he'd witness events "which would fill the whole land with intense excitement, moral and political, and would bring the institution itself of Masonry almost to the verge of destruction." Indeed, it's not a stretch to say the Freemason Lodge 433 of Batavia, New York, in the fall of 1826 changed the course of American history entirely.

Hopkins proceeded through the three levels of Freemasonry quickly, completing them in a matter of weeks. He then undertook the more difficult task of earning the Royal Arch degree, which came with a different oath: keep each other's secrets—murder and treason not excepted.

Perhaps this level of secrecy was warranted. At the end of the ceremony, Hopkins received the "Grand Omnific Royal Arch Word," which was none other than the very name of God. Surely such a thing is worth protecting. And no sooner had Hopkins joined the exalted ranks of the Royal Arch Masons than he was informed by the brother who'd initiated him that there was trouble afoot in Batavia, and that the Masons may have to take the law into their own hands.

The matter concerned another Mason named William Morgan. Morgan was a veteran of the War of 1812, a bricklayer from Virginia who'd settled down in Batavia. Morgan was a generally well-liked, outgoing member of the community. About fifty years old (with a wife, Lucinda, that was half his age), he was actively involved in Masonry: it was Morgan who'd helped instruct Samuel Greene in learning his rites as he was preparing to take the oaths. Greene would later recall how his wife, listening to the two men from the other room, would remark after Morgan left, "Husband, husband, how can you be so great a fool as to repeat such stuff as that?"

It was perhaps his wife's gentle ridicule that led Greene to gradually disassociate from the Masons; he'd more or less stopped going to meetings, and had resolved to drift away from the organization, when he first got wind of the suspicions around Morgan. Rather than cut ties altogether, he decided to start attending meetings again so he could keep tabs on what was happening and also, he later claimed, so he could do what he could to prevent any violence from happening.

Morgan had become disillusioned with the fraternity in New York, in particular due to the tight grip it had on local power and politics, and he'd resolved to do the unthinkable: publish the group's secret oaths and rites. He'd lined up a publisher, David Miller, and was working on exposing the Masons' secrets for the whole world to see. And the men of Lodge 433 were resolved to prevent this from happening, by any means necessary.

In his history of the Freemasons, Jasper Ridley suggests that the events that unfolded in upstate New York that September reveal something broader about the Masons—that they never were in fact the homogenous group we imagine them to be. The Masons, Ridley comments, "do what they do, not because they are Freemasons, but because of the social surroundings in which they live. British noblemen and members of the Royal Family who became Freemasons continue to behave like British noblemen and members of the Royal Family, just as French, Italian, Spanish, and Latin America revolutionaries who became Freemasons continue to act like French, Italian, Spanish, and Latin America revolutionaries." And, Ridley concludes, "Hoodlums and petty local bosses in the small towns of up-state New York in 1826 happened in many cases to be Freemasons, but they continued to act like hoodlums and petty local bosses in the small towns of up-state New York." To this one can add that when the hoodlums have locked up control of local government, sometimes things get out of hand.

As Samuel Greene would later explain, a curious air of detached conspiracy settled over the lodge that summer. It was clear to everyone what needed to be done, and yet no one could say the thing outright. So conversations, Greene noticed, got increasingly "roundabout and half-enigmatical." The brothers would denounce Morgan as a "wicked and perjured wretch," deserving of those penalties for breaking one's oath, and then someone would chime in and say something like, "all honest Masons would see" that these penalties had to be "executed." Yet no one would come out and say what they specifically planned to do.

"But the most curious talk that went on there was of a broken kind," Greene recalled, with "one man uttering part of a sentence, and another taking it up and carrying it on, and then another, as though, by dividing up the sentence in this way, no one was specially responsible for it." It sounded something like this:

"Should one of your neighbors kill another, and be proved
    guilty of murder in the first degree . . ."
". . . and should he be sentenced by the judge . . ."
". . . to be hung by the neck till he is dead, dead, dead . . ."
". . . do you think the country would lay it to heart?"
"No; would not met rather rejoice that the country was rid of
    the murderer?"
"Morgan has violated the laws of the most moral, benevolent,
    and I had almost said Christian institution . . ."
". . . and should he be taken away . . ."
". . . and executed, would Masons lay it to heart?"
"No; would they not rather rejoice that there could be found
    no track or trace of so vile a wretch as he?"

Conspiracy in the air, the brothers seemed to get a further boost from the governor of New York, De Witt Clinton, himself a Mason. At a lodge meeting, a letter supposedly from Clinton was read aloud, in which the governor ordered them to "suppress the secrets of Masonry at the expense of blood and treasure," and reassuring them that "if you are detected you shall be protected. If you are convicted you shall be pardoned, for I have the pardoning power."

Protected by the powerful, and possessed of a near-religious zeal, they set out to suppress Morgan's betrayal. At first they tried harassment. David Miller was besieged with frivolous legal suits, and Morgan was arrested on Saturday, August 19, on trumped up charges and kept in jail through Monday before being released. While he was imprisoned, Morgan's lodgings were ransacked by those looking for his manuscript. But Morgan and Miller were unbowed, and so, on September 10, arsonists attempted to set fire to Miller's printing office. The fires were quickly extinguished, but by then the Masons were resolved to keep their secrets at all costs.

The morning after the fire, Morgan was arrested once again, this time on a phony charge of a two-dollar debt. Taken to Canandaigua, he was held overnight until a man Morgan had never seen before arrived to pay his bail and have him released. Morgan's initial relief turned to terror as he understood there were worse things than the law—as he was taken from the jail he saw a carriage waiting for him, and he began to scream "Murder! Murder!" as he was shoved roughly inside. It was the last time William Morgan was ever seen alive.

M en like Greene and Hopkins watched this growing hysteria with terror and alarm; they understood both the depravity of their brothers' actions and the grip that Freemasonry held over the community, knowing that they could not publicly denounce these events without being targeted themselves. Hopkins in particular felt torn because of the oaths he had taken; wasn't the breaking of an oath nearly as bad a sin as keeping silent about a murder?

It was hard to say that there even was a murder. William Morgan's body was never found. The conspirators would later hint that he had been driven first to Rochester, and then west to the empty Fort Niagara. Some Masons maintained that he had been taken to the Canadian border and told never to return to the United States, but most privately agreed that he had been killed. This is certainly what Greene was told.

Above all, for Greene, Hopkins, and the others aghast at what had happened, it was important that it not be seen simply as a random mob who'd been excited to some horrible action. Greene stressed that "these men, who were the leaders in this plot against Morgan and Miller, were men of standing and character. They were at the time holding the most important offices in church and state." They were judges and justices, sheriffs and constables, military officers of high standing, religious leaders and politicians. What had occurred was "no mad freak of low and drunken fellows. Everything had been considered and determined upon by the very highest authorities in the masonic councils."

The men named in the original kidnapping—Loton Lawson, Nicholas Chesebro, and Edward Sawyer—were all eventually tried and convicted of kidnapping and spent time in prison, but no one confessed to the murder itself and thus there could be no trial for murder, no final justice for William Morgan. (In a curious postscript, Morgan's widow, Lucinda, would later end up involved in the nascent Church of Jesus Christ of Latter Day Saints, and may have been, though sources disagree, one of Mormonism's founder Joseph Smith's many wives.)

But the absence of a corpse was, in retrospect, a crucial part of what came next. Small societies of amateur sleuths started to form to try to unravel the mystery of what had happened to William Morgan. Groups of concerned citizens began to meet in various towns along the route of the abduction. These "Morgan Committees" were initially only invested in the question of whether or not Morgan (or at least his corpse) could be recovered. But well-placed Masons in law enforcement and public office continually frustrated these attempts, and the Morgan Committee members began to see that the problem was wider than just one man's disappearance. Masons had so thoroughly infiltrated American government—at least at the local level—that they held a monopoly on power, preventing the usual mechanism of justice from working.

Opponents began to speak out more openly against Freemasonry in general. They began to denounce the fraternity as a cult, and as having undue influence. Hidden, behind the scenes, pulling the strings, the Freemasons had distorted American democracy and had to be stopped. Apostates like Hopkins and Greene broke their silence, giving public lectures about the dangers of Freemasonry and secret societies. On July 4, 1928, the citizens of Le Roy, New York, published their "Declaration of Independence from the Masonic Institution." The movement had grown far beyond the question of William Morgan. At stake now was nothing less than the question of democracy itself—could a secret group be allowed to implement its own system of justice?

And this was how America's first genuine third party—the Anti-Masonic Party—was born.

The early years of the republic had seen the rise and fall of the Federalists, and the Democratic-Republican Party of Jefferson split into Andrew Jackson's Democrats and the opposition Whig Party. But the Anti-Masonic party was the first sustained third party, the first organized political movement that spontaneously grew out of a frustration with the two major parties—the Democrats and the Whigs—and their failure to deal with the Masons. (Historian William Preston Vaughn has referred to the Morgan episode as the era's Watergate.)

It was the first major populist crusade, spurred not by politically connected men but in opposition to them. "We are indeed engaged in a fearful warfare, with the wise, the wealthy, and the powerful of the earth," Anti-Mason Joseph Ritner wrote to Albert H. Tracy in September 1829, "and I have little doubt, with the Prince of Darkness himself." Nowadays we tend to treat fears of the Illuminati and fears of Freemasonry as one and the same: both are envisioned as shadowy, secret organizations that manipulate events from behind the scenes. But in the beginning, each of these panics was spurred by completely different motivations. The Illuminati panic, fomented largely by clergymen like Barruel and Morse, and embraced by established elites like Morse and Dwight, was born largely of a concern that the masses could not be trusted with philosophy. Those in power feared what would happen if the traditional loci of power were abandoned, and they saw in the possibility of radical democracy not progress but conspiracy. It was a panic of the elites.

The Anti-Masonic movement, however, was the opposite. The agitators were those sick of the increasingly undemocratic power of the Masons, and the belief that the only way to get ahead in America was through backroom networking at your local lodge. Anti-Masonry was not born, as Richard Hofstadter would claim, of paranoia, and despite the suspicion they had for the Masons, they were hardly an example of what Hofstadter would deem "the paranoid style." It is better to say they were simply responding to the question of what democracy could be and what it should look like.

The movement was a surprising success. One of the first populist uprisings against entrenched interests in America, Anti-Masonry's message resonated among the public. No one had really, up until that point, given that much thought to the Masons' power; it was accepted more or less as a way of life. Now those seeking justice for William Morgan had spurred people to wonder if the Masons truly were a force for good in the country. What the Anti-Masons successfully called into question was the very notion of a social organization. Why did one need a club or a secret group when democracy is best done out in the open? What had seemed second nature to men like Benjamin Franklin was now permanently tainted.

But now, forced to publicly account for themselves, the Masons had little by way of defense. They tried to maintain that their secrecy was mostly harmless, focused on the betterment of humanity, but the actions of Lodge 433 had called all that into sharp question. It turned out to be remarkably easy to cast suspicion on Freemasonry. Whatever secrets they were protecting, outsiders assumed, must be worth killing over. As Henry Dana Ward wrote in *The Anti-masonic Review and Magazine*: "It is impossible, however, that a society should accumulate funds, build splendid halls, command the precious time of the statesman, hold in subservience the pen of the scholar, try the intellects of the orator, gain the support of the divine, and yet be merely frivolous. . . . There is something earnest in all this, but the object is concealed."

Add to this Freemasonry's ambivalent relationship to Christianity—claiming to be in harmony with the religion while maintaining a separateness and developing its own rites and rituals—which led to accusations that the organization was an attempt to undermine religion from within.

As Anti-Masonry spread, parishioners refused communion from Masonic clergy, or stopped attending services conducted by Masons altogether. Masonic membership plummeted over the course of the decade; enrollments were cut nearly in half, and almost no new lodges were opened. Where it had once been an asset to be a Mason in America, it now became a liability. Within a few years, the Anti-Masonic Movement had grown to the point where it ran a candidate for president in the election of 1832. William Wirt did not stand a realistic chance of winning the White House, of course, but it marked a major shift in public opinion that such a candidacy could exist at all.

Anti-Masons did more than just end the power and influence of the Masonic fraternity in the early nineteenth century. They also set the template for how a reform movement would work. Even as the formal party flamed out, their goal of undermining Freemasonry largely succeeded. Never again would the fraternity have the same levels of acceptance. It had gone from being seen as a benign organization, one at times even vital to the new republic, to a shadowy organization that, no matter what it did subsequently, could never fully rid itself of the suspicion of outsiders.

On an early day in May, I set out to trace William Morgan's fateful last journey. Virtually nothing is left standing out here from 1826, so at first I had little sense of what I was doing, other than driving through a series of small towns in upstate New York. The only destination I had in mind was the Batavia Cemetery.

It was midday by the time I arrived and, hungry, I went first to the Pub Coffee Hub across the street from the old cemetery. My barista Harley told me what he could remember of the story—he learned it growing up in Boy Scouts, the kind of thing that gets told over the campfire, and while he didn't know all the details ("He was a journalist, maybe?"), the story seems to still circulate. We talked about whether or not the Masons are a shadowy group of conspiracists or just a bunch of old men; Harley was inclined to believe the latter, but then said to me, "I suppose if you have secrets, everyone has to cover for everyone. So I can see how it might get out of hand."

Harley suggested I check out the men's clothing store on Main Street next to the pizza place, which is in a former Masonic building. How much of the lore and mystery of the Masons comes from this simple fact: that the buildings endure, that the stone lingers, the symbols embedded in façades that never wear away. Some of our fascination with the Masons comes from the fact that they embedded their symbols into buildings at a different time, and those buildings have become culturally distant while being physically present. These are not the same kind of structures as Stonehenge or the Great Pyramid of Giza, ancient constructions whose meaning and purpose can seem at times wholly alien to us. The Masonic buildings are recent enough to not be entirely mysterious, yet are culturally unfamiliar. Conspiracy theories often arise in such a space, from the anxiety caused by our estrangement from the middle past.

It's not just the men's clothing store in Batavia—as I continued my drive following Morgan's fatal last journey, I kept seeing lodges, both former buildings that have been repurposed or those still in active use. A rickety wooden building in Stafford off Route 5, with a small plaque indicating it was once a lodge; a seemingly still-operating lodge in Caledonia with a hair salon tenant; a physical therapy office in Lima whose building still reads MASONIC HALL in large letters.

The Olive Branch Freemason Lodge of Le Roy, New York, is a little bit off the main route, so I pulled into the parking lot to have a look around. Nearly two hundred years ago, the citizens of this town had published their "Declaration of Independence from the Masonic Institution," and perhaps that's why the current lodge is much newer; its look was plain, with nothing but utilitarian brick and siding. As I was about to leave, a truck pulled up and an older man in a Mason cap got out.

He'd seen me taking pictures, and now he eyed me suspiciously, asking if he could help. Steve told me he'd been a Mason for forty years, that it was the best thing he'd ever been a part of. When I asked him about the various conspiracy theories surrounding the Masons, he told me bluntly, "Don't believe everything you read on the Internet. If it's negative, it's probably written by someone who was rejected for one reason or another."

Then I asked him about William Morgan and the cenotaph in the Batavia Cemetery. At the mention of the name, Steve visibly stiffened. There was a long pause, before he said at last, "I don't know what to tell you." His voice was almost trembling. "It's an entirely honorable organization."

Not long after that, he excused himself, and I got back in my car to continue my drive. The timbre of his voice stayed with me, though. It had been almost two hundred years since William Morgan's disappearance, but up here, those wounds still seemed quite fresh.

PART TWO

Deep-Laid Schemes

When the familiar political landscape, with all its party loyalty and logrolling compromise, has been reflected in chiaroscuro, even the most innocent shapes have assumed an ominous meaning.

—David Brion Davis, *The Slave Power Conspiracy and the Paranoid Style*

FIVE

Mysteries of Iniquity

I n a place like Manhattan, there's always something waiting just below the surface. Collect Pond Park, a small green respite in lower Manhattan, seems initially unremarkable—one more small municipal park in a massive city full of them—but it boasts a particularly rich history, its past full of notorious events that have accrued over time like sediment. Once home to a Lenape village, the Dutch and English settlers used it as a source of recreation and a community hub in the seventeenth and eighteenth centuries, until its waters became so polluted it was hastily filled in during the early 1800s. It became, in quick succession, a real-estate boondoggle, a slum (the notorious Five Points), and the site of the Tombs, Manhattan's elaborate prison complex. Today, the Tombs has been replaced by the more modern Manhattan Detention Complex, and Collect Pond Park is surrounded by court buildings and office complexes (city hall itself is nearby). A block away is another park named for Thomas Paine, who detested slavery and helped give voice to the early idea of America as a home of liberty, and Lorenzo Pace's mammoth black granite monument, *Triumph of the Human Spirit*, erected in 2000 to memorialize the 427 unknown and anonymous enslaved people whose remains were excavated here in 1991.

Nearby, the towering façade of the supreme court building reads
THE TRUE ADMINISTRATION OF JUSTICE IS THE FIRMEST PILLAR OF
GOOD GOVERNMENT. But nowhere in Collect Pond Park will one find
mention of the thirty-four people executed here during the summer of
1741. Thirty Black men and four whites were hanged or burned alive
during a year of mass panic and hysteria, mostly on hearsay and coerced
testimony. The Salem witch trials were still living memory, but Massachusetts would be outdone by New York in its feverish search for
conspiracy and subversion.

The trouble began with an ordinary robbery. On the night of February 28, 1741, three enslaved men named Prince, Cuffee, and
Caesar robbed a shop near the East River docks, making off with jew-
elry and other items that they fenced at a tavern owned by John and
Sarah Hughson. They were quickly found and arrested, their trial set
for April. Meanwhile, though, strange fires began to break out all over
New York City: the garrison at Fort George, where the governor's house
was, caught fire on March 18, and more fires soon followed.

George Clarke, the governor, didn't think much of it at first. "For
some time after the fort was burned," he later recalled, "I had no other
thoughts of it, than it was an accident." But as more fires broke out,
rumors began to spread. Slavery had already been banned in Spain's
colonies, but occasionally Black Spaniards were kidnapped and sold
into slavery in the British colonies, and there were whispers that the fires
had been started by such men as revenge for their loss of freedom. It was
also possible that the fires had been set to commemorate an earlier slave
uprising in 1712, since the first fire fell on the anniversary of that earlier
event.

New York City at the time was as close to a literal tinderbox as a city
could be. The city's buildings were unusually tall by contemporary
standards, reaching to four and five stories, and made of wood and

thatched roofs, vulnerable to fire both deliberate and accidental. Fire was a regular and almost unremarkable (if often tragic) fact of life. It wouldn't be until the end of the eighteenth century that the city would outlaw wood construction in new buildings and begin to work toward an infrastructure solution to an infrastructure problem. But in the absence of fixing the problem, accusations of conspiracy worked to deflect attention.

By the time Prince, Cuffee, and Caesar went to trial for burglary, there were strong suspicions that they were somehow involved in the fires, now universally believed to be deliberate arson. Daniel Horsmanden, one of the trial judges, had already concluded that "some villainous Confederacy of latent Enemies amongst us" were behind them. Eventually, he found a witness who, under threat and coercion, testified that the three burglars had conspired with the tavern owners John and Sarah Hughson to burn down the entire city of New York.

Hughson and his wife, Sarah, were soon arrested, but the arrests didn't stop there, and by the time Caesar, Prince, and Cuffee (who Attorney General Richard Bradley referred to at one point as "Monsters in Iniquity") were executed at the Collect Pond for the burglary, they had already been implicated in a much wider conspiracy. In the end over a 150 people were arrested, and over eighty confessed to involvement in an absurd plot: Hughson supposedly had gathered dozens of enslaved people at his tavern, served them a lavish feast, and then made them swear an oath of secrecy before revealing his plan to overthrow the governor and install Caesar as the new ruler of New York.

By the summer's end, thirty-four people had been executed, including a random Anglican priest accused of secretly being a Catholic and the mastermind behind it all. ("The Old proverb has herein . . . been verifyed," wrote Horsmanden afterward. "That there is Scarce a plot but a priest is at the Bottom of it.") As he went to the gallows protesting his innocence, the plot had been foiled and the natural order had been restored. All it took were the deaths of nearly three dozen people.

Most had been hanged, but several had been burned alive and Caesar had been gibbeted, his body left to rot as a warning to all would-be conspirators and to encourage others, in Horsmanden's words, "to unfold this mystery of iniquity."

But what actually did happen? Jill Lepore, attempting to make sense of it in her book *New York Burning*, focuses on an event Horsmanden had kept out of the trial record: Three years before the fires, the same three men who had committed the original burglary had also robbed a distillery and made off with a quantity of gin. Calling themselves the "Geneva Club," they were ridiculed in the press as "Black Freemasons."

Masonry was new and still largely a mystery to many. Suppose, Lepore suggests, that Hughson and his friends read these reports of his friends being labeled Black Freemasons and took up the idea of a secret society as something of a joke? "Maybe Hughson found Masonry ridiculous," Lepore suggests, "fancy gentlemen in ruffles wearing artisans' aprons and swearing oaths of spooky secrecy, and mocked it mercilessly, parodying Masonic rituals and pledges." Perhaps Hughson really did ask others to take an oath—not as a deadly serious rite but as a frivolous joke. It would explain, for example, why numerous enslaved people confessed to the strange, almost offhand way that Hughson had invited them to join his conspiracy. Perhaps there was no conspiracy, just a joke that carried on too long, and eventually reached the notice of those who failed to recognize it as such. "The plot," suggests Lepore, "was, essentially, a prank that grew out of proportion."

The story of the Insurrection Panic of 1741 in New York City goes a long way in explaining how Americans had begun to understand secrecy. As evidenced by how savagely authorities came down on a rumor of a secret meeting of enslaved men, Freemasonry and Hughson's parody of it make clear that the question of who was allowed to meet in secret was a tightly controlled matter. While white, propertied men could gather in private, fraternal groups, lower-class whites and Black men— particularly those enslaved—could not. The country was already using fears of secret societies to demarcate the relationship between public and private: who could have a private life and who could not. Who could enjoy the freedoms of democracy, and whose lives were to be open and subject to public scrutiny at all times.

Nearly a hundred years later, this same ground became the site of a major riot that ran through Manhattan like an arsonist's fire. The Collect Pond had long since been filled in, and the area was now known as the Five Points. Local landmarks included the once-spectacular Chatham Garden Theatre, which had fallen into disrepute before it had been leased by Lewis Tappan, an ardent abolitionist whose brother Arthur would become the first president of the American Anti-Slavery Society. Lewis Tappan converted the theater into the Chatham Street Chapel, where abolitionist preachers spoke and Black congregations gathered.

In July 1834, riots sparked by white agitators in response to the Tappan brothers' abolitionist work broke out here, starting at the Chatham Street Chapel before spreading out in all directions. For five days a riot raged, one that seemed in retrospect surprisingly well-organized (couriers passed handbills between various segments of the mob to keep them abreast of latest developments, and sentries were posted to warn the violent throng of approaching cops). Private residences of Black New Yorkers were destroyed, as were churches that ministered to them (along with white targets, as the mob's fire continued to look for new fuel), and only the arrival of the 27th Infantry finally ended the destruction.

Arthur Tappan espoused a belief in Slave Power, a malevolent conspiracy by which a small cabal of enslavers had taken control of the American government and were perverting democracy to serve their ends. In 1850, Tappan warned that if California were not allowed to enter the Union as a Free State, the Slave Power would "secure its permanent ascendancy on the North American continent," a success that would be a "triumph of evil, involving the subjection of North American interests to the aristocracy of the South, and a mighty empire to the various curses attendant upon human bondage." It was a belief shared by ardent, fire-breathing abolitionists like Tappan and journalist William Lloyd Garrison, as well as more mainstream politicians like Abraham Lincoln. As William Goodell, the Abolitionist Party's presidential candidate in 1852, described the conspiracy theory, it involved the question of "whether civil government shall serve and protect human rights, or whether a ruthless despotism, displacing civil government (properly so-called) shall be wielded by the Slave Power for the subjugation of freemen." The conspiracy issue wasn't just a question of the rights of the enslaved; adherents to the Slave Power thesis saw their own personal civil liberties as freemen—their rights to exercise free speech, and to hold their elected representatives accountable to them—all at risk under this regime of collaborators whose fealty to profiting from slavery threatened to destroy the very principles of the country. White Northerners, many of whom believed that slavery should have died out of its own accord decades earlier, instead saw its pernicious spread creep slowly westward, and increasingly turned to this conspiracy theory to make sense of what was happening.

Nor would this be the last riot fed by conspiracy theories to consume the Five Points in the years before the Civil War. In 1857, riots broke out here between two notorious street gangs, the Bowery Boys and the Dead Rabbits. The Bowery Boys were still smarting over the loss of one of their great heroes, William Poole, better known as Bill the Butcher, whose last words were famously reported as, "I die a true American." Skirmishes between the Irish Dead Rabbits and the anti-immigrant Bowery Boys broke out first on the evening of July 4, 1857, and by the next morning had exploded into one of the largest gang wars New York had ever seen. Hundreds of participants overwhelmed the cops sent in to break them up, laying waste to each other and much of lower Manhattan before nightfall and the militia arrived.

The Bowery Boys were the violent arm of the Know Nothing Party, a nativist organization that had appeared from nowhere to dominate American politics in the early 1850s. The Know Nothings operated under the conviction that America had been infiltrated by a secret network of Catholics, who bore ultimate allegiance not to the laws of the country and the Constitution, but to the pope in the Vatican. While there had been anti-Catholic conspiracy theories in America since Protestants first colonized the land here, they had long been abstract, more opposed to the idea of Catholicism than Catholics themselves, since their numbers were few.

The Know Nothings, also known as the American Party, famously got their name from their secrecy; when asked about their allegiance, they were instructed to reply that they "knew nothing." It was, in other words, a secret conspiracy that sprung up to combat what it perceived as a secret conspiracy. And for a brief moment in the 1850s, the movement reshaped the American political and cultural landscape.

These three conspiracy theories—that enslaved Americans were on the verge of overthrowing white America; that enslavers had infiltrated the government and subverted the will of the people to serve their selfish, immoral needs; and that Catholics were working to undermine democracy and destroy the cultural foundations of American Protestantism— each consumed different parts of the American public in the decades leading up to the Civil War. Each involved more than just political differences or racist attitudes, and instead theorized that one's ideological and racial opponents were part of a massive conspiracy, a secret cabal whose aim was the end of American democracy itself.

At the time, the United States was a country defined by three internal contradictions: it wanted the land of its indigenous population but it did not want the people themselves; it wanted the labor of enslaved Black Americans but did not want their participation in civic life; and it wanted the labor of Irish and German immigrants but did not want their culture. The United States, in other words, had become untenable:

the move to expand westward ran straight into the desire to balance out a nation split in half by slavery; compromise followed compromise, a perpetually more complicated series of trade-offs that satisfied fewer and fewer stakeholders. Increasingly, Americans sought narratives that would explain away these hypocrisies and contradictions, that would offer a clear and convincing narrative to explain these decisions not in terms of the sausage making of politics, but as a grand struggle of Good versus Evil.

These three conspiracy theories were intertwined and have to be seen together. Even though the anti-Catholic paranoia of the Know Nothings may seem a mere sideshow when compared to the conspiracies surrounding slavery, it is an integral part of the story of the events that led to the Civil War. For one, Know Nothings and others opposed to immigrants were actively courted by both pro- and anti-slavery factions, each attempting to fold the nativist narrative into their own.

Through the 1830s and 1840s, these beliefs often found expression in show trials and mass executions, riots, and moral panics. By the 1850s, though, the various brands of paranoia had given birth to two new political parties and had overtaken a third. Through the decade, culminating in the presidential election of 1860, voters were asked not whether they believed in conspiracy theories, but rather which candidate's conspiracy theory most closely matched their own worldview.

SIX

"Do Not Open Your Lips"

E ven today, no one is even sure precisely where the name originated. Some have traced it to an account from 1839, when a
young Black man was caught "lurking" around the Capitol in
Washington, D.C.—when asked how he got there, he said that he had
been sent North by a "railroad which went underground all the way to
Boston."

Through a loose network of formerly enslaved and free Black Americans, along with their white allies, thousands of enslaved Americans made
their way north in the decades before the Civil War, moving sometimes
surreptitiously, sometimes out in the open, on railways and ships, in wag-
ons and freight, toward freedom. It is impossible now to know for certain
how many people made their way out of slavery on the Underground
Railroad; as with Freemasonry, both supporters and detractors had an
investment in embellishing its impact. In the North, abolitionists drama-
tized the plight of those seeking refuge and to play up their own heroic
efforts. In the South, enslavers argued that the Underground Railroad
was nothing short of a grand conspiracy of subversive lawbreakers—the
higher the numbers, the greater the threat to the country.

There was never a literal railroad, but the term stuck because it resonated with strange grace and radiance. Wherever the term came from, once America had seized upon it, it became a powerful metaphor. There were "stations" and "conductors"; Jermain Loguen, who'd escaped slavery and made it to Canada in 1834, returned regularly to Syracuse, New York, to help others, raising funds by referring to himself as a "depot on the Underground Railroad." A group of enslaved people held in prison in New York City were slated to be returned to the South when they were broken out by a group of abolitionists; the papers at the time reported that the underground railroad "runs directly under the prison in New York, and . . . the slaves let themselves down through a stone trap-door into one of the cars."

But it wasn't just the idea of a railroad—there was also the underground. Tucked back in a small neighborhood not far from the Brooklyn Bridge, among rows of expensive brownstones, is Plymouth Church, which became known as the "Grand Central Depot" of the Underground Railroad, for its prominence in the abolitionist cause. There, Henry Ward Beecher held "mock slave auctions" to raise money to buy emancipation, and fugitives were brought there on multiple occasions. Plymouth Church (architecturally unchanged since its founding) has no closets or offices in the main church, nor does it have an attic; all it has is a simple basement, consisting of a series of low brick walls and archways. Lois Rosebrooks, who led tours of the church for decades before her retirement in 2015, says that though we can't say for sure, if fugitives were hidden in the church on their way to safety, it would have likely been in the basement.

The first half of the nineteenth century was a time of increasing interest in the subterranean. It was a hidden world, where nothing was as it seemed and everything was a front for a criminal organization. The whole city was just a cryptogram waiting to be decoded. The most popular book in the country in 1845 was George Lippard's serial novel, *The Quaker City: or, The Monks of Monk Hall.* Part of a new genre of "city mysteries" novels, it portrayed a secret world of villainy, where a criminal underground operated out of a literal underground catacomb beneath the titular building. Monk Hall is described as a "large and magnificent mansion," ostensibly a private residence, but within its doors, young professionals—law students, doctors, merchant's clerks—are enticed with gambling and prostitution, gradually becoming ensnared in a criminal web run by the novel's archvillain, Devil-Bug. Below Monk Hall's three-story façade is a three-level basement, each floor separated by hidden trapdoors, leading further into the depths of depravity.

The surface world was not to be trusted, and ordinary explanations no longer sufficed. In the decades leading up to the Civil War, everything was connected, nothing was as it seemed. The newly urban world demanded an eye that saw beyond surfaces and sought out hidden networks. The Underground Railroad was just one more subterranean plot, one more secret network of lawbreakers chiseling out the foundations of the country. As the nation found itself unable to avoid a confrontation over slavery, this paranoid vision shaped that narrative, too. Those who sought their freedom, Southerners believed, did not work alone, nor were they capable of imagining liberty for themselves without being controlled by their abolitionist puppet masters.

If there was a single term to describe the mood in the South in the years leading up to the Civil War, it was "paranoid." Southern enslavers feared abolitionists, and they feared those they enslaved. They lived in a state of perpetual terror, albeit one that could never be openly referenced. The "peculiar institution" depended on a peculiar kind of denial, one in which the grossly unnatural condition of bondage had to be misrecognized as a benign, divinely sanctioned institution. Southerners reassured themselves that they treated the people they kept in bondage well, and, as such, the enslaved had no cause to complain, and were even happy in their lot. The absurdity of such a position only reinforced its absolute necessity.

Contrary to the stories enslavers would tell themselves, that Black men and women were happy being enslaved, escapes were so common that printers sold stereotype "runaway slave" icons to newspapers to be used in classified ads by enslavers. There was even a "medical" term for the desire to escape: *drapetomania*. The reality was obvious everywhere you looked, but no one could name it outright. As a result, the South became infused with, and ultimately gripped by, conspiracy theories— conspiracy theories that were born out of attempts to explain away this obvious discrepancy. If enslaved people were naturally happy being in bondage, as Southerners anxiously tried to tell themselves, then their desire to run away must be the result of external provocations.

In an 1835 speech, future president and Virginian John Tyler captured much of the prevailing sense of paranoia and fear of the day. "The unexpected evil is now upon us," he cried; "it has invaded our firesides, and under our own roofs is sharpening the dagger for midnight assassination, and exciting cruelty and bloodshed." Men like Arthur Tappan and William Lloyd Garrison had perverted the post office to their ends, and they hid behind religion in an attempt to foment anarchy. With an abuser's logic, Tyler argued that abolitionists were not "friends" to enslaved Americans but their "enemies," since their agitations drove enslavers to crack down harshly on those in bondage. Even worse, for Tyler, was the number of women who seemed to have joined the crusade: "woman is to be made the instrument of destroying our political paradise, the Union of these States," he lamented; "she is to be made the presiding genius over the councils of insurrection and civil discord." For not only were women joining the abolitionist crusade to divide the Union, they were indoctrinating their children, so now "the youthful imagination is filled with horror against us and our children by images and pictures exhibited in the nursery."

Tyler's tirade (along with many other similar outbursts) was in part driven by massive technological advances happening during the time that had dramatically changed the landscape. The introduction of the steam engine to printing presses allowed for a new proliferation of periodicals, including (but of course by no means limited to) anti-slavery texts. The American Anti-Slavery Society was distributing 122,000 pieces of literature in 1834; a year later, that number had increased almost tenfold, to 1,100,000. Using mailing lists provided by sympathizers and the postal service, Garrison and Tappan could wallpaper the South with abolitionist arguments. Southerners couldn't understand how such a "mere handful of obscure persons" (in Tyler's words) could disseminate so much material, and ultimately decided that there must be money coming from abroad, alleging that foreign saboteurs were in league with abolitionists. (This, of course, wouldn't be the last time a new technology would spur a flood of new conspiracy theories, as evidenced by the proliferation of paranoia brought on by the Internet and social media.)

Rather than see this printing innovation as proof of American ingenuity, slavers took it as proof of subversion; any attack on them was an attack on the United States itself. W. W. Sleigh's *Abolitionism Exposed!* conceived of America as "the cradle of republicanism," and as such a bane on the existence of European monarchies, who stirred up abolitionism dissent from afar to bring down democracy. Unlike Tyler, Sleigh suggested that American abolitionists were in fact "actuated by the purest motives of doing good to all," but were being manipulated by "some crafty, designing persons . . . behind the curtain." Either way, though, proponents of slavery accused abolitionists and their allies of bringing factionalism into American politics, sowing discord as an attempt to bring down the Union, and implicitly reaching back to Washington's Farewell Address, which had explicitly warned of such troubles.

And this is why the idea of the Underground Railroad became so powerful. On the one hand, it's fair to say that it *was* a secret, subversive society, dedicated to breaking the law and overturning the United States Constitution. William H. Seward spoke for many when he said that "there is a higher law than the Constitution." Complying with the Fugitive Slave Act, abolitionists like him believed, conflicted with the "laws of God." But while a veteran of the Underground Railroad would later describe it as a "deep-laid scheme," it's not wholly accurate to describe it as a secret society; it was more a loose network of like-minded figures working, sometimes independently and sometimes in tandem. There was no central organizing committee or enduring structure; at its height it was never more than a semi-ad hoc network of loose confederates, all united behind the same ideal. It was safer this way, anyway; a highly centralized group could have easily been brought down, whereas a guerilla network of unconnected cells stood a much more robust chance of persevering. The idea of a highly organized system of tunnels, codes, safe houses, and networks is mostly a fiction, but a useful one.

This organization was its strength, and its limitation. For one thing, the secrecy—while necessary—also put an upper limit on what could be accomplished. Because anti-abolitionist mobs broke up meetings, chased down lecturers, and destroyed property, much of this work had to be clandestine; Anthony Lane, treasurer of the New York Vigilance Committee, later recalled that they "dare not" advertise their meetings publicly, since fugitives often attended, and thus meetings could have been easy targets for slave catchers. Such secrecy often hampered fundraising and prevented the kind of widespread coordination that Southern conspiracy mongers assumed was happening.

But even when offered the chance for a more robust conspiracy, abolitionists rejected it. John Brown had at one point proposed a fortified series of underground railroad depots that could be used for a massive, sustained operation of emancipation, but sharing his idea with trusted sympathizers gained him little support. What abolitionists wanted was less a highly coordinated and organized network than the idea of such a thing, something that gave them common cause and purpose. Among these disparate and loosely affiliated actors, the concept of the Underground Railroad gave a concreteness to an otherwise ad hoc and fragmented group.

But it also had the side effect of allowing for an imaginary villain among enslavers, a shadowy organization of lawbreakers, to which one could attach all manner of conspiracy theories. As with the Illuminati, the less directly visible the Underground Railroad was, the more work it could be accused of accomplishing behind the scenes. And by shifting the focus from the problem of America itself to some kind of phantom attacker, they could hope to provide a cause that all (white) Americans needed to unite behind. Virginia secessionist Edward Ruffin lamented in 1857 of the "ability of the abolitionists to operate on our slaves, to infuse discontent, and to seduce them to abscond, or to rebel. . . ." There were "organized associations for stealing slaves, and exciting insurrection and massacre," he warned, that "have now every facility to enter the country, and to sojourn wherever they can best operate." No Northerner could be trusted, since any "pretext of business is enough to serve to account for their presence; and there is no neighborhood in the Southern States into which Yankees have not penetrated." Similarly, William Henry Drayton of South Carolina wrote of abolitionist "conspirators, at their midnight meetings, where the bubbling cauldron of abolition was filled with its pestilential materials, and the fire beneath kindled by the breath of the fanatics. . . ." And the *Mississippian* worried of how "the conspiracies detected among the slaves in Tennessee, Kentucky, South Carolina, and Texas show that the vile emissaries of abolition, working like moles under the ground, have been secretly breathing the poison of insubordination into their minds."

Again and again, conspiracy theories about secret societies became a way to massage these hypocrisies and smooth over their prickly surfaces. Perhaps the hypocrisy was not with slavery. Perhaps America itself was fine, but some subversive element had gotten in there, twisting the facts and confusing the weaker brained. Perhaps what seemed like a contradiction was only the machination of wily abolitionists, stirring up trouble.

If Southern forces were amplifying rather than downplaying the effectiveness of the Underground Railroad, it was in no small part because it gave them freer license to implement anti-American crackdowns and administer extralegal violence. It also allowed them to massage their own cognitive dissonance. America's founding—as a nation of democracy and liberty where men and women were forcibly kept in bondage—involved a hypocrisy so rank it could never be fully acknowledged outright and could only be approached obliquely. Conspiracy theories—particularly those involving secret, subversive societies—were absolutely essential as one of many tools that enslavers and their sympathetic allies used to avoid confronting the country's original sin.

Southern leaders regularly used conspiracy theories surrounding slave insurrections to attempt to curtail First Amendment freedoms. In 1829, a Black clothing dealer named David Walker authored a pamphlet titled *An Appeal to the Colored Citizens of the World*; when a parcel of sixty copies showed up in a Savannah warehouse that December, there was an immediate panic and ensuing crackdown. It hardly mattered that most enslaved Americans were illiterate; the presence of the pamphlet and other abolitionist materials led to severe restrictions on what could be mailed through the post office and distributed in the South. Such conspiracy theories were hardly spontaneous, inchoate eruptions of emotion. They were deployed to achieve specific aims, often thought through well in advance. In the North, where enslavers could not control the post office or the press, they turned to sympathetic Democrats to instigate mobs and riots. Georgia Democrat John Forsyth wrote to presidential hopeful Martin Van Buren in 1835 with just such a request, suggesting that "a little more mob discipline of the white incendiaries would be wholesome. . . . and the sooner you set the imps to work the better."

The main goal of these conspiracy theories seemed to have been twofold: to reassure Southern enslavers that what they were doing was morally right, and to justify any act of violence or suppression necessary to maintain slavery. Such seemingly anti-American crackdowns on free speech in the South could only be logically maintained if they were cast as a reaction to an anti-American subversive element. In cases where those in power felt the need to suppress such inconvenient thought, the question was how to do this without seemingly reneging on that promise of free speech and open debate. Whispers of subversive societies offered the best and most expedient way of accomplishing this; alleging extra-democratic instigators whose speech was simply out of bounds allowed for suppression without fear of cognitive dissonance.

These conspiracy theories were a durable and omnipresent aspect of Southern culture during slavery. But to what extent were they motivated by the reality on the ground? How typical were the events that took place in Charleston, South Carolina, in 1822, when the freed carpenter Denmark Vesey was accused of masterminding a savage, murderous conspiracy that almost took place?

On May 25, 1822, Peter Prioleau, an enslaved person in the house of Colonel John Prioleau, went to his friend, a free Black man named William Pencil, concerning a strange interaction: another man had approached him and told him he was a member of a secret group: "We are determined to shake off our bondage," he told Prioleau, "and for this purpose we stand on a firm foundation. Many have joined, and if you go with me, I will show you the man, who has the list of names, who will take yours down." Prioleau was afraid and uncertain what to do; Pencil advised him to tell his master about this supposed plot.

At first, authorities failed to take these whispers seriously—the white community was incredulous that their beloved, "well-treated" people they enslaved could be conspiring to liberate themselves. Gradually, though, a violent conspiracy was unearthed: a group of Black Charlestonians, both enslaved and free, had been conspiring for months, perhaps years, to launch a violent insurrection: on July 14, those enslaved who were working in houses would rise up and murder their enslavers, while fires would be set throughout the town. As white people fled into the streets, they were all to be murdered: the men, the women, the children.

The conspirators had acquired a large store of weapons and incendiaries, as well as white powdered wigs that they planned to use to disguise themselves as whites to further sow chaos in the conflagration. Entreaties had been made to the government of Haiti regarding safe harbor for the insurrectionists. As the plot was uncovered, authorities discovered that the mastermind was an unlikely figure: a freed Black man named Denmark Vesey.

Vesey had been born into slavery in the Caribbean but had bought his freedom when he was in his early thirties after winning a lottery in Charleston. He established a prosperous trade as a carpenter and himself as a local community leader. Respected among the whites in Charleston, he was a singular figurehead in the Black community: he spoke multiple languages and helped found an African Methodist Episcopal church, which became one of the largest Black congregations in the country. Vesey had his freedom; he could have left the United States for Haiti or elsewhere. But he believed in liberation; according to one of his conspirators, Vesey had told them "he had not a will" to leave America; he wanted to "stay and see what he could do for his fellow creatures."

It would cost him his life. In a rushed and secret trial, the accused were swiftly tried and convicted; on July 2, six men were hanged, including Vesey. None had confessed to insurrection and each maintained his innocence. As July wore on, more people were rounded up, tried in haste, and convicted; by the time the panic had subsided, sixty-seven men had been convicted of conspiracy, thirty-five had been executed, and thirty-one more were deported.

In 1964, historian Robert C. Wade published a reconsideration of the events of 1822 and suggested that, just as with Salem in 1692 and New York in 1741, the Vesey conspiracy was largely a fiction, imagined by a hysterical white population terrified of the very people they'd held in forced bondage, who wanted an excuse to pass more draconian laws preventing public gatherings by Black Carolinians. As with the 1741 trial, we only have a record that is clearly biased and paranoid, and so the tendency is to assume that there was no conspiracy, and that everything was the fiction of feverish minds. But this reappraisal has not held up to contemporary scrutiny. Historians have carefully debunked Wade's hypothesis, and reconstructed the severe lethality of Vesey's plot. While it is clearly the case that the conspirators' guilt was steamrolled through a kangaroo court, it also seems to be the case that, more than likely, they were in fact guilty of a planned conspiracy.

While America has birthed a seemingly endless series of moral panics based on scant evidence, Lenora Warren, a scholar who studies abolitionism, insurrection, and the politics of resistance, notes that slave uprisings were in fact quite common, along with smaller forms of guerilla action that were constant. And yet insurrection—even famous ones like Vesey's—has largely disappeared from the public record.

There's a reason we default to the Salem witch trials as the paramount moral panic of American history—because we can unequivocally reject the superstition over witches and fears of paranormal activity, it's easy to tell that story as one lacking any moral ambiguity: the men and women executed in 1692 were innocent, and the trial is a singular travesty of justice. Slave insurrections, though, are different, in that they both were occasions for wild hysteria, moral panic, and outsized reactions by a white justice system, while at the same time being actual instances of violence by enslaved Americans against their tormentors.

As Warren notes, it was largely the abolitionists who were invested in playing down the reality of slave insurrection. If there was a real threat of violence, white Northerners (even those opposed to slavery) assumed Southerners were justified in using physical restraint and even corporal punishment. And so in order to heighten the barbarism of such tactics, abolitionists took to portraying enslaved people as docile and harmless, unable or unwilling to fight back or stand up for themselves. (One of the most iconic anti-slavery images of the period, the Wedgewood Medallion, shows a supplicant slave on his knees in prayer, a picture of Christian piety and nonviolence.)

But that meant, Warren explains, "making insurrectionists into monsters," because abolitionists could not afford to talk about insurrections "as having political efficacy." As she writes in her book *Fire on the Water: Sailors, Slaves, and Insurrection in Early American Literature, 1789–1886*, insurrectionist violence would remain "a conundrum for the abolitionists by displaying evidence of the slaves' innate savagery, and bolstering pro-slavery arguments against emancipation." Fundamentally, Warren argues, the South was a landscape not of chattel slavery—that is, one where there was a stable equilibrium—but rather one of constant war between victor and captive. There was never a moment at which enslaved people were not looking for liberation, and never a moment when they didn't feel that the violence done to them did not merit an equal response. Insurrection and conspiracy were a viable and appropriate response from the very moment of bondage. Denying the reality of slavery as constant warfare, and of conspiratorial uprisings as a constant guerilla engagement in this war, allows space for slavery to be somehow considered a natural state of affairs, which, of course, it never was. Rather, it's more accurate, Warren argues, to say that the "conditions that produce insurrection isn't this sort of various gradations of depredation and violence, but it is the act of being enslaved itself." The denial of this fact created in the South a kind of perpetual hysteria, where Southern leaders were constantly both downplaying insurrection while obsessing over it.

What can appear from a contemporary lens as conspiracy theories and paranoia may not be the best fit for what happened in the South under slavery. "The problem with terms like 'conspiracy theorist' or 'terrorist' in applying them to slave insurrection," Warren told me, "is that if you are an enslaved person, there is no such thing as paranoia, and the assumptions you're making about your life or the fears you have are valid." On the other side, though, for enslavers "there's a certain logic in being afraid of the people you are oppressing. And so the unnaturalness of that relationship collapses these things on themselves."

One thing a history of secret societies and conspiracy theories reveals is how much of American history simply *cannot be known*, because it is, itself, secreted away. At the heart of the story of Denmark Vesey is silence. Both Vesey and one of his chief conspirators, Peter Poyas, were both recorded as saying to their condemned comrades, "Do not open your lips; die silent as you shall see me do." Vesey denied his executioners the satisfaction of a confession, something they could use to complete their narrative of insurrection (so, too, had the first men executed in the 1741 panic, Caesar and Prince, dying as they did "very stubbornly"). But Vesey also refused to offer a protestation of innocence, something that abolitionists and later historians could have used to depict him as a meek martyr.

As with Horsmanden's record of the 1741 panic, the judges involved in executing Vesey and his comrades wrote a heavily biased trial record. Lionel Kennedy and Thomas Parker, both magistrates on the city court, coauthored a manuscript entitled *An Official Report of the Trials of the Sundry Negroes, Charged with an Attempt to Raise an Insurrection in the State of South-Carolina*. But within a few years of its publication, it was withdrawn, and whites who owned copies were advised to destroy the book. A Northerner staying in Charleston before the war inquired about the book to her hosts, and was told, she later recalled, that "the only copy in the house, after being carefully kept for years under lock and key, had been burnt at last, lest it should reach the dangerous eyes of slaves. The same thing had happened, it was added, in many families." Even the official record—the one that sought to erase his voice entirely—itself had to be eventually erased. There is something about Vesey's story, it seemed, that was so threatening, so terrifying, that even propaganda could not shape and control it.

SEVEN

In the Convent's Crypt

I t is one thing to be in a very old building, to feel the weight of history in its beams and rafters, how it sighs with age at every step. It is quite another to be on the spot where there was once a great building of consequence, where now barely a trace remains. The Gold Star Memorial Library in Somerville, Massachusetts, faces Broadway, a major thoroughfare that still connects this small city to Boston and Cambridge. Flanked by restaurants, cell phone stores, and barbershops, it's a small building the size of a post office, and easy to miss. On the grounds of the library is a prominent granite memorial dedicated to "the veterans of world wars." There is a smaller granite monument in the garden in memory of "Cate Weaver, who loved literature and treasured books." One has to seek out the third granite stone for the only indication that something happened here in 1834. Sitting off to the side, it reads simply:

PLOUGHED HILL
FORTIFIED AND BOMBARDED IN 1775–1776
SITE OF URSULINE CONVENT
FOUNDED 1820 AND OPENED 1826

BURNED 1834

HILL DUG DOWN 1875 TO 1897

ERECTED BY

MT. BENEDICT COUNCIL NO 75

It's a strange name, "Ploughed Hill"—a hill that's been ploughed, a place name testifying to its own erasure. But this is perhaps fitting: in a city known for meticulously preserving its history, it seems almost intentional that there's so little to be said about what happened here. Boston is a city that prides itself on a spectacular riot, the Boston Tea Party, and yet another great riot on August 11, 1834, when the Catholic Ursuline convent on Mount Benedict was burned to the ground, barely merits a mention.

As with slavery, anti-Catholicism had been fundamental to the founding of American democracy. America was built on a kind of philosophical aversion to Catholicism, a sense that the religion was inimical to what the founders were trying to accomplish. But in the decades leading up to the Civil War, anti-Catholic attitudes exploded, becoming a question of national obsession. Immigration trends had been steady for the first few decades of the United States' history, averaging around 10,000 a year, but in the late 1820s and early 1830s, this number began to grow, exceeding 50,000 new immigrants a year by the mid-1830s. This number continued to shoot up at an exponential rate, ultimately peaking in the 1850s, when 1854 alone saw more than 400,000 new immigrants. The majority of these were Irish and Germans, and native-born Americans saw the demographics of their cities begin to shift in unprecedented ways; before long, cities like Chicago, New York, and Detroit had more immigrants than native-born Americans. But it was more than just the number of new arrivals; America's long-standing attitude toward welcoming foreigners began to strain as the number of new Catholics began to outpace that of Protestants.

This rapid shift led to a new focus on, and eventual distrust of,

Catholicism. It gave way to a paranoia that was no longer merely an intellectual discussion about what did or did not make a good citizen; "Catholic" was now a rumor and a slur that permeated all levels of American culture. Conspiracy theories that arose in reaction to this shift cannot be seen as a sideshow or a diversion from the question of slavery and the paranoia that swirled around it. Rather, anti-Catholic conspiracy theories, which were obsessively framed around the threat of white Protestants finding themselves "enslaved" at the hands of the pope, were a means of preserving a sense of white unity as the question of actual slavery continued to drive apart the country. Anti-Catholic conspiracists repeatedly used the fear of Catholic mind control to shift the discussion away from slavery—while whites might disagree on whether or not Black Americans should be enslaved, they could all agree that none of them wanted that fate for themselves.

Anti-Catholic conspiracies also became a template for a moral panic that remains with us today. The dangerous, trans- and homophobic attacks of recent years that accuse the LGBTQi community (and their political and cultural allies) of being "groomers" is itself virtually unchanged from the anti-Catholic attacks of the 1830s. The target is new (but still, as it was then, a vulnerable minority) but the slander is the same: a cabal of sexual deviants are attempting to gain control of the education of young people. Making sense of conservative pedophilia accusations leveled at the Democratic establishment at large, both from fringe actors like QAnon and its proponents (including Congressional representative Marjorie Taylor Greene), begins with what happened at Ploughed Hill in 1834.

M uch of seventeenth- and eighteenth-century political thought revolved around a central question: Was it possible to have a community without some kind of sovereign force—God or a king—enforcing people's behavior? Political philosopher Mark Lilla calls this

"The Great Separation": an attempt to divorce politics from theology, and to find a way to imagine political participation that wasn't ruled by a divine authority. Democracy was conceived to be that answer.

Catholics, Protestants feared, could not be trusted to participate in representative democracy, since they were taught to defer to religious authorities. Rather than act as autonomous citizens making an informed decision about which politicians or policies they'd support in the public sphere, it was feared they had an ingrained tendency to act as a bloc in accordance with the wishes of the pope. (This "philosophical" aspect of anti-Catholicism, which targeted not the individuals so much as the idea that people could be controlled by a religious authority not bound by American sovereignty, helps explain why it was so easily repackaged in more recent times against Muslim immigrants and the specter of Sharia law.)

Representative of this kind of "philosophical" anti-Catholicism was someone like Texas senator Sam Houston, who stressed a belief in freedom of religion while at the same time suggesting that Catholicism was incompatible with democracy. "We make war upon no sect," he said in November 1855, while also asserting the need to resist "the political influence of Pope or Priest." More fundamentally, he wondered aloud, "Are not their doctrines opposed to republication institutions?" One only had to look at Mexico, Houston went on: "The Mexicans have expelled despotism, why are they not free? Because priestcraft rules, and civil liberty is subordinate. There is no freedom where the Catholic Church predominates." Houston seemed to believe genuinely in the idea that Catholicism was by its nature inimical to the Jacksonian democracy that he championed, where virtuous, disinterested men made decisions in the best interest of the people, free of corruption or foreign influence. Such leaders could only be chosen by those trained in the principles of republicanism, and he favored a twenty-one-year naturalization period for immigrants, which would, he argued, be enough time for them to shed their knee-jerk subservience to foreign religious leaders.

Gradually, this political need to conceptualize Catholics as somehow "other" took on a concrete form: an increasing obsession with the convent. In the first decades of the nineteenth century, city mysteries like George Lippard's *The Quaker City* became more and more popular: they imagined a subterranean world beneath the surface of the city, a place of crime and debauchery behind false fronts and down hidden staircases. This genre soon included a popular series of books—some purported to be memoirs, some pure fiction—involving convents. Books, including Scipio de Ricci's *Female Convents: Secrets of Nunneries Disclosed* and Richard Baxter's *Jesuit Juggling: Forty Popish Frauds Detected and Disclosed* (among dozens of others), all detailed a nightmare world of women in bondage, lecherous priests, and unwanted infants murdered and buried in cellars.

In these "memoirs," the convent was revealed to be not a place of piety and devotion but a secret den of illicit sex and infanticide. George Bourne's novel *Lorette: The History of Louise, Daughter of a Canadian Nun; Exhibiting the Interior of Female Convents* described the convent as "the *sepulchre of goodness*, and the *castle of misery*. Within its unsanctified domain, youth withers; knowledge is extinguished; usefulness is entombed; and religion expires." Nor was this attitude relegated to fiction or sensationalist faux memoir; it was accepted fact. "Convents," the Harrisburg *Herald* reported in November 1854, "are the very hot-beds of lust debauchery."

Conspiracy theories always breed strange architectural imaginings. It starts with something like the rumors of illicit sex between priests and nuns, and from there the allegations of unwanted pregnancies. But there are no children around, so the infants must have been murdered. Where are the bodies buried? You start to imagine deeper catacombs, hidden structures, sub-basements, and labyrinths—or else how to explain the lack of evidence of your conspiracy theory? The idea of the subterranean, the house with secrets—all this becomes an architectural necessity to explain where the dead are hidden.

These books were popular because they were both titillating and moralizing. They could promise a world of illicit sex and fantasy while at the same time decrying such a world. For all their lurid detail, there was a heavy hand to the moral worldview here. There was a fear, after all, for the women educated in such environments, even if they weren't Catholics. Scipio de Ricci told his readers that the "sole object of all monastic institutions in America is merely to proselyte youth of the influential classes of society, and especially females; as the Roman priests are conscious that by this means they shall silently but effectually attain the control of public affairs." The convent was a space distinct from the home, and thus an affront to the role of Protestant woman as a mother and wife.

Part of the essential American narrative that had developed in the early days of the Republic was the notion that American women were perpetually under threat. They were not granted participation in American democracy, of course, but still they were envisioned as the keepers of democracy itself, since it was their job to raise sons and inject values into them. This is what scholar Linda Kerber has called republican motherhood: the complicated way in which women were held up as the vessels of American ideals even as they were denied access to political power. As such, those worried about secret subversion often fretted about the susceptibility of women to moral decay and degeneration, and assumed that foreign conspirators would target them as the key to bringing down America itself.

What might have begun in the eighteenth century as philosophical anti-Catholicism—the idea that Catholics were not prepared to be citizens in representative democracy, and that in fact religious authority was incompatible with American democracy altogether—gradually gave way to a nativist bigotry that saw Catholics as foreign invaders, direct subjects of the pope in Rome, who would bring about sexual immorality and the degradation of the family.

It was only a matter of time until these salacious rumors and simmering xenophobia burst forth into something tangible.

The Ursuline convent had opened in 1820, and quickly established itself as a leading school for the young women of Boston's elite. But it was far from the city center, across the Charles River, and it rose up on Mount Benedict, where it loomed over its neighbors, mostly brick-makers and other working-class laborers. Protestant and wary of elites, these neighbors struggled with the Ursuline nuns, particularly the mother superior. Sister Mary Edmond St. George (born Mary Anne Moffatt) had repeatedly clashed with her neighbors, and was known for her fierce, independent attitude. As one John Buzzell would later say of St. George, "She was the sauciest woman I ever heard talk."

These local tensions were fueled by the rise of national anti-Catholic sentiment, and by the flood of lurid bestsellers about sexual depravity in nunneries. So when, on the night of July 28, 1834, a woman named Elizabeth Harrison (also known as Mary John, who had taught music there for twelve years) fled the convent and took refuge with a local neighbor, the community were quick to see confirmation of their deepest suspicions. Harrison was taken to her to her brother in Cambridge, and there, distraught, she said that she didn't want to return to Mount Benedict. But within a few hours, Bishop Fenwick had arrived and was able to comfort the young woman, convincing her to return. The next morning, she went back to the convent willingly, but some claimed that she had said she would only stay for a few weeks.

Years of anti-Catholic fearmongering now had a narrative to cling to: a young woman being held against her will by a haughty mother superior who refused to submit to male authority. Rumors and distortions swirled around Harrison's condition. On August 8, a local newspaper ran an article headlined "MYSTERIOUS," relating the story in brief but ending on a suspicious note: "After some time spent in the Nunnery, she became dissatisfied, and made her escape from the institution—but was afterward persuaded to return, being told that if she would continue but three weeks longer, she would be dismissed with honor. At the end of that time, a few days since, her friends called for her, she was not to be found, and much alarm is excited in consequence." That same weekend, Lyman Beecher (father of Harriett Beecher Stowe and abolitionist Henry Ward Beecher) delivered a series of anti-Catholic sermons in Boston, and though he would later claim he had no influence on the events to follow, it was clear that there was something in the air.

The decision to riot seemed to have developed rather leisurely. There was some genuine concern about Harrison's status, it seems, but that was mingled with a long-simmering resentment toward these women who seemed to look down on their laboring neighbors. Men in the neighborhood began to talk openly of securing Harrison's rescue and burning down the convent. Placards and posters appeared throughout the city that read:

> GO AHEAD. To Arms! To Arms! Ye brace and free the
> Avenging Sword unshield! Leave not one stone upon another
> of that cursed Nunnery that prostitutes female virtue and
> liberty under the garb of Holy Religion

A week before the riot, local farmer Alvah Kelley was asked if there was a plan to attack the convent; "in a cool deliberate manner," Kelley replied that if Mary John was not "liberated" from her confinement within a few days, the entire nunnery would come down.

When enough time had elapsed, neighbors increased pressure on both the convent and on local officials for proof that Harrison was alive and unharmed, having convinced themselves she was being held against her will or worse. Early in the evening on August 11, the mother superior allowed several groups of prominent men a tour of the convent; they found nothing amiss and Harrison apparently happy and fine. Satisfied, the group prepared a report to this effect to be published in the papers the following morning. But by the time it was published, the Ursuline Convent was a smoking ruin.

After the fact finders had left, a crowd had built. By eleven o'clock they had lit several barrels of tar on fire in a neighboring field to provide ready incendiaries and torches. St. George, sensing what was in the offing, threatened the rabble, telling them "the Bishop has twenty thousand Irishmen at his command in Boston who will whip you all into the sea," but this only infuriated them. Around midnight, they stormed the convent; after making sure the nuns and their pupils had all been evacuated, they ransacked the place, in search of the hidden crypts where the bodies of infants were buried, and in search of what they assumed would be Harrison's corpse.

As it became clear law enforcement was going to make no effort to put down the mob, the scene turned carnivalesque; John Buzzell broke into Fenwick's retreat and draped himself with the bishop's vestments. They broke into the crypt, looking for the infant corpses of unwanted pregnancies or the body of Harrison herself. Disappointed in their search, they instead satisfied themselves by overturning a few of the coffins, desecrating the remains inside. Finally, they set the convent on fire. One of the nuns, Louisa Whitney, would later describe the mob's cheery violence as the work of "amiable ruffians"; the *Christian Examiner* would describe the scene as "a sort of diabolical frolic, as if such an atrocity were no more than the kindling of a great bonfire."

Having destroyed the nuns' homes, the rioters seemed to think they had acted philanthropically. The morning after, some of the men told Whitney, "We've spoiled your prison for you. You won't never have to go back no more." Whitney was incredulous: "The general sentiment of the mob seemed to be that they had done us a great favor in destroying the Convent, for which we ought to be grateful to them."

It was a cognitive dissonance born of years of conspiratorial musings and distortions. American Protestants had come to see Catholicism as a cryptic rite not unlike the Illuminati: an organization that not only worked in secret, but which demanded complete fealty and worked to disrupt traditional values of family and male authority. Its rites were bizarre to outsiders: mystical and bordering on the occult.

In the wake of the riot, multiple men were arrested, but they would face no serious punishment. There was a widespread acquiescence to what had happened, and it marked the beginning of a more serious turn in America's anti-Catholic history. Anti-Catholicism became increasingly mainstream, and an increasingly successful political position. A book supposedly by an ex-nun, Maria Monk (but actually written by a group of Protestant preachers, including the nephew of Timothy Dwight), *Awful Disclosures of the Hotel Dieu Nunnery of Montreal*, yet another pornographic morality tale, appeared soon after and became the best-selling book ever published in the United States—a title it would retain until *Uncle Tom's Cabin* appeared in 1852.

The following year, two enormously successful books would appear: Lyman Beecher's *A Plea for the West* and Samuel F. B. Morse's *Foreign Conspiracy Against the Liberties of the United States*. Both appeared in 1835 and both were reprinted several times over the next two decades. (Morse's had originally appeared pseudonymously as a series of articles in the *New York Observer*, but after their success he came forward as the author and collected them in book form—it became a national bestseller and went through seven editions over the next two decades.) Both books warned that Protestant America was on the verge of being caught unawares ("We must awake, or we are lost," writes Morse; "this giant nation sleepeth and must be awaked," offers Beecher) by a new George III: the pope in Rome. America's increasing obsession with Catholic conspiracy theories was just getting started.

EIGHT

Fresh from the Loins
of the People

When moral panics arise, they need an outlet. If the courts are on the side of the paranoid, as happened in Salem in 1692, the fire quickly becomes a legal farce, with innocent people rounded up, tried on flimsy evidence and convicted and often executed. When those in the grip of a moral panic do not have access to the courts, however, they turn to riots. Contrary to Martin Luther King, Jr.'s famous comment that the riot is the language of the unheard, the riot can also be the language of the powerful. Many of the anti-abolitionist riots in the North in the decades before the Civil War were instigated by and composed of middle-class merchants, manufacturers, and professionals (just as many of the participants of the January 6, 2021, insurrectionist riot on Capitol Hill were real estate agents, small-business owners, and other prosperous members of the white middle class).

Curiously, though, while a moral panic that has the support of the legal system will almost inevitably go no further than a frenzy of trials that eventually runs out of scapegoats and winds down, riots are almost always just the beginning. Having made their voices heard through violence, rioters gripped with a moral panic will often attempt to translate that energy into direct political action. And they are often successful in the short term, particularly with despoiling the status quo and upending existing political parties. It's only when such movements try to establish durable, lasting political power that they stumble.

In the 1850s, an unspoken question began to circulate among many American nativists: Could the raw and terrifying power that drove the Ursuline Convent riot be transformed into a political party? Nativist sentiment had continued to pulse in the background of American culture long past the events of 1834. A riot here or there simply wasn't enough. What was needed was a way to channel this rage, this xenophobia, this excitement, into a durable locus of power.

Answers began to appear in the form of strange codes in places like Philadelphia, where, in 1854, one could find pieces of colored paper cut into specific shapes littered on the sidewalks like confetti. Sometimes they were squares, or perhaps diamonds, cut from posters and handbills. Sometimes cryptic messages would be published in local newspapers, such as this one, which appeared in *Philadelphia Telegraph* on April 22, 1854:

K N—iv—iii—7 — 10

o———o

What were they? Notices for the most secret of secret societies, so secret that even the name suggested obfuscation: the Know Nothings. The name came to stand in for a variety of smaller nativist groups, some of whose names changed regularly (all of which would eventually merge into what became known first as the Native American party and, after 1855, the American Party). But it was as the Know Nothings—a name that simultaneously suggested ignorance and deep obscurity—that they were best known.

Lurking in the background as a murky secret society, the Know

Nothings began drastically reshaping the political landscape in 1852, and emerged as a full-blown political party in 1854, notching electoral successes throughout the country: the governorships of eight states and the mayorships of cities such as Boston, Philadelphia, and Chicago, along with thousands of other state legislators.

There are any number of theories as to how the Know Nothings rose to power so quickly, seemingly out of nowhere—a bizarre, fringe group that suddenly overtook America. Their slogan, "Americans must rule America," was directed specifically at immigrants, whom they argued lacked the intellectual temperament to participate in representative democracy. But their focus was Catholics: "We are not now contending against foreigners, but against the principles of Roman Catholicism and its devotees," one Know Nothing newspaper explained. They described Catholicism as a "canker-worm," capable of turning a "free, enlightened and independent" United States into a country "enthralled, ignorant, and debased." The Know Nothings welcomed those opposed to slavery, Temperance crusaders, and those fed up with corruption, but more than anything else, anti-Catholic nativism was the core of the movement.

Their chief criticism of Catholics was the belief that they took their marching orders from a foreign power—the pope. "It is the constant plotting of these Jesuitical craftsmen that we resist," one Know Nothing explained, since their goal was "to unite Church and State, and render both subservient to the nod of the Pope." Republican democracy required an informed citizenry, educated and capable of making informed decisions. Blind subservience to a hierarchy of leaders flew in the face of this principle. And yet, the great strength of the Know Nothings came from their organizational structure, and the mandate that all members vote for candidates decided upon by the organization's leadership. In their history, then, one can tease out the evolution of America's incredibly complicated relationship to secret societies and paranoia about conspiracy, and how increasingly reactionary movements began to mimic the supposed threats that terrified them.

The Ursuline Convent Riot had been the first overt expression of anti-Catholic nativism, and in the years since then Catholics had been coming to the United States in even greater numbers. More violence was inevitable. But in addition to riots and mob brutality, nativists began to look to political organizing to find a means of blunting Catholic influence in America. The first seeds of a nativist political movement arose in 1839, when New York governor William Seward learned that Irish families were keeping their children out of schools that used the King James Bible instead of the preferred Irish Catholic Douay-Rheims version. Seward tried to allow the formation of parochial schools, so that Catholic children could at least get an education, a move that prompted a strong anti-Catholic backlash. The American Republican Party, founded in New York by nativists in 1843, called for mandating the King James Version of the Bible in all American schools, as well as a twenty-one-year probationary period before an immigrant could vote. A year later, the Order of United Americans was formed "for the purpose of more effectually securing our country from the dangers of foreign influence," with specific goals that included keeping the King James Bible in schools. Its start was not auspicious. As the nascent political movement spread, it soon reached Philadelphia, where religious tensions ran hotter than in New York; in July 1844, a riot broke out so violent it left even those New Yorkers with anti-Catholic tendencies mortified. George Templeton Strong wrote upon learning the news that "I shan't be caught voting a 'Native' ticket again in such a hurry," summing up the general feeling as the American Republican Party's support collapsed.

But while nativism remained too toxic for mainstream party politics, it continued to build throughout the country, nurtured in an increasingly friendly climate for conspiracy theories. More and more they became acceptable rhetorical moves to explain the country's contradictions,

particularly when they involved the projection of internal American con-
flicts onto external, foreign forces. Just as Augustin Barruel had turned
to the foreign, Bavarian Illuminati to explain what had happened in
France, American nativists used fantasies of meddling by Rome to explain social and economic ills within the country. As the pressures of
the slavery question drove deeper into the American consciousness, the
need to transfer that anxiety onto outside agitators grew stronger. One
Bostonian wrote to Charles Sumner in May 1854 that "this Catholic
power is felt to be at the North a more dangerous power than the Slave
Power and therefore absorbs all other considerations."

The Order of United Americans had been a largely public organization, but in 1850, a New Yorker named Charles B. Allen founded a new
nativist group, the Order of the Star Spangled Banner, which would
quickly cannibalize the OUA and become the boldest attempt yet to
control American domestic policy through a secret organization (it was
Allen's group that would eventually form the nucleus of the Native
American political party). Allen's Order of the Star Spangled Banner,
which he himself only ever referred to as "the council," "the Order,"
the "wigwam," required absolute secrecy and absolute loyalty—you could
not admit that you were a member. If you were asked about it, you replied that you Knew Nothing.

Lodges met in secret, either in halls rented from existing fraternal
organizations or under false pretenses, such as in the guise of Temperance meetings. Induction rituals were stolen almost entirely from the
Freemasons, with the exception that Know Nothings could not be a
Catholic or be married to one. A prospective candidate for membership
would enter the anteroom of the lodge's meeting place and would there
be asked if he believed in a Supreme Being, if he was at least twenty-one
years old, and if he had any connection to Catholicism. He would then
swear an oath to secrecy and be required to swear that he would only
vote for native-born Protestants, "to the exclusion of all foreigners and
aliens, and Roman Catholics in particular, without regard to party pre-

dilections." Having passed these tests, he would enter the inner sanctum, and then take another oath swearing to abide by all decisions of the lodge's leadership, before being taught a series of secret codes, handshakes, and other signs.

The initial purpose of this organization, according to one leader, was not to put forward candidates themselves but rather influence outcomes and ensure favored candidates won. In this, they were wildly successful. In 1854, New Hampshire, Massachusetts, Rhode Island, Connecticut, New York, and Kentucky all elected politicians aligned with the Know Nothings to statewide office. Texas, Maryland, Delaware, Virginia, Georgia, Alabama, Mississippi, and Louisiana also elected Know Nothings. In congressional elections, Know Nothing–backed candidates won fifty-one House seats, including all eleven seats of Massachusetts's delegation. Their success depended not just on the moribund nature of the existing Democrat and Whig parties, but their secrecy. Chambersburg, Pennsylvania, was so solidly Whig that the opposition Democrats often did not bother to field candidates. But in 1854, the Whigs were defeated by a Know Nothing slate that had not been publicly known to exist before its sudden win. In San Francisco, Know Nothings swept the city elections only three months after forming their first lodge. In Philadelphia, the Democrats were confident of victory until the Whig candidate for mayor, Robert T. Conrad, began adopting a Know Nothing platform, and handily beat his Democratic opponent. "I take it for granted that hereafter, no foreigner or *Catholic* can be elected to any office in this city," complained one bitter Democrat.

The success of the Know Nothings had to do with their appeal among the middle class. While there were some attracted to the Know Nothings as a result of economic anxiety—people who saw cheap immigrant labor as a threat to their own livelihoods—the group attracted plenty of middle-class professionals as well. Skilled workers—carpenters, machinists, shipwrights, engineers, and so on—along with merchants and manufacturers made up the bulk of the ranks of Know Nothing lodges, whose general demographic profile skewed slightly more well-off than the general population. They were by and large not wealthy, but nor were they poor—they were relatively well educated and economically secure. It is a common misconception about subscribers to conspiracy theories that they are uneducated—a convenient narrative that sidesteps the real issues. The initial narrative surrounding the coalition that elected Donald Trump in 2016, for example, was that his supporters were working class and subscribed to his racist and paranoid beliefs out of "economic anxiety," but subsequent polling revealed that a third of Trump voters made over $100,000 a year.

The Know Nothings also drew heavily from those opposed to slavery, either on moral grounds or because Northern farmers had a hard time competing with the large-scale operations of Southern plantations. And then there was the Kansas–Nebraska Act of 1854. The compromise had been engineered by Stephen Douglas, who wanted to push through the transcontinental railroad; in order to get Southern support for Kansas's and Nebraska's statehoods, he agreed to repeal the Missouri Compromise barring slavery above the Mason–Dixon line. The move, in turn, enraged Northerners aghast at the further encroachment of slavery and the increasing power of Southern slaveholders. In Philadelphia, one of Conrad's supporters claimed it was not just nativism that brought him victory: "It is [an] *anti-Nebraska, anti-Catholic triumph,*" wrote the Harrisburg *Herald.*

The Know Nothings capitalized on the anger of the Kansas–Nebraska Act—quickly outpacing both the established Whigs and the upstart Free Soil parties to become the main political vehicle for opposing Southern slave power. But abolitionists recognized that throwing their lot in with the Know Nothings meant subordinating what they perceived as the real crisis of America to one they considered at best a distraction. "This election," one writer lamented after the Know Nothing successes of 1854, "has demonstrated that, by a majority, Roman Catholicism is feared more than American slavery." Just when white men were "beginning to see how slavery was mixed up with all their concerns," wrote another, "there 'comes cranking in' this new Agitation, frightening honest people out of their wits with fears of the Pope."

Anti-Catholic bigotry helped deflect and displace the root problem of American democracy: what to do about slavery. It did so in part by relying heavily on the rhetoric of slavery itself. Literature from Maria Monk's *Awful Disclosures* to Lyman Ward Beecher's *A Plea for the West* described Catholicism as an "enslaving" force, something that would render its victims entirely subjugated to the whims of the pope.

Threaded through this was a more generalized anti-establishment sentiment: one that rebelled against established politicians, established church leaders, and established Slave Power. They sought in their political candidates someone who was, in the words of one Know Nothing, "fresh from the loins of the people—a mechanic—able and jealous of the religious hierarchy of Rome."

Because they were not their own party, the Know Nothings had success electing Whigs, Democrats, and independents; in some contests, the winning slate would be a hodgepodge of party affiliations, as the Know Nothings separately evaluated each candidate and chose the one most aligned with their nativist views. "Democrats have been elected in some of the strongest Whig counties, and Whigs from Democratic counties," a writer in the Harrisburg *Keystone* explained that October. In Boston, Jerome V. C. Smith was elected mayor with the largest popular vote ever cast in a mayoral race; the *Boston Post* noted that his base was "composed of as many colors as Joseph's coat—abolitionists, free-soilers, Whigs, 'Native Americans,' a few democrats etc." It was, the writer griped, "one of the most reprehensible coalitions" ever assembled.

Principally, the Know Nothings emerged as an organization devoted to combating what they perceived to be another secret group. Though the nativists feared a religious sect that operated in secret without having to answer to the general public about their aims and motives, the Know Nothings themselves operated in strict secrecy. Just as nativists feared that Catholics voted as a bloc, doing what they were told without thinking for themselves, the Know Nothings, too, demanded strict allegiance on voting matters. This hypocrisy did not go unnoticed; Whig politician Charles Francis Adams was among many who detested the Know Nothings for their structure, declaring that the "essence of the secret obligations which bind these men together" was nothing less than "immoral, anti social, and unchristian—productive of nothing but fraud, corruption and treachery." But it worked. As one Democrat complained to James Buchanan: "These 'Know nothings' act in perfect concert, it would seem, but where they meet, or how they are organized, no one can tell."

The Know Nothings' success came in part from the malleability that secrecy conferred: without a public face and public policies, they could adapt themselves from state to state, tailoring their message as needed. In the North, lodges leaned heavily into their anti-slavery plank, as well as their anti-immigrant policies; Southern Know Nothings, on the other hand, pushed Temperance issues and concerns about corruption.

This fluidity powered their success and their mystique. Until May 1854, membership had been relatively stable, but that year the ranks of the Know Nothings soared from fifty thousand members to over a million by October. Not just a movement or a political party, it was also a pop culture fad: stores hawked Know Nothing candy and tea, Know Nothing cigars, even Know Nothing toothpicks and soap. The popular *The Know Nothing Almanac and True Americans' Manual* offered information on eclipses and tidal cycles, alongside scaremongering about immigrant crime rates and advertisements for anti-Catholic literature. Newspapers rushed out exposés attempting to unmask the group, play up their bizarre antics, and pin down their policy positions. But the controversy only drove their success as a reaction to politics as usual, and the media circus only increased: that same year, a clipper ship named after the group was christened in New York City.

Once in power, they had surprising legislative success; in Massachusetts and Connecticut, newly elected Know Nothing governors disbanded several state militias that were composed primarily of immigrants; Maine passed a law prohibiting immigrants from making up more than a third of any state militia. Massachusetts and Maryland also formed "nunnery committees" to inspect convents for secret sexual misconduct (the Massachusetts committee ran into scandal, predictably, when it was revealed that the chairman was himself engaging in sexual impropriety, using taxpayer money to pay for his mistress's lodgings). They imposed literacy tests and tried to wrest property away from the church, mandating that church holdings be governed by a board of trustees instead of the bishops themselves. The only major policy they fell short on was the institution of a twenty-one-year period between naturalization and voting, the most radical of their goals. But even the Know Nothings were not immune from politics as usual, descending into intraparty bickering and scandal that reminded voters that they were little different from the Whigs or the Democrats.

The anti-party had now itself become a party, and there the troubles of the Know Nothings (now reorganized officially as the American Party) began. Attempting to build on their regional successes to win the presidency, they faltered and fell apart. Organized as a fraternal organization built around a series of networked lodges, there was no central party apparatus, and no easy way to scale up from local successes to national victories. A national convention in Philadelphia in June 1855 turned out disastrously as delegates compromised on the question of slavery, enacting the same kind of backroom dealing on a party level that voters detested in Washington, D.C. While nativism had provided the heat that drove much of the Know Nothings' early successes, the more sustained and vexing question of slavery continued to assert itself; as North Carolina politician, Whig-turned-Know-Nothing Kenneth Rayner, lamented in June 1856, "the cursed question of '*slavery*' is at the bottom of all our troubles."

There's only so far your tentacles can spread without a public platform. The *New York Herald* had marveled in 1855 that "Know Nothingism presents the phenomenon of a powerful party without leaders . . . a splendid army without so much as a single field officer." But leaderless armies do not win wars, and the decentralized nature of the Know Nothings—borne of their desire for secrecy—put an upper limit on their ability to seize power. They could not offer a unified message without a visible leadership structure, and they could not enforce message discipline when anyone could claim the mantle of a secret fraternity.

The status of the Know Nothings in 1854 offers a good data point for understanding the limits of power even the most effective secret societies can actually have on democratic politics. At some point, secrecy becomes a hindrance: it allows for false rumors to spread and it impedes organizing. For all the conspiracy theories surrounding Freemasons, or secret cabals of Jews, able to pull the strings behind the scene, the closest historical analogue to such a scheme is the Know Nothings, who had unexpected but distinctly limited success in using secrecy to advance a series of political goals. But such success could only be measured by the reach of individual lodges and word of mouth. To be fair, in 1854 that reach was still far, but it was not far enough to reach the White House. To control the nation, the Know Nothings needed to unite under a common banner, one visible enough to attract new adherents, and one public enough that its message could not be distorted by rumor and lie. And in coming out, the Know Nothings imploded.

The Know Nothings would also embody a core contradiction that would limit the national effectiveness of such movements. Like others who would come after them (the Klan of the 1920s and the Trumpist wing of the Republican Party), the Know Nothings wanted two contradictory things simultaneously. They wanted the anarchic freedom that came with riots, embracing a destructive and bacchanalian liberation. But they also wanted political power, to be part of the establishment, to be insiders while retaining an outsider status. This contradiction turns out to be a great way to seize power but a terrible way to hold on to it, and the Know Nothings couldn't hope to replicate their successes of 1854.

Lastly, the Know Nothings suggest that scapegoats and conspiracy theories can only get you so far. When America was gripped in a legitimate crisis brought on by slavery, anti-Catholic conspiracies worked for a time to distract the public and to project internal divisions on to external foes. Journalist Charles A. Dana succinctly captured the growing mood of the second half of the 1850s when he wrote in 1854 that "neither the Pope nor the foreigners ever can govern the country or endanger its liberties, but the slaveholders and slavetraders *do* govern it, and threaten to put an end to all government but theirs."

Successful as an agitation, they could not seize the mantle of governing, and in a few short years they were eclipsed by another party—Abraham Lincoln's Republicans—who were far more effective at mobilizing conspiracy theories for political ends.

NINE

A Piece of Machinery,
So to Speak

Was the Slave Power conspiracy really a conspiracy? Was there, in other words, a secret, organized plot by enslavers that operated behind the scenes to dominate and control American politics and shape the nation's history? And was such a belief driven by paranoia, or was it a simple recognition of the structure of the antebellum United States?

By the mid-1850s, the Slave Power conspiracy had become a defining belief among abolitionists, Free Soilers, and others opposed to slavery. Northerners came to believe that America would have long ago achieved its promise as a pure and united beacon for liberty had it not been for an organized cabal of enslavers who kept their thumb on the scale of justice and secretly pulled strings to their own benefit. Further, this cabal's manic love of slavery didn't simply deprive Black Americans of liberty; slavery was so vital to them that they were willing to trample on the rights of non-slaveholding whites. This was more than just a moral or philosophical disagreement; it was a totalizing conception of the nation's history as a whole, based in a belief of a plot hatched by aristocratic oligarchs to pervert the entire functioning of the state. Anything and everything that happened could be interpreted in the light of this theory. As bad as slavery itself was, Northerners worried, it was only the beginning.

It's easy enough, in an age of perpetual suspicion of government (on both the right and left) to see this less as a conspiracy theory than just a description of how the world worked. But the Slave Power theory was a definitive outlier in terms of how Americans viewed the workings of history, since, for the most part, government was always the target of conspirators, not its agent. The idea that the workings of government were the result of conspiracy was a new and deeply unsettling prospect.

Adherents to this belief conceived of the Slave Power as a parasite within the existing federal government, a Deep State of slaveholders. Ohio Senator Salmon P. Chase described Washington as "a Federal Government controlled by the slave power"; Charles Sumner of Massachusetts fretted that "none, from the President to the lowest border postmaster, should decline to be its tool." For *New-York Evening Post* editor William Cullen Bryant, the slaveholders of the South had "everything in their own way. They rule in the great national election of President. . . . They rule in the United States Senate. . . . They rule in the House of Representatives." Another editorial in the *Post* intimated that there was something distinctly *un-American* about it all, darkly ruminating on the Slave Power's "policy of supporting its interests by strange process of law, imitated from the practice of arbitrary governments of Europe."

The self-published writer John Smith Dye went as far as to argue, in his 1864 book *The Adder's Den; Or, Secrets of the Great Conspiracy to Overthrow Liberty in America*, that Slave Power conspirators had attempted to assassinate multiple presidents and succeeded twice. Dye suggested that former vice president John C. Calhoun had hired a mentally unstable house painter to assassinate president Andrew Jackson (the assassin, Richard Lawrence, failed only because the powder in his pistols was too damp to light), all because Jackson had asserted federal power over South Carolina when it proposed to stop paying federal taxes it feared would benefit the North. But, Dye argued, the Slave Power had been successful in bringing down William Henry Harrison, who'd stated during his campaign that he would not bring Texas into the Union as a slave state. Harrison in fact died of pneumonia, but Dye alleged that the real cause of death had been arsenic poisoning, thus clearing the way for slaveholding Freemason John Tyler. Zachary Taylor also, by Dye's reckoning, succumbed to Slave Power assassins, and the cabal so successfully intimidated James Buchanan that the fifteenth president "became more than ever the tool of the slave power."

Dye's book was a success when it was published in 1864, and even more so when it was brought back in print in the wake of Lincoln's assassination. And while such paranoid versions of American history found a ready audience, more moderate versions of the Slave Power theory were widely believed and shared. The person perhaps most famously associated with this idea was Salmon P. Chase, who, in Eric Foner's words, did more than anyone to articulate "the idea that southern slaveholders, organized politically as a Slave Power, were conspiring to dominate the national government, reverse the policy of the Founding Fathers, and make slavery the ruling interest of the republic." In attempting to wean the Democratic party off slavery, he proposed an Independent Democracy Party, the aims of which would be to "denationalize slavery; to divorce the General Government from slavery; to rescue the Government and its administration from the control of the Slave Power," and "to put its example and influence perpetually and actively on the side of Freedom at home and abroad," among other issues not related to slavery. It's noteworthy that his emphasis was not on abolition per se, but rather the idea that the country was beholden to a subversive, insidious power from which it needed to free itself. Slave Power worked, rhetorically at least, just as Freemasonry or the Illuminati had in other eras: a secret cabal of powerful men who pulled the strings and dominated the federal government, perverting the natural course of liberty to devious ends.

By the mid-1850s, any Southern aggression against the North was seen by many not as an isolated incident, but as part of this larger plot. When a fight broke out in the House of Representatives between John C. Breckenridge (a pro-slavery Democrat from Kentucky) and Francis B. Cutting of New York, leading to a duel in March 1854, anti-slavery media outlets were quick to see Breckenridge's outbursts as something sinister, "part of a well-considered plan," the *Tribune* reported, "to pursue by intimidation and violence every independent northern Democrat who dares to defy the mandates of the Slaveocracy."

Nor was this something reserved for partisan papers and the paranoid fringes. One of the most celebrated and important speeches of American history, Abraham Lincoln's "A House Divided" speech, delivered on June 16, 1858, at the Illinois statehouse after Lincoln received a U.S. Senate nomination, is itself a masterwork of conspiratorial musings, some subtle, some less so. While it would yield a number of statements that would come to be canonized ("A house divided against itself cannot stand," and "I believe this government cannot endure, permanently half *slave* and half *free*" among them), Lincoln's speech also advanced the idea of a Slave Power conspiracy destroying America. "Let any one who doubts," Lincoln stated,

> carefully contemplate that now almost complete legal combination—a piece of *machinery* so to speak—compounded of the Nebraska doctrine, and the Dred Scott decision. Let him consider not only *what work* the machinery is adapted to do, and *how well* adapted; but also, let him study the *history* of its construction, and trace, if he can, or rather *fail*, if he can, to trace the evidences of its design, and concert of action, among its chief bosses, from the beginning.

Lincoln himself seemed aware that he was playing with fire, at least on some level. "At the Republican State Convention at Springfield I made a speech," he wrote after the fact. "In it I arrange a string of incon-testable facts which, I think, prove the existence of a conspiracy to na-tionalize slavery. The evidence was circumstantial only; but nevertheless it seemed inconsistent with every other hypothesis, save that of the ex-istence of such a conspiracy. I believe the facts can be explained today on no other hypothesis." Lincoln then concludes by hedging his bets: "I have not affirmed that a conspiracy does exist. I have only stated the evidence, and affirmed my belief in its existence," ending in a sort of "just asking questions" rhetorical pose, encouraging the listener to be-lieve in the conspiracy while disclaiming any responsibility for it.

But is this Slavocracy conspiracy just another term for capitalism? People with power are able to affect legislation and increase their power and wealth. Democracy is imperfect, and money buys lobbyists and public relations campaigns, and can sway the votes of politicians. This is distasteful, often corrupt—but is it a conspiracy in the same way as Watergate or Iran–Contra? Were slave-owning interests in the first half of the nineteenth century an aberrant intrusion into the workings of democracy, or was it just awful business as usual? To talk about the Slave Power conspiracy, then, is, on some level, to talk about what that word "conspiracy" really means, and when it diverges from the unjust but predictable workings of capitalism and becomes something else en-tirely.

For many proponents of the Slave Power conspiracy theory, enslavers had corrupted the project of American democracy, a stain on the country that had thrown the entire idea of liberty in doubt. Among the most strident voices was the famed abolitionist William Lloyd Garrison. "For more than two centuries, slavery has polluted the American soil," he lamented. "From the adoption of the American Constitution, it has declared war and peace, instituted and destroyed national banks and tariffs, controlled the army and navy, prescribed the policy of government, ruled both houses of Congress, occupied the Presidential chair, governed the political parties, distributed offices of trust and emolument among its worshippers, fettered Northern industry and enterprise, and trampled liberty of speech and conscience in the dust." Garrison offered perhaps the most paranoid vision of American history, in which all events and decisions were determined by Slave Power.

American political history to this point had been a series of half-hearted compromises, stopgap measures, and abdications of responsibility, to the point that it looked like an incoherent mishmash to most observers. To subscribers of the Slave Power conspiracy theory, however, there was a way to make sense of the legislative chaos: it was not the work of imperfect men refusing to deal with the elephant in the room. Instead, it was the effort of men working in perfect harmony to achieve their long-held objective of spreading the crime of slavery across the continent. The American project had been conceived as something genuinely different, something that would stand as a beacon of liberty for the world, a perfect experiment. To face the harsh realities of its flaws and contradictions was a sobering proposition. But if one could find an enemy, something nonessential to democracy itself, something that had nonetheless infected it, then that might explain everything. As William Goodell argued, slavery was "the simple key," with which the historian could "unlock the otherwise inexplicable labyrinths of American politics for the last sixty years": wars, financial panics, immigration could all be explained by the Slave Power.

And while this indeed smacks of paranoia, historian David Brion Davis may be right that sometimes such paranoia is necessary. "We might conclude," he wrote in 1970, "that the image of the Slave Power was a necessary means for arousing the fears and galvanizing the will of the North to face a genuine moral and political challenge. There is something almost providential in the way that the paranoid style, for all its irrationality, finally enabled significant numbers of Americans to perceive the evil of an institution which had long been intertwined with the promise of American life." As a conspiracy theory, the Slave Power thesis cut powerfully through a rhetorical conundrum many in the North had found themselves in. Overturning slavery would, on its face, require violating the Constitution—the beloved and sacrosanct ruling principle of the nation. But, if Northerners believed that the Slaveocracy had fundamentally corrupted the American project through extralegal or conspiratorial means, then abolishing it could restore—rather than violate—the Constitution's principles.

Making sense of Lincoln's ascendancy to the presidency requires a recognition that not all Slave Power conspiracy theories were created equal. In fact, the rise of the Republican Party out of the ashes of the Whigs and the Know Nothings would not have happened in such a quick and startling fashion had not its leaders—including Lincoln, Salmon P. Chase, and Charles Sumner—not worked to cultivate and refine the apocalyptic and paranoid rhetoric of figures like Garrison into something more palatable to the mainstream.

As the issue of slavery grew more intractable through the decades, it went from being a problem to be solved through compromise, dialogue, and legislation to a fundamental flaw, a tragic and insurmountable problem—a feeling shared by both sides. The gradual but unstoppable shift in abolitionist thinking from the radical pacificism of men like Garrison to those like John Brown, who were willing to use violence, reflected an awareness in the abolitionist movement that there was no salvaging the United States so long as slavery existed. The South, likewise, had come to see abolition as a similarly tragic flaw of the country, one that left no room for compromise. As abolitionist Wendell Phillips put it, "Disunion must and will come. Calhoun wants it at one end of the Union—Garrison wants it at the other."

This binary continues to drive contemporary politics. In the twenty-first century, it's fairly easy to recognize how this tragic view of history has come to shape both left *and* right political positions: though they disagree on the root of the problem, both the GOP of Donald Trump and the progressive arm of the Left often speak of the American project as fatally doomed and needing an entire reboot from scratch. The political message of Joe Biden in 2020, on the other hand (and many other politicians who've come before him), focused instead on the idea of misunderstanding: if the two sides of the divide could just learn to speak openly and listen to each other, these seeming disagreements could be resolved.

Lincoln and his Republicans favored this position as well. The rise of the Republican Party out of the ashes of the Whigs and the Know Nothings ultimately came not from their repudiation of conspiracy theories, but rather their ability to shape conspiratorial musings into a positive political program. They refused the line of men like Garrison, who argued that the entire project of American democracy had been corrupted by slavery and thus was failed. Instead, they suggested that, while imperiled by slavery, America could yet fulfill its promise.

Chase, one of the loudest voices alleging conspiracy, gradually tailored back the scope of Slave Power, moving the Republican position away from the theological mode of radical abolitionists to a position that saw a solution in the technocratic workings of government. He rejected the apocalyptic cast of Garrison's conspiracism, arguing instead that Slave Power was the work of an ordinary syndicate driven by banal motives such as greed and self-interest. Lincoln also narrowed the scope of his conspiracies, focusing on specific actions like the Kansas–Nebraska Act and the Supreme Court's *Dred Scott* decision rather than the whole of slavery. These were, he averred, the work of a small, dangerous cabal whose machinations threatened to undo American democracy. But they were outliers, and as such represented not an overwhelming, omnipotent malevolent conspiracy but one that could be fought.

This distinction between formulations of conspiracy theories—the tragic and insurmountable on one side, the perpetual misunderstanding that can yet be worked out on the other—suggests also the degree to which we often fail to recognize the latter as conspiracy theories at all.

Even though Lincoln's "A House Divided" speech has all the hallmarks of a conspiracy theory, we tend not to see Lincoln in the same camp as the deeply paranoid. Perhaps this is because it is only once a conspiracy theory has assumed the tragic mode that it stands out as conspiratorial to the mainstream. In this way, one can, via a taxonomy of conspiracy theories, see the enduring belief that America is ultimately a unified, centrist body whose disagreements are largely based on misunderstanding. The extent to which this belief endures and dominates political discourse highlights the degree to which conspiracy narratives can be openly paranoid, but so long as they hold out the promise of compromise and resolution, they will remain acceptable.

The Republicans' rapid ascent to a major political party also relied on another set of conspiracy theories, since they built their popular support out of the waning fortunes of the Know Nothings. The question that increasingly dominated the 1850s wasn't whether or not conspiracy theories might rise up from the margins and overtake the sensible middle, but simply which conspiracy theory would win out over the others.

Almost as soon as they had achieved any kind of power, the Know Nothings were split by two rival conspiracy theories: Slave Power and anti-Catholicism. They knew that *someone* was pulling the strings, but there was a constant tension among the ranks as to who was the ultimate villain. Throughout the country, Know Nothing politicians tended to emphasize one issue over the other, depending on local biases: in the cities, the anti-Catholic issue played well among those competing for jobs with Irish immigrants, while in rural areas, small farmers were more exercised about the agricultural domination of large Southern plantations.

The Republicans worked to find a way to use this nativism to their advantage. In Ohio in 1854, Democrats had tried to recruit German and Irish immigrants into the party in order to counteract hostility toward the Kansas–Nebraska Act, but Know Nothings had swept to power anyway, capitalizing on a public sentiment opposed to both slavery and immigrants. Those in the anti-slavery movement understood quickly that they needed to break their reliance on the nativists, however: "The proscriptive spirit of Know-Nothingism, and its dis-equalizing spirit," wrote E. S. Hamlin, a friend of Chase, "are in sympathy with the spirit of slaveholding."

The goal was to break Know Nothingism without losing the good-will of those opposed to slavery. When Chase ran for governor of Ohio in 1856, he welcomed Know Nothings to the new Republican Party with open arms. But he did so without making any concessions to nativist conspiracy theories about Catholics or foreigners; the July 1856 convention formally organizing the Republican Party in Ohio devoted itself entirely to an anti-slavery platform. Chase and his allies had simultaneously welcomed Know Nothings as delegates while depriving nativist concerns of any oxygen in this new party. When Chase won the governorship that fall, he did so with heavy Know Nothing support, but he also managed to hollow out the upstart party, and redirected its remnants away from an anti-Catholic conspiracy theory to one focused on Slave Power.

The evaporation of the Know Nothings' support doesn't signal the end of nativist conspiracy theories, but it does suggest that in the 1850s even anti-Catholic nativists understood that slavery was a more central issue. And it suggests that the Republicans were able to successfully argue the fundamental fact that it was enslavers—not Catholics—who were the fundamental threat to the United States. They did so not by rejecting conspiracy theories, but by turning them to their own advantage.

TEN

The Mystic Red

On July 4, 1860, family members and supporters of John Brown gathered at his farm in North Elba, New York, to honor the abolitionist who'd been hastily executed the previous December after his botched raid on Harper's Ferry. Henry David Thoreau was invited but could not attend, so he sent a remembrance instead, in which he concluded that Brown "is more alive than he ever was. He has earned immortality. . . . He is no longer working in secret. He works in public, and in the clearest light that shines on this land." Thoreau was not wrong; tributes and memorials had broken out across the country, all honoring a criminal who'd plotted in secret to violently violate the laws of the state of Virginia.

To Southerners, this was intolerable, and the outpouring of support for Brown's raid was proof that it wasn't a fluke, that there still might be active conspiracies afoot targeting enslavers and what they perceived to be their way of life. As the election of 1860 approached, the whole country seemed to be sitting atop a powder keg, and nowhere was this more literally true than in Texas. During a scorching hot summer, amidst a punishing drought, strange fires broke out across the state. On July 8, the hottest day of the month, a fire consumed eighteen buildings in downtown Dallas. There were no fatalities, but it caused an estimated $300,000 in damages (equivalent to nearly $5 million today). The fires were still raging in Dallas when a separate fire broke out in Denton, Texas, forty miles to the north—soon another fire had started in Point Pilot. In nearby Waxahachie, a house burned to the ground, while a mill caught fire in Collin County.

As with the fires of New York City in 1741, there was a fairly plausible explanation at work: that summer had seen the introduction of a new kind of match, one that used phosphorous and was unstable at high temperatures and had a history of spontaneous combustion. And at first, no one suspected arson—why would arsonists work in the middle of the day, when they'd be most likely to be spotted and people would be at the ready to douse the flames?

Such lucid reasoning would not last. On July 9, Otis G. Welch of Denton, Texas, mused, "How the two fires originated at the same time in the two towns is wrapped in mystery, though we have but little doubt that they must be the work of an incendiary." Murmurs of a conspiracy involving enslaved people seemed to be confirmed on July 12, after a small fire broke out on Crill Miller's farm five miles west of Dallas. In the aftermath, a slave named Bruce said at first that he'd seen three white men start it, but under heavy interrogation, he changed his story and claimed another slave, Spence, had paid him a dollar to start it.

No one was more responsible for fanning the flames than Charles R. Pryor. Born in Virginia and trained as a doctor, he had moved to Dallas in 1850, following his older brother (who would become the city's first mayor in 1856). There, he contributed articles to the *Dallas Herald*; when its editor died in 1859, Pryor took over the paper. Fervently pro-slavery, Pryor used the *Herald* as an organ to promote slavery and to rail against Northerners and "submissionist" Southerners like Sam Houston who favored harmony with the Union over the South's right to slavery.

The *Herald*'s presses were destroyed during the July 8 fire, but Pryor quickly rallied, and soon began dashing off feverish announcements of a growing plot that had only barely been averted. The fires, he claimed to have learned, were the work of "certain Abolition preachers, who were expelled from the country last year, to devastate, with fire and assassination, the whole of Northern Texas, and when it was reduced to a helpless condition, a general revolt of the slaves, aided by the white men of the North in our midst . . ." The fires were just the beginning of open war: "The stores throughout the country containing powder and lead were to be burned, with the grain, and thus reduce [*sic*] this portion of the country to helplessness," Pryor stated. "When this was accomplished, assistance was expected from the Indians and Abolitionists." Beyond an attempt to cripple infrastructure, Pryor concluded, "many of our most prominent citizens were singled out for assassination whenever they made their escape from their burning homes." Wells were to be poisoned to kill anyone who escaped the fires, and the white women who lived were to be parceled out amongst the mutineers. Pryor closed out one letter to a colleague on a darkly ominous note:

> You and all Bonham are in as much danger as we are. Be on your guard, and make these facts known by issuing extras to be sent in every direction. All business has ceased, and the country is terribly excited.

Pryor's letters were widely reprinted and circulated throughout the South, adding to the fervor. Any fire, no matter how obviously accidental, was further proof of a massive conspiracy to set all of Texas aflame. The *San Antonio Herald* labeled the revelations "one of the most diabolical plans that was ever conceived in the most depraved age or country, by the foulest fiends in human shape." Months before the 1860 election, Texas had become 1741 New York City all over again.

As with that earlier panic, retribution was swift and devoid of due process. There was a proposal to hang every enslaved person involved in the fires; a correspondent in Fort Worth wrote to a New York paper to warn its readers to "be not surprised when I tell you that we will hang every man who does not live above suspicion. Necessity now reverses the rule, for it is better for us to hang ninety-nine innocent (suspicious) men than to let one guilty one pass." A vigilante committee was formed, and enslaved people throughout the town were rounded up, interrogated, and, in some cases, tried. But there was a limit to the number of executions the committee could carry out: enslavers worried about the dramatic loss of income and "property" such a mass execution would represent (indeed, a man owned by the richest man in Dallas was tried and released after the man who held him in bondage intervened). In the end, only three men were hanged, but hundreds of enslaved people were whipped.

Unable to execute those in bondage for fear of losing their investment, Southerners turned their ire, predictably, to abolitionists. On August 19, Richard Broadwright and his nephew were hanged in Robertson County for "tampering with slaves." The open distrust of Northerners now reached utter paranoia. Guadalupe County passed a "citizens' resolution" that read: "We hold persons born and educated North of Mason and Dixon line, whose antecedents are not known, and whose means of support are not visible, as enemies to our peace and welfare until the contrary is proved, and advise them, if they have a prudent regard for their personal safety to give us a wide berth, as they will be dealt with according to a law which we have established for our own protection." The *New York Herald* ran a letter from a correspondent that advised that "Texas is no place for Northern people just now, especially for itinerant pedlars, and so forth. Such a class had better keep away. Their necks would be in great danger of breaking."

Among the more horrific outcomes was the sad fate of Anthony Bewley. Bewley was a Methodist minister from Tennessee who had joined the Northern Methodist missionary program, hoping to spread its influence in Texas. Hardly an outspoken abolitionist, he was careful to make his views known mainly to those who already agreed with him.

But simply allying himself with the Northern conference was enough to raise suspicion, and he failed to make inroads in a heavily pro-slavery state—he left in failure in 1859 but was coaxed to return a year later, in late spring of 1860. But in less than a month, he had learned of Pryor's allegations against enslaved Texans and abolitionists and knew that his family was in danger. He took his family north, making it as far as southern Missouri before a posse caught up with him, hoping to cash in on a $1,000 reward. Dragged back to Texas, Bewley—whose only crime was his association with the North—was hanged on September 13, and then buried in a grave so shallow his knees protruded from the ground. Three weeks later his corpse was exhumed and his skeleton was used to decorate the roof of a local storehouse, where children would crawl up and contort it into various positions, mocking "old Bewley," the "old abolitionist."

To linger on the death and treatment of a white abolitionist is not to deny that the reality for those enslaved in Texas was on many levels far, far worse. It is only to note that in the racist logic of slavery, white abolitionists held a special place. There was a limited amount of harm whites could inflict on the people they owned before they began to "damage their property," for one. For another, Southerners attacked abolitionists precisely because they saw them as ringleaders and masterminds, in an attempt to convince themselves that those they kept in bondage had neither the intellect nor the inclination to foment revolt. They weren't just convenient scapegoats; they were the hinge that allowed the entire conspiracy theory to make sense.

Northern newspapers decried the execution, claiming that Bewley wasn't even an abolitionist, or if he was, he was of the "mildest" kind. Southerners, meanwhile, maintained that not only was Bewley's fate deserved, but that he was part of a larger conspiracy of which there was now evidence. Soon enough, a letter appeared, supposedly dropped by one of the conspirators. Written by a "William Bailey," it gave a name to this plotting organization: "I found many friends who had been initiated," this "Bailey" wrote, "and understand the Mystic-Red." It seemed to confirm suspicions of a devious plot, spelled out in conveniently explicit terms: "If we can break Southern merchants and millers, and have their places filled by honest Republicans, Texas will be an easy prey, if we only do our duty." Texas, it seemed, along with the election of Lincoln, was key to destroying slavery: "LINCOLN will certainly be elected; we will then have the Indian nation, cost what it will. Squatter Sovereignty will prevail there, as it has in Kansas; that accomplished, we have at least one more step to take—but one more struggle to make—that is, free Texas. We will then have a connected link from the Lakes to the Gulf. Slavery will then be surrounded by land and by water, and soon sting itself to death."

The only people buying this were those who already wanted to believe it. When the letter was reprinted in the *New York Times*, it appeared under the headline "A Curious Document—An Evident Forgery." The *Times* wasted no serious consideration of the letter itself: "the following document," ran the story "purporting to be a copy of a letter written by an Abolitionist in Texas, we find in the Austin State Gazette. It needs no explanation. Its bogus character is sufficiently apparent." The forgery becomes all the more preposterous when you recognize that someone who was openly trying to sabotage the Union would hardly have supported Lincoln. Lincoln had been chosen by the Republicans as a safe, moderate, and compromise candidate, someone committed to the preservation of the Union, even if that meant tolerating slavery for the time being. That the Mystic Red never existed beyond this forged letter mattered less than the fact that the mere invention of some cryptic name gave a nefarious tinge to the abolitionist movement, confirming a belief that such work was inherently subterranean and somehow "anti-American."

It is important that this feels repetitive, that the unfolding of events mirrors New York City in 1741 to an almost uncomfortable degree. It is important to face the fact that the arc of history does not always bend to justice, and in many ways it does not really bend at all. You have to be able to see American history as a series of panics, almost rote in their unfolding, see them again and again to the point of ad nauseum, to be able to see past Salem and the McCarthy hearings. Those two events, held up as outliers and anomalies, were just two points on a straight line composed of a dozen similar points. We have to move beyond this forgetting, and recognize that these events unfold over and over again in a painfully similar manner.

Conspiracy theories, after all, feed on historical amnesia. They depend on your belief that what is happening now has never happened before. They present repetition as novelty. When a moral panic dissipates, its traces are forgotten in a forceful act of collective amnesia. If you are going to make sense of the history, you have to stick with the sense of déjà vu; you have to run in circles if you're going to get anywhere.

By the time of the election, the Southern pathology had been entirely overtaken by conspiracy theories. Nowhere was this more true than in South Carolina, where conspiracy theories were more or less public policy. Militia and patrol groups were assembled regularly for the defense against the domination of "mongrel tyrants who mean . . . to reduce you and your wives and your daughters on a level with the very slaves you buy and sell." Congressman Laurence M. Keitt fretted in an 1860 letter to a friend, "If Lincoln is elected—what then? I am in earnest. I'd cut loose through fire and blood if necessary—See—poison in the wells in Texas and fire for the Houses in Alabama—Our Negroes are being enlisted in politics—With poison and fire how can we stand it?"

Everywhere Southerners looked, they saw John Brown: his raid may have been unsuccessful, but it stirred increasingly paranoid musings about "Abolition Fanaticks" who were moving on all fronts against the Southern way of life. "John Brown's work is yet going on," read the

August 31, 1860, edition of the Fayetteville *Arkansian*. He may have been captured and executed, but "there were more left unhung . . . and these are now laying waste the towns of Texas, and others are ready elsewhere to burn other towns." It seemed impossible for anyone to accept Harper's Ferry had been a lone, isolated act of violence and not the opening salvo to some larger plot. "What meant the note alluding to depradations in Texas, found in the camp of the traitorous Brown?" the *Dallas Herald* asked, concocting a fictitious piece of communication in an attempt to tie the fires to abolitionists. Thoreau was right: Brown lived on and had achieved immortality. That his failure only *strengthened* fears of abolitionists suggests the degree to which conspiracy theories had become a way of life: all had become false flags, feints, and fifth columns. The ability of Southern enslavers to manage their constant cognitive dissonance with conspiracy theories had reached its breaking point.

As historian Steven A. Channing explains, Southern conspiracy theories were not a case of delusional thinking. "The people of South Carolina were not being brainwashed," he writes, "at least in the usual meaning of that term. They were not being forcibly persuaded to give up basic political and social beliefs in favor of a contrasting set of attitudes. What was being accomplished, consciously or not, was the construction of a psychological set, a predisposition to perceive, interpret, and react to an external event in a predetermined fashion." The mindset of so many South Carolinians in the year before the war reveals an important aspect of conspiracy theories. In the months leading up to the Civil War, in other words, these paranoid fantasies worked to reduce the options down to a single outcome. Conspiracy theories, by design, exist to ameliorate chaos, confusion, disorder, and ambiguity. They reduce the wild uncertainties of the world into a coherent set of machinations by malevolent forces, and in doing so they suggest that only one course of action remains: resistance to this malevolent force.

They also reduce the available option of responses. They destroy nuance both in the processing of information and in the area of problem-solving. They appeal in part because they make the world simple. They do not change minds, but they reduce the possible interpretations of the facts at hand. Anything that happens at all, no matter how unexpected, is a further confirmation of the basic plot, even if superficially it may seem otherwise. Conspiracy theories help drive polarization and partisanship, becoming the means by which difficult thinking can be swept away in favor of seeing the world not in its surface complexity but in the sole, subterranean answer. All possible new developments reinforce a single outcome, and in this case that outcome was disunion and war. At moments when America seems to be reaching toward its stated ideals of equality and liberty, ideals that can at times require difficult work, new ways of thinking, and a willingness to embrace complexity, conspiracists respond with a story of doubt and unease.

It may not be enough to say that the root of the Civil War was slavery. Rather, the root of the Civil War was the default paranoid state engendered by slavery. As Channing puts it, "Secession was the product of logical reasoning within a framework of irrational perception." The Civil War was undeniably the result of America's original sin of slavery, which had finally reached a point where it could no longer be contained or ignored. But decades of deferral had created a nation divided by two competing conspiracy theories, each of which saw a hidden hand manipulating national history for its own devious ends. One by one, such paranoid musings eliminated the possibilities for any kind of outcome save bloodshed—and on April 12, 1861, bloodshed is what the nation got.

PART THREE

National Indigestion

⁓

Hyacinth stared. "But isn't he tremendously deep in—"
What should he call the mystery?

"Deep in what?"

"Well, in what's going on beneath the surface.
Doesn't he belong to important things?"

—Henry James, *The Princess Casamassima*

ELEVEN

Abraham Lincoln's Secret Confidant

After the Civil War, the demographic makeup of the United States underwent significant changes. One way to put it would be to say that after the Civil War, the United States experienced an unprecedented period of innovation, and efforts were soon underway to create new laws to control the millions of innovations. Another way, perhaps, would be to say that after the Civil War, the United States experienced an unprecedented growth spurt, and had to scurry to create new laws that would give it a chance to digest the millions of innovations.

On the surface, these two phrases may seem to more or less convey the same meaning. But in 2009, researchers offered these statements to two different groups of people and then followed them with a series of questions about immigration and the minimum wage. The group who was given the second prompt tended to respond with generally negative attitudes toward foreigners, immigrants, and working-class laborers. The key is in those subtle metaphors: "growth spurt," "scurrying," "digest." When America is seen as a body, it changes how we feel about immigrants. And a hallmark of anti-immigration sentiment has been to invoke, repeatedly, the idea of indigestible groups of people. Researchers

Mark J. Landau, Daniel Sullivan, and Jeff Greenberg concluded that "activating motivation to protect one's own body against contamination will result in more negative immigration attitudes, but only when the United States is metaphorically framed as a body."

Referring to immigrants as "indigestible" has been a mainstay of xenophobic attitudes throughout the country's history, particularly in the wake of the Civil War. In 1877, the US Congress referred to Chinese immigrants as an "indigestible mass;" The Irish of nineteenth-century Boston, per one historian, were "a massive lump in the community, undigested, undigestible." White supremacist Alma White wrote in 1925 that "The Jew is insoluble and indigestible; and when he grows in numbers and power till he becomes a menace to Christianity and the whole moral fabric, drastic measures will have to be taken to counteract his destructive work, and more especially when he is in alliance with the old papal machine." This rhetorical flourish has continued, more or less unabated, through to the current day; the only thing that changes is the given target of abuse. In 2018, Fox News host Tucker Carlson whipped up xenophobia by arguing that American immigration trends represented "more change than human beings are designed to digest."

But just because demagogues treat immigrant groups as perennially foreign, unsuited to American ways of life, and unable to participate in democracy doesn't mean that foreigners are useless to those demagogues. Rather, precisely because nativists could paint immigrants as a lumpen mass of aliens united by their ethnic ties—bound together and estranged from cultural and political participation—such groups became increasingly identified with secret societies: dark, hidden combinations, people whose allegiance lay anywhere other than the country they now called home.

Because we so often see conspiracists as raving, paranoid fringe actors, ranting on YouTube channels, it can be easy to miss the fact that the goal of any conspiracy theory is to soothe, calm, and reassure. American immigration numbers are driven by a host of different, complicated factors, with ethnic groups coming to the United States from a variety of countries for a myriad of reasons. Conspiracy theories boil all that down to a simple cause-and-effect mechanism, a battle between good and evil, and offer the listener a clear place in that binary. They take the guesswork out of world affairs and eliminate the confusion that comes from not knowing exactly why things are happening. In lieu of facts, they offer simplicity.

Antebellum Catholic conspiracy theories were given new life in the wake of the Civil War, as the numbers of Catholic immigrants continued to rise. By 1850, Catholics made up 5 percent of the American population; by 1906 that number was 17 percent. These trends deeply worried nativists, especially now that they didn't have slavery as a cause to rally around. And so the strange document that began circulating among the middle-west states of the United States in 1893 may have seemed at first terrifying, but it promised the key to understanding the rapid demographic and religious change in America at the turn of the century. Titled "Instructions to the Catholics. Platform of the Papal Party as Laid Down by the Pope. Pecci's Hands Busy In American Affairs," it was purported to have been written by a conclave of eight archbishops and Cardinal James Gibbons, at a meeting that took place on August 5, 1890 (Pecci was the surname of the then-pope, Leo XIII). It warned of grave dangers for Catholics in America—namely education and the English language. The pamphlet argued that the best way to restore the glory of Rome would be to ensure that "the people must not think; that is a privilege that belongs only to the pope, who by divine right is the only person appointed by God to do the political and religious thinking of this world." It singled out "the rapid diffusion of the English language," and proclaimed itself opposed "to any system of schools that teaches the youth more than Roman catechism, or that teaches the young to think—it is unnecessary, a waste of time and money."

Accordingly, the anonymous tract called for the destruction of "the free public schools of this Protestant nation." But it went further: "In order to find employment for the many thousands of the faithful who are coming daily to swell the ranks of our Catholic army," its authors advised, "we must secure control of all the cities, railways, manufactories, mines, steam and sailing vessels—above all the press—in fact, every enterprise requiring labor, in order to furnish our newcomers employment; this will render it necessary to remove or crowd out the American heretics who are now employed."

As though this vision was not unsettling enough, "Instructions to the Catholics" was often circulated with another text, this one purported to be a papal encyclical of Leo XIII, "given at St. Peter's on December 25, 1891, in the fifteenth year of our Pontificate." In this encyclical, the pope announced "the people of the United States to have forfeited all right to rule said republic, and also all dominion, dignity, and privileges appertaining to it." Citizens of the United States were henceforth relieved of any obligations resulting from taking any oath of loyalty to the US government; anyone who retained allegiance to the United States, however, was in for trouble: "on or about the feast of Ignatius Loyola, in the year of our Lord 1893," the encyclical concluded, "*it will be the duty of the faithful to exterminate all heretics found within the jurisdiction of the United States.*"

One text calling for a ban on the English language, another for the extermination of all non-Catholics—both were, obviously, gross forgeries—but obvious to whom? Both forgeries were the work of the American Protective Association, a virulently anti-Catholic organization that flourished in the end of the nineteenth century during a time of paranoia and suspicion. Founded in 1887 by Henry Francis Bowers in Clinton, Iowa, the APA emerged as a response to the fear that Catholics were voting at the ballot box en masse, tipping elections under orders from their clergy. While the APA's stated principles claimed that they rejected all forms of discrimination, in practice they were devoted to prohibiting Catholics from holding office or gaining employment.

The APA saw the machinations of diabolical Catholics everywhere, in every arena of social and political unrest. Among the many tools the Catholics were supposedly employing to destabilize America was their ability to orchestrate runs on banks, leading to credit instability, financial panic, and economic depressions.

By 1893, when the bogus encyclical first began appearing in APA newspapers across the country, the organization had 70,000 members spread out over twenty-two states. A year later, their membership had swelled to half a million. However absurd these propaganda tactics may seem now, they had their desired effect—rallying new members and giving a structure to people's inchoate fear of foreigners. The false encyclical was reprinted throughout the country, and both pamphlets were handed out at rallies nationwide. Their ubiquity was enough that numerous newspapers had to publicly refute their authenticity, taking pains to debunk the claims within. New York's *Christian Advocate*, a Methodist periodical, wrote: "We do not know of a more transparent fraud. We are astonished that any human being acquainted with the methods of the Roman Catholic Church could have believed either the Pope or his advisers such dull idiots as this document would prove them to be." It is the work, the *Advocate* concluded, of someone "whose mendacity has intoxicated his own mind to such a degree that, though he obviously wanted to lie, he could not do it shrewdly."

The APA didn't form its own political party as the Know Nothings had; instead, they worked largely with the Republican party, pressuring them from running Catholic candidates and to adding anti-Catholic legislation to their party platform. By the mid-1890s, they had a membership in the thousands, but when presidential hopeful William McKinley refused to meet with them in 1896, they turned on the Republicans, and their movement subsequently flamed out.

But they had still managed to tap into existing xenophobia and understood that for those virulently opposed to Catholicism, it hardly mattered whether or not the conspiratorial pamphlets they distributed were authentic or not. As the Catholic lawyer and historian Humphrey J. Desmond explained, "Perhaps half of the A. P. A. membership in 1893, believed the document genuine. Those who knew it to be a forgery defended it on the ground that if it was not edited by the Catholic hierarchy, it nevertheless came close to being actual Catholic teachings."

This kind of hate-filled rhetoric was not without consequence. Tensions between Protestants and Catholics erupted into violence throughout the country in the 1890s. On July 4, 1894, two saloon keepers in Butte, Montana, displayed APA banners in their windows, sparking a riot that lasted all day and necessitated bringing in the National Guard from Helena; during the melee, two people were killed, including a police officer.

The number of anti-Catholic riots that the country endured with an almost stubborn regularity—coupled with the fact that many today are largely unknown to the contemporary public—is a reminder of how moral panics are most useful when they are almost immediately forgotten afterward. Their purpose, after all, has always been to resist and stifle progressive change, both in controlling attitudes about "indigestible" new immigrant populations, but also in off-loading internal contradictions onto external forces. By constantly exhorting people to unite behind a common enemy, such conspiracies shift the focus away from internal tensions like slavery and racism. But this magic trick only works when it flashes up like a burst of phosphorous, blinding and shocking, only to disappear a moment later. The dismissal of such outbreaks of violence as merely irrational and uncontained emotion, rather than a durable and regular part of American democracy, is a fundamental misunderstanding of American history—for conspiracies and moral panics are the great unseen engine of the country.

The forged pamphlets were by no means the strangest material published by the APA. That honor may belong to the work of Protestant minister and ex-Catholic priest Charles Paschal Télesphore

Chiniquy. Chiniquy was born in Canada in 1809; he was ordained as a Catholic priest in 1833 and was active in the Temperance movement, convincing some 400,000 Canadians to take a temperance pledge, contributing to a crash in the Canadian liquor industry. An effective and engaging speaker, he came to Illinois in 1851 to work with French Canadian immigrants. Shortly after arriving in the United States, however, he accused a land speculator of perjury, sparking a lengthy legal trial. At one point, Chiniquy retained the services of a still largely unknown lawyer named Abraham Lincoln, who helped him settle out of court.

Meanwhile, Chiniquy was excommunicated from the Catholic Church, and after attempting to start his own religious sect, he joined the Presbyterians in 1860. As he became an increasingly vocal critic of the Catholic Church, his former lawyer went on to bigger and better things. It's impossible to prove beyond a shadow of a doubt whether he ever had any further communication with Lincoln, though no positive evidence has ever emerged. That didn't stop Chiniquy, however, from claiming that Lincoln was his "most devoted and noblest friend," and that the ex-priest had become the only person with whom Lincoln could "speak freely."

And about what, according to Chiniquy, was Lincoln so eager to speak freely? The Catholic Church, and specifically a secret conspiracy by Jesuits to bring down the United States. In a wild, almost entirely fictitious memoir he published in 1885, *Fifty Years in the Church of Rome*, Chiniquy claimed that he made repeated trips to the White House during Lincoln's presidency, where the two bosom buddies discussed the growing threat of the Catholic Church. In this telling, it was Lincoln's legal work on behalf of the apostate that had first drawn the ire of the church; "ten or twelve Jesuits from Chicago and St. Louis" had attended the trial, eager to see Chiniquy lose, and when Lincoln's legal brilliance delivered a victory instead, the Jesuits had become enraged and swore revenge.

Fifty Years in the Church of Rome is filled with bizarre claims ventriloquized via the president about the Catholic Church. It is not against "the Americans of the South, alone, I am fighting," Lincoln tells Chiniquy at one point, "it is more against the Pope of Rome." He goes on:

> Till lately, I was in favour of the unlimited liberty of conscience as our constitution gives it to the Roman Catholics. But now, it seems to me that, sooner or later, the people will be forced to put a restriction to that clause towards the Papists. Is it not an act of folly to absolute liberty of conscience to a set of men who are publicly sworn to cut our throats the very day they have their opportunity for doing it? Is it right to give the privilege of citizenship to men who are the sworn and public enemies of our constitution, our laws, our liberties, and our lives?

To say this strains credulity is a bit of an understatement; Lincoln was many things, but a dedicated anti-Papist he was not. He did, however, at one point declare his enmity for the Know Nothings and their nativism. "As a nation, we began by declaring that '*all men are equal.*' We now practically read it 'all men are created equal, *except negroes,*'" he wrote to his friend Joshua Speed in 1855. "When the Know-Nothings get control, it will read 'all men are created equal, except negroes, *and foreigners, and catholics.*' When it comes to this I should prefer emigration to some country where they make no pretence of loving liberty—to Russia, for instance, where despotism can be taken pure, and without the base alloy of hypocrisy."

It wasn't just that Chiniquy's evidence was thin, or nonexistent; one of the hallmarks of conspiracy theories surrounding secret societies is that the *less* evidence there is, the *more* powerful the supposed conspiracy—the lack of evidence necessarily presupposes the absolute omnipotence of the conspirators to eliminate all traces. And lest one entirely dismiss this fabulist, *Fifty Years in the Church of Rome* was a bestseller and went through some forty editions. As with the *Awful Disclosures* of Maria Monk and other anti-Catholic agitprop, it found its audience.

Why was something so obviously false so readily accepted by so many? Chiniquy's conspiracy theory about Jesuit assassins has to be understood in a postwar America that was still reeling from a horrific conflict and still trying to make sense of it. What Chiniquy's Catholic conspiracy offered readers was a way of shifting the conversation away from slavery, away from Reconstruction, away from how the country might now accommodate emancipation and Black Americans finally taking a step toward equality. If the Civil War was not about slavery, but was rather the result of secret Catholic agitation, then these questions could all be avoided.

What Catholics offered America in the second half of the nineteenth century was increasingly a way to sidestep America's contradictions, to explain any and all shortcomings in the American democratic system. If Catholics, indigestible and anti-democratic, were undermining the regular workings of democracy, then inequity and inequality all could be understood. As historian Michael J. Sobiech put it, "After a conflict in which white Americans fought white Americans over the enslavement of African Americans, emancipation and full citizenship for black citizens gave way to Jim Crow; white Americans sought to forge a (white) union that would never divide again by, in part, forgetting (and segregating) the freed blacks." Chiniquy's shift in focus away from questions of slavery and emancipation offered an easy route for those looking to make sense of the war. The entire bloody conflict had all been a misunderstanding, one prompted by Catholic saboteurs, and to think it had anything to do with slavery was to fall for their misdirection.

In the wake of the Lost Cause narrative, it would seem increasingly impossible to reunite the country: the secessionist losers argued that they were not in the wrong, and that there was no need for any kind of concession, change in behavior, or modulation of the South's guided narratives of racial hierarchy. In the face of this open contradiction of how America read the Civil War, conspiracy theories about supposedly foreign infiltrators—Catholics and Jews—allowed for a way out. What had happened between 1861 and 1865 was not a crucible to settle, once and for all, an inherent contradiction in America; it was as if the country had been seized by an excessive mania wholly exterior to it, a brief and unfortunate delusional state. Pinning the blame on Catholic saboteurs allowed (white, Protestant) Americans an easy solution that sidestepped any soul-searching and excused a refusal to change behavior. The anti-Catholic conspiracy theories of the postwar era became an important means for distorting the causes and meanings of the Civil War, making space for the Lost Cause narrative not only among Southern whites, but also among their Northern counterparts, who were more eager to see kinship in white Protestants from other states than they were the Catholic immigrants and freed Blacks in their own communities—especially as these groups represented economic competition.

It is tempting to look at the electoral failures of the Anti-Masons and the Know Nothings and conclude that conspiracy theories cannot penetrate the mainstream, and that they exist only on the fringes. This, certainly, is the conclusion Richard Hofstadter drew when he articulated a history of American paranoia, asserting that a "sensible middle" was vital to keep the American project on track. It may be more accurate to suggest instead that conspiracists have learned through trial and error that they were far more effective by operating in the fringes, and that over time they more or less willingly abandoned the middle in order to increase their power. The goal of the conspiracist is not to claim the middle and seize power; it is, instead, to operate a guerilla war from the margins. The goal is not to effect change but to resist it; to keep America in a state of un-advancement, where social goals and progressive policies cannot be implemented.

Further, conspiracists work to benefit from and enhance the very idea of a "sensible middle." It is the sensible middle who agree that

American democracy is fundamentally sound and doesn't need a radical overhaul. It is the sensible middle who ignores the pleas of America's most marginalized groups, advising them that there are existing routes to equality that don't need tweaking. Conspiracy theories—particularly those about secret groups—have the most weight and effect as a means of preventing change. You can use a conspiracy theory to drive a riot or depress turnout, but it's much more difficult to use a conspiracy theory to make progress in this country. What Chiniquy and the APA helped accomplish was to re-create a "sensible middle" in the wake of the Civil War: a sensible middle of white Protestants who had briefly been misled into a war of brother against brother, over something as "inconsequential" as emancipation and civil rights for Black Americans.

By cementing a narrative that the country was under attack, conspiracists could band together white Protestants under a common cause—healing the divisions of the Civil War under a common enemy. Abolitionists had once helped fill this role, but in the decades immediately after the end of the Civil War, Catholic immigrants became the preferred target. The influx of immigration during the postwar period, then, turned out to be a boon in the sense that it provided an easy target that conspiracists could use to redirect American fear and paranoia. And as those immigrants and their allies began to argue for better working conditions and an improved quality of life, these conspiracy theories would continue to prove their usefulness.

TWELVE

The Man Who Threw the Bomb

I n the decades after the Civil War, two sensational trials—one in Pennsylvania's coal country in 1876, the other a decade later in Chicago—demonstrated not only the power of conspiracy theories to marshal paranoia around secret groups, but how that power could be used to blunt and roll back the burgeoning labor movement in the United States. What happened in the anthracite coal region of Pennsylvania was an early test case for a new kind of conspiracy theory. It recycled long-standing fears of fraternal organizations and fused them with anti-immigrant sentiments, then projected them on to a labor union composed largely of Irish immigrants seeking better working conditions and pay—proving the ease with which whispers of conspiracy could be used to blunt progressive change at a crucial moment in America's labor history.

The story of the Molly Maguires is so steeped in legend and propaganda that it's almost impossible to tell it at all. Like most secret societies, we do not have any clear historical record of when they became active in the United States, what exactly they were involved in, or who comprised their membership. We cannot even say definitively that they existed at all—at least as an organized conspiracy. The threats and violence attributed to the Molly Maguires may have been part of a concerted agenda, or it may have been a smattering of isolated incidents by individuals claiming the mantle for their own ends. The main source of information we have about their inner workings comes from a Pinkerton agent paid to infiltrate them and whose veracity is dubious at best.

In Ireland, the name "Molly Maguires" had been one of many similar, often interchangeable terms for various groups that had fought for tenants' rights in rural counties, engaging in a low-key guerilla war against English landowners and their agents. It's not clear when or how they first began appearing in the United States, nor how organized they ever were, but the first mention of the Molly Maguires on American soil came from the *Miners' Journal*, a regional Pennsylvania newspaper whose editor, Benjamin Bannan, first wrote in October 1857 of "the order of 'Molly Maguires,' a secret Roman Catholic association which the Democracy is using for political purposes."

Bannan's *Miners' Journal* covered news in what became known as anthracite coal country, a mountainous swath of land in eastern Pennsylvania that included Carbon and Schuylkill counties. It was one of several places in America that received an influx of Irish laborers in the wake of the Great Famine. These unskilled laborers, who often still spoke Gaelic and imported their traditions and customs to the region, found work in the dirty coal mines, usually under Welsh and English immigrants, who quickly ascended to the ranks of skilled miners.

Where Bannan got his information was hard to say, but he saw the specter of the Molly Maguires behind various acts of violence in coal country. He connected this secret terrorist organization to a public fraternal organization, the Ancient Order of the Hibernians, which had been founded in 1836 and, for all intents and purposes, looked like any other fraternal organization. The AOH was established as a benevolent organization for Irish Catholic immigrants, requiring dues in exchange for social connections and emergency funds. But, like other secret societies, it kept its membership rolls secret.

There is no direct evidence to support Bannan's claims that the Molly Maguires were engaging in election fraud, but he became increasingly vocal in his belief that the violence in Schuylkill County was not the result of individuals but part of a secret network of conspiratorial terrorists. When George K. Smith, a mine owner, was assassinated in his home on November 5, 1863, Bannan blamed the Molly Maguires, an accusation picked up by the *New York Times*, who reported that Smith had "incurred the hatred of the Irish miners by his opposition to their secret organization, which had for its object the exclusion of all the workmen of other countries." The specter of the Molly Maguires allowed for the conflation of multiple kinds of different violence: petty violence including robbery; personal enmity and drunken rage; and retributive justice, in which Irish immigrants took the law into their own hands to settle scores or otherwise act to correct what they perceived as injustices.

At the time, mine ownership had been consolidating, and one man in particular, Franklin B. Gowen, had his eyes on a monopoly. Having been elected president of the Reading Railroad, Gowen now wanted to establish dominion over the anthracite coal region, but this required breaking the miner's union, the Workingmen's Benevolent Association (WBA). And that, Gowen came to realize, required the Molly Maguires.

In 1873, Gowen hired Allan Pinkerton to break the union, and Pinkerton, who understood that there was a strong solidarity among the Irish laborers, tasked an Irish agent in his employ, James McParland, to go undercover and infiltrate the Irish community. McParland spent two years posing as a man named James McKenna. During that time, the union went on strike and threats of violence began appearing, targeting scabs and mine owners, all signed "The Molly Maguires." While the WBA was advocating a peaceful work stoppage, so-called coffin notices were found warning that "Any blackleg that takes a Union Mans job while He is standing for His Rights will have a hard Road to travel and if he dont he will have to suffer the consequences," a threat followed by a crude image of a dead man inside a coffin. Mine superintendents and foremen turned up dead—though it was impossible to say if these killings were the work of sporadic, individual acts of violence or a coordinated conspiracy. It hardly mattered; local newspapers grew increasingly bold in equating all the strikers with the mysterious Molly Maguires.

Historians still debate to what extent McParland was an impartial observer during this time, gathering facts and intel, or an outright agent provocateur. What is clear is that by 1875, the strike had been broken, the WBA had been crushed, and murders attributed to the Molly Maguires had dramatically increased. Having broken the political power of the WBA, Pinkerton turned to taking on the Molly Maguires themselves. In an August letter, he advised the creation of a group of vigilantes to take them out, and at some point that fall sent a list of suspects and their addresses to "The Vigilance Committee of the Anthracite Coal Region." When the Molly Maguires meet, he instructed, "then surround and deal summarily with them. Get off quietly. All should be securely masked." On December 10, 1875, the house of the widow Margaret O'Donnell, home to several suspected Molly Maguires, was surrounded by a group of thirty men. In the assault, Margaret O'Donnell was beaten, and her daughter Ellen was shot and killed as she came down the stairs. Ellen's husband, Charles McAllister, was able to escape, but others were less fortunate: Margaret's sons Charles and James, along with a man named James McAllister, were rounded up for arrest, but in the chaos they managed to break free. In the escape, McAllister was shot in the arm but got away, while Charles O'Donnell was shot in the head at least fifteen times.

Nor did the railroad barons stop there. Members of the Ancient Order of the Hibernians were arrested for the murders of a mine boss named John P. Jones and a police officer, Benjamin Yost. The trials of the Molly Maguires were some of the great show trials in American history—almost entirely devoid of the legal safeguards that the United

States prides itself on. Normal order was virtually suspended: a private corporation, the railroad, had hired a private detective firm, the Pinkertons, to gather evidence; the trial was prosecuted by the railroad's lawyers based on the testimony of private investigators like McParland (as historian Harold Aurand dryly notes, "the state provided only the courtroom and the hangman").

Chief to the prosecution's case was the assertion that the Ancient Order of the Hibernians, the WBA, and the Molly Maguires were interchangeable entities. Any crime attributed to the Molly Maguires, they argued, was proof of the culpability of the AOH or the WBA. Conversely, membership in the AOH made one culpable for the crimes of the Molly Maguires. Which is how, for example, Alexander Campbell, treasurer of the Storm Hill Hibernian lodge, was tried, convicted, and executed for murder. Campbell had not been present at the murder of Jones, and the prosecution made no attempt to prove that he was; it was enough that he was a member of the AOH. In all, twenty men were hanged, most on flimsy or nonexistent evidence.

What focusing on the specter of the Molly Maguires allowed for was to effectively render moot any and all legitimate labor grievances of the WBA. This was Gowen's most effective contribution to American capitalism. What happened in anthracite coal country in the 1870s was not borne of irrational exuberance or some unpredictable explosion of passion and fear. It was ultimately a carefully stage-managed attempt to rebrand legitimate disputes of class warfare and inequity as violent terrorist free-for-alls.

The Molly Maguires never engendered the same kind of panic and paranoia that had accompanied other panics—for one, Pennsylvania coal country was made up of too many Irish immigrants, who understood from the outset that they were all targets. But scapegoating worked as a legal mechanism, one which allowed for the rapid deployment of collective punishment toward not just possible suspects, but labor organizers and anyone else remotely conceived of as troublesome. It was less about whipping up paranoia and hysteria and more a proof-of-concept for a certain kind of argument.

First as tragedy, then as food and drinks. On a trip to the town now known as Jim Thorpe, Pennsylvania, I visited the jail where four of the Molly Maguires had been martyred on "Black Thursday," June 21, 1877. One of them, AOH treasurer Alexander Campbell, supposedly left a handprint on the wall of his cell as he was being dragged to his death; the handprint, a lasting image of the injustice of those trials, is still there today.

The door to the cell is closed, but you can peer through the bars and see the print on the wall—it's been circled so you won't miss it. I couldn't truly make out a hand; it looked more like a large gray smudge about ten inches in diameter. We were allowed to photograph everything but the handprint itself. The story we were told is that past wardens tried to wash it off and paint over it, but that it remains indelible and permanent. (Yet apparently using a camera—even one without a flash—can supposedly damage it.)

Afterward, I ended up at the popular local Irish pub just down the road, Molly Maguire's Pub & Steakhouse. Over a passable Caesar salad and a Guinness, I tried to strike up a conversation with the locals and ask about the bar's name. The recorded narration at the jail tour speaks of the importance of never forgetting the history of what happened here, but the servers and the other patrons that I talk to had no idea about the Molly Maguires, nor the connection to the pub's name. I quickly gave up once it became clear to me how odd my line of questioning was. Of all the generic Irish bar names throughout the United States, who would ever think to ask why a given bar is called O'Tooles, or Finnegan's, or O'Connor's? Similarly, for the people here, Molly Maguire's is just another generic Irish name, one meant to connote conviviality and good spirits. Even in a town with so much dedicated to keeping the story alive, it seemed, the thread that binds us to the past was fragile and tenuous at best, and the work done to keep that delicate thread intact was always on the verge of failing.

The story, however, lives on in other ways. The Scottish writer Arthur Conan Doyle was already an international celebrity when he met McParland in the early 1910s and was impressed by his story. He repeatedly pressed for details of the case, which he turned into the last of four Sherlock Holmes novels, *The Valley of Fear*. In it, Holmes is summoned to the English countryside, where a man named Douglas has been found dead, presumedly by an assassin belonging to a secret society, who has blasted off enough of Douglas's face that he's only recognizable by his clothes. Eventually, however, Holmes deduces that Douglas is alive, and that after murdering the assassin himself, he faked his own death hoping that the secret society would leave him in peace. The second half of the novel tells of Douglas's earlier history as an undercover informant in a Pennsylvania coal company, where he falls in with a brutish band of Irish terrorists who use a fraternal organization as a cover for their murderous activities.

The turn of the century was the heyday for this new kind of narrative, the detective story, which reached its apex with Sherlock Holmes. The mechanism of the detective story is predicated on the ability of the detective to recognize ordinary, seemingly inconsequential details that reveal a deeper laid plot. In the detective story, the seemingly benign order to the world is in fact a fiction, and the protagonist is the one who can see through that fiction and plumb the depths below. As the reader begins to understand that the surface world's law and order is illusory, the detective reveals a subterranean world of order, one in which sinister figures dominate and the true order is crime itself. In a successful resolution, the detective restores order by defeating or arresting the criminal, and that initial realm of law and order can be reconstituted once again.

The detective genre was well suited to fears of secret societies, since such conspiracy theories are predicated fundamentally on an idea of a hidden order that lies below the surface order. And these stories became increasingly popular in an age where more and more audiences were primed to believe that secret groups like the Molly Maguires were carrying out coordinated plans hidden from sight. In Conan Doyle's retelling of the Molly Maguire unrest, gone are any aspects of labor history and the idea that any of the violence in coal country may have originated in legitimate grievances.

The trials in anthracite coal country demonstrated an incredibly effective way to scapegoat immigrants for labor problems, by hypothesizing about secret groups and underground networks. The elegance of such theories is that anyone can be a target. Anyone who was Irish, or Catholic, might be accused of membership in some subversive group, a group whose orders came from abroad and whose true goal was the dissolution of America and its fragile democracy. What Gowen and others had seen was that these same accusations could now be used against organized labor, as well. The executions themselves are easily on par with Salem in terms of a gross miscarriage of justice and a stain on our legal history. That it has been forgotten is a travesty, but perhaps part of the reason is because it was such a useful strategy—after all, the same play was used less than a decade later, to a much more devastating effect.

On the evening of May 4, 1886, labor leaders had assembled a hasty rally in Haymarket Square in Chicago. A light rain was falling, but still a crowd of between six hundred and three thousand workers had gathered to hear a series of socialist and anarchist speakers. The platform, hastily arranged, was an open hay wagon on Des Plaines Street, just around the corner from square itself. While the mood in the city had been tense all day, the atmosphere that night was calm; the mayor of Chicago, Carter Harrison Sr., had stopped by to observe the proceedings but soon left after he became convinced nothing would happen. Three men spoke that night—August Spies, a German-born Socialist and editor of the radical labor newspaper the *Arbeiter-Zeitung*; Albert Parsons, a Southern-born anarchist and longtime activist on behalf of the formerly enslaved; and teamster and lay preacher Samuel Fielden.

The mood that night was still raw from the previous day's events. Strikers at the nearby McCormick Reaper Works, locked out since February, had attacked scabbing workers leaving the plant, and had been met by a brutal police response, resulting in a melee that left at least two striking workers dead (later estimates would claim there were six fatalities altogether).

After the violence, Spies had returned to his office at the *Arbeiter-Zeitung* distraught. "I knew from experience of the past" he later testified, "that this butchering of people was done for the express purpose of defeating the eight-hour movement." Spies was a Socialist, believing that the redress for inequality was a strong government able to protect citizens' rights. This brand of socialism had received a boost from the Civil War, where it became clear that the only viable means of attacking slavery was a strong government. With Reconstruction, that lesson had only been reinforced: Southern slave states, left to their own devices, would simply carry on slavery by another name unless the federal government stepped in and enforced Black Americans' rights. Anarchists like Albert Parsons, on the other hand, increasingly saw big government as the problem, not the solution. In lieu of a strong, central government working to protect citizens' rights, anarchists favored decentralized, local power, believing that individual communities were better equipped to provide for the needs of their members. But both socialists and anarchists saw themselves as working toward the same basic thing—the fundamental American ethos of equal treatment under the law.

By 10:00 p.m. on the night of the fourth it had begun to rain and most of the crowd had dispersed, some to a nearby tavern frequented by anarchists. Samuel Fielden was the last speaker that night, and as he finished, a wall of police—176 men—approached, seeming to have materialized out of thin air. They moved in to the square, and William Ward, the police captain, commanded the crowd to "immediately and peaceably disperse." Fielden shot back, "But we are peaceable," but then quickly demurred. "All right, we will go," he told Ward.

It was just at that moment that a lit object arced out of the crowd and into the air toward the police. One of them shouted, "Look out. Boys, for God's sake, there is a shell," but it was too late—the bomb exploded, and all hell broke loose.

The explosion threw everything into chaos, scattering the cops, who immediately returned fire. In the aftermath it would be impossible to know exactly what had happened—how many bystanders were killed by cops and how many cops were shot by friendly fire. As a witness later recounted in the *Tribune*, the police, "goaded by madness," were "as dangerous as any mob of Communists, for they were blinded by passion and unable to distinguish between peaceful citizen and Nihilist assassin." When the smoke cleared, one police officer was dead and six others had been mortally wounded.

As with the Molly Maguires, a fundamental problem presents itself to the historian. There is no compelling evidence, one way or another, of who threw the bomb at Haymarket, and barring some miraculous archival discovery, there never will be. It remains one of the great unsolved mysteries in American history. Which is not to say that there aren't a host of theories and those who claim with absolute certainty that they know who was responsible. But who you believe threw the bomb that night is less a matter of fact and more a matter of who you see as the aggressors that day.

At the time, of course, there was little doubt among the general public that an anarchist did it. Chicago businessmen openly called for the lynching of the speakers, pledging the "willing hands" of the city's stock traders. The slain policemen were lionized as heroes in the press, and even labor journalists turned their back on those they believed responsible, arguing that Parsons in particular should be "summarily dealt with," due no more consideration than "wild beasts."

Certainly, there is ample rhetoric from anarchists advocating the use of a recent invention, dynamite. Albert Parsons's wife, Lucy, argued, "The voice of dynamite is the voice of force, the only voice which tyranny has ever been able to understand." For those predisposed to believe that an anarchist—either acting alone or in coordination with others—was responsible for the bomb, this was clear evidence: almost all of the most vocal and prominent leaders in the anarchist movement repeatedly invoked the use of dynamite as an acceptable tactic. Gerhardt Lizius, city editor of *Arbeiter-Zeitung*, spoke for many anarchists with his enthusiastic praise: "Dynamite! Of all the good stuff, this is the stuff."

Historian Timothy Messer-Kruse has concluded that the saboteur was an anarchist named Rudolph Schnaubelt, who fled to Canada and escaped prosecution. But there are plenty of people convinced that the bomb was thrown by someone else: an agent provocateur, perhaps a Pinkerton agent or another cop. After all, the revelations out of Schuylkill County had made it clear that Pinkertons were infiltrating the labor movement, and the fact that McParland's undercover work had neatly coincided with a rapid uptick in Molly Maguire violence that he either provoked, or—if nothing else—failed to stop despite foreknowledge, made it clear to many anarchists of the day (and many labor historians since) that it was quite possible, perhaps even probable, that some combination of law enforcement, Pinkertons, or another hired gun for the factory owners threw the bomb to discredit the anarchists and the labor movement. Howard Zinn's *A People's History of the United States* tentatively agrees with Messer-Kruse about Schnaubelt, yet disagrees about his motives: "Some evidence came out that a man named Rudolph Schnaubelt, supposedly an anarchist, was actually an agent of the police, an *agent provocateur*, hired to throw the bomb and thus enable the arrest of hundreds, the destruction of the revolutionary leadership in Chicago," Zinn writes, but then cautions, "but to this day it has not been discovered who threw the bomb."

In short, both explanations are plausible but neither seems definitive, at least based on the evidence at hand. Any conclusions about what happened that night have to encompass multiple possible suspects, which makes definitive statements about what happened and what it means all but impossible.

At the time, though, everyone thought they knew who was responsible. Paranoia became the order of the day, as police rounded up anarchist suspects all over the city. Every day brought new breathless reports of more suspects, more bomb-making material, more seditious literature. Spies and Schwab were at work the following day on the next edition of their paper when they were arrested, along with the entire staff of the *Arbeiter-Zeitung*. Bomb-making material was found in Spies's office, though he insisted the cops had planted it there. Police came for Albert Parsons's wife Lucy, too. Albert shaved his mustache and fled. Bars known to be frequented by anarchists were closed.

The witch hunt was led by Captain Michael J. Schaack, an ardent foe of anarchists and trade unionists, who was convinced from the very start that some "network of conspiracy extended in every direction," as he would later write in his memoirs of the incident. Schaack and his men set out to round up anyone remotely associated with anarchism or socialism, relying on warrantless searches, intimidation, and his "sweatbox": a small, pitch-black wooden container where suspects would be locked in for hours at a time.

With the ringleaders arraigned, the cops pressed on; every day, it seemed, brought news of more subversives arrested, more caches of weapons discovered. Panic gripped the city, what journalist Brand Whitlock would later call "one of the strangest frenzies of fear that ever distracted a whole community." Police closed down saloons they labeled the "headquarters" of foreigners. Immigrants were rounded up by the dozens and arraigned under the theory that anyone who had spoken in favor of violence against the police could be considered an accomplice of the bombing and eligible for the death penalty. Economist Richard Ely labeled it simply Chicago's "period of police terrorism." Chicagoans became convinced that their entire city had been infiltrated by seditious aliens who had no place in America. "If men can pass their lives among us," worried Professor David Swing, "and never be touched by one ray of religious, social, or political truth, what can we say of America and what of Chicago?"

Ultimately, eight men were tried for the Haymarket bombing, all anarchists and Socialists, including Spies, Schwab, Fielden, and Parsons (who had safely escaped but, in a fatal miscalculation, later turned himself in). All were convicted, all but one sentenced to death, and four (Spies, Parsons, George Engel, and Adolph Fischer) were eventually hanged (Louis Lingg committed suicide in his cell). The last three surviving defendants were pardoned in 1893 by Governor John Peter Altgeld, whose statement suggested that the actual bomber may have had nothing to do with anarchism at all but may have simply had a grudge against the Chicago police, who by then had a long-standing history of brutality.

Though they were charged with murder and accused of conspiracy, the prosecutor, Julius Grinnell, made clear in his opening remarks that the trial was not going to be about the bomber himself, who may or may not have been in the courtroom. "It is not necessary in this kind of case," he told the jury, "that the individual who commits the particular offense—for instance 2, the man who threw the bomb—to be in court at all. He need not even be indicted."

The police were routinely rounding up suspects every day, including people who, they claimed, had bomb-making materials. Why not indict any of them for the bombing? How had they been unable, in such a massive dragnet, to locate a suspect for the actual attack? Even supposing rampant corruption, if they failed to turn up evidence on the killer themselves, why not fabricate it? How could they not find some informant willing to name a name? Why not trump up false charges to pin it on someone?

It was common knowledge, Captain Schaack would later claim, that "the thrower of the bomb was not simply a Guiteau-like crank, but that there must have been a deliberate, organized conspiracy, of which he was a duly constituted agent." Convicting a single actor was far less valuable than uncovering the story of what Assistant States Attorney Francis W. Walker proclaimed in his closing arguments, that there "has been a conspiracy existing in this community to overthrow the law of the State of Illinois by force, for years and years." What is most staggering about the Haymarket Trials is how they were explicitly designed to shift the focus away from the actual criminal offense. Even more so than the trials of the Molly Maguires, the Haymarket Trials used a mutual understanding of a wide-ranging conspiracy to attempt to transfigure a lone act of violence into the work of a secret, coordinated network of subversives.

It was, in a real sense, absolutely vital to the prosecution's case that they *not* try someone for an isolated incident of violence. What was vital was that they try anarchism as a concept. What they were after was not an individual who had committed a heinous act but rather a spectral conspiracy, the mere thought of which had upended the entire city. Chicagoans had begun to see bomb-wielding anarchists everywhere they looked. They didn't need one lone bomber brought to justice; they wanted proof that the law was taking out an entire subterranean network. And the law obliged.

The goal of both the Haymarket Trials and the Molly Maguires trial was to destroy the labor movement by elevating history into myth. In order to do this, you needed a place where the facts were simply unknowable and where in the absence of facts you had nothing but beliefs, and then you needed to enter those beliefs as facts in the courtroom. The creation of secret societies was the preeminent means of doing this. Their invocation short-circuited the basic functioning of the legal system, because to invoke a secret society was to announce that oaths could not be trusted, documentation could not be taken at face value, and that everything innocuous secretly held deeper truths—even those diametrically opposed to the surface story.

Having accomplished this sleight of hand, the prosecution was free to shift the discussion of inequality to a discussion of violence. And in the wake of the Haymarket bombing, the American labor movement was set back decades. The goal of the McCormick strikers had been an eight-hour workday, a policy that seemed on the verge of being realized until that night at the Haymarket. In the wake of that disaster, the United States would not establish the right to an eight-hour workday for everyone until the Fair Labor Standards Act of 1938.

THIRTEEN

A Matter of Trusts

E phraim Benezet is a poor farmer, one who's struggled to get by and lost nearly everything to "grasshoppers, poor crops, 'pools,' 'trusts,' 'rings,' 'high prices for what we bought, low prices for what we sold,' 'burning the candle at both ends,' increasing taxation to support a lot of office-holding non-producers; an increasing family, with another lot of non-producers to support, much beloved, however, of their progenitors; debt, pinching economy, and, at last, that conditional sale of the homestead which is disguised under the name of a 'mortgage.'" What's worse, his sweetheart, Sophie Hetherington, has fallen into disgrace after the bank forecloses on her family's farm. One night in a dream he is visited by an old man who calls himself "The Pity of God," who displays before him a golden flask, in which is a "clear, amber-colored liquid," a drop of which is sufficient to change anything to gold.

Thus begins Ignatius Donnelly's strange 1892 novel, *The Golden Bottle.* In it, Benezet uses his magical device to "redeem mankind": after rescuing Sophie, he establishes a regional bank that lends at 2 percent and functions as a sub-federal reserve, ushering in an age of universal prosperity among the people. Attacked by plutocrats who own the Supreme Court and try to foil his schemes, Benezet builds his own media empire, his own rail system, his own towns. He ultimately gets elected president, then launches an apocalyptic war against Europe that ushers in the new millennium and a "Universal Republic" of Jesus Christ.

The notion that East Coast bankers and their politician puppets were preventing ordinary working Americans from realizing their dreams is an old conspiracy, and one that lingers with us to this day. This, despite the fact that it doesn't initially look like other conspiracy theories surrounding secret cabals. Bankers are hardly a protected class, after all; they are not a religious or ethnic minority, and they are not, as a group, particularly marginalized—quite the opposite in fact.

Their emergence as a target for conspiracy theories in the late nineteenth and early twentieth century reflects the beginning of a major shift in American paranoia. Previously, only the Slave Power had come close to being conceptualized as a dominant conspiracy *within* the government. But with the populist movements of the late nineteenth century, banking conspiracies began to reinvigorate the Slave Power narrative. Slavery was no longer the primary economic motive of course, but otherwise it was the same: powerful capitalists controlled too much of the federal government and had begun to deny ordinary Americans their basic democratic rights in an all-out pursuit for ill-gotten wealth.

There's certainly some amount of truth to this; there always has been. Power and wealth tend to breed corruption, and American's financial sector is hardly an outlier in this regard. But the increasingly elaborate and mythical corruption and malevolence attributed to Wall Street at the time augurs a psychological need that goes beyond recognizing that the playing field is uneven. We use conspiracy theories, after all, not just to demonize critiques of capitalism, but also to manage the cognitive dissonance that comes with being subject to capitalism. But at the dawn of the twentieth century, this meant seeing the federal government not just as a victim of conspiracy, but as an active participant—and in this shift one gets a glimpse of how such conspiracy theories persist even as the world around them changes.

The Federal Reserve has long attracted the eye of paranoid cranks because of the very circuitous process of its birth. Unlike its counterparts in Europe, the United States lacked a central bank for much of its early history, aside from two brief periods. In both cases, the central bank was allowed to wither, failing to receive congressional reauthorization out of a fear of centralized government. As a result, during its first hundred and twenty years of its existence, the country had been buffeted by almost constant economic panics and financial depressions.

Between 1873 and 1907, America suffered five severe banking crises and twenty lesser panics. The financial system was defined, above all, to prevent inflation, which meant restricting the amount of currency in circulation, and thus restricting the liquidity of the financial markets. Currency was pegged to the gold standard (every bill in circulation was backed by gold held by the government in reserve), which meant that during moments of financial crisis, the government was unable to introduce more currency to stabilize the markets, so when panics hit, they hit hard. What bank reserves there were on hand to ease bank runs and panics were too far spread out amongst many little banks to be of any use; one economist likened the system to a town without a fire department but with a bucket of water in each household to put out fires. These economic shocks had long since been politicized, but the truth of the matter was simply that the American banking system—hobbled by a long-standing distrust of centralized government, laissez-faire to the point of chaos—was a mess.

By the 1890s, the dysfunction had coalesced around the gold standard: at a crossroads, all of the nation's hopes and fears, it seemed, came down to whether or not the country would stay on the gold standard. The status quo tended to favor Wall Street and the Northeast; the agrarian

South and West, on the other hand, desperately wanted off the gold standard so that the currency markets could inject more liquidity into the system. Agriculture, in particular, is an economy that deals in booms and busts, and having ready access to credit is necessary to maintain a smooth-functioning industry.

Economic populists repeatedly demanded moving off the gold standard, most famously in William Jennings Bryan's "Cross of Gold" speech. Delivered at the Democratic National Convention in 1896, Bryan argued that the country needed a bimetallism standard (accepting silver as a backing for currency as well as gold), and the rhetorical strength of his speech was enough to garner him the nomination for the presidency (though he lost to William McKinley). The gold standard, meanwhile, was championed by those with capital; those most invested in the gold standard were the Wall Street bankers like J. P. Morgan and their allies in Washington, D. C.

Because credit was loose in the Northeast and scarce in the Midwest, bank policy resulted in an uneven distribution of the future; those in New York could envision a prosperous United States as it strained to measure up to Europe, while those farther afield saw only a backward nation unnecessarily hobbling its citizens.

Without Benezet's magic bottle to save the American economy, Washington had no choice but to turn to Wall Street. Because the American banking system itself was so tenuous, the government relied ultimately on private bankers to keep the nation out of complete financial ruin. In 1895, the government was forced to secretly buy gold reserves from J. P. Morgan just to stay solvent. Morgan, himself no altruist, of course made a profit on the transaction, which would lead to accusations of conspiracy among the moneyed interests of Wall Street. The following year, William Jennings Bryan's presidential campaign further forced the issue; even though he was unsuccessful at winning the presidency, those on Wall Street could see a reckoning was coming.

For the next decade, though, they struggled over what to do. Among those stridently in favor of the gold standard was Nelson Aldrich, a Republican senator from Rhode Island and a major party boss. Populists despised Aldrich, who was instrumental in killing any monetary reforms that didn't benefit corporate interests. At a stalemate in the 1890s, it would take another crisis in 1907 to finally spur the government to action. In the fall of 1906, the Bank of England raised its interest rate from 3.5 percent to 6 percent; Germany's Reichsbank raised its rate as well. Capital flowed out of the US back to Europe. This and other measures by the Bank of England caused a tightening of credit in the United States; the next year, a copper magnate's attempt to artificially manipulate the price of copper on Wall Street caused a full-born panic. Banks failed, their crises cascading into one another in a manner reminiscent of the panic that would lead to the Great Recession of 2008.

Once again, dissent broke along regional lines; the further west you went, the more agreement there was that the banking sector was responsible for this crisis, and that they were unworthy of so much power. A Wisconsin senator, Robert M. La Follette, charged that a "group of financiers who withhold and dispense prosperity" had "deliberately brought on the late panic, to serve their own ends." Most were in agreement that the Panic of 1907 had resulted from Wall Street's greed, and that even now the crisis was being manipulated so bankers could make money off the chaos. Looking back from a century's vantage point, it's hard to disagree.

Despite his aversion to central banking, the 1906 crash finally persuaded Senator Aldrich to do something. A fact-finding mission to England and Europe to see how other countries handled economic policy was a sobering rebuke to his long-held principles. Every other advanced economy worked with a central bank that provided confidence in the market and liquidity as needed, and all without having to keep on hand the amount of bank reserves that Aldrich assumed the US needed. Humbled, he resolved to create a new banking system that would emulate what he'd seen across the Atlantic and bring stability to the American economy. In doing so, one might have assumed, the conspiracy theories would finally end.

But the exact opposite happened—Aldrich's plan would only further stoke the fires of conspiracy.

Aldrich decided that his plan had to be hatched in secret, so in November 1910, he arranged a secret meeting at Jekyll Island, Georgia—one that would involve himself, Henry Davison (senior partner at J.P. Morgan & Company), the economist Paul Warburg, Frank Vanderlip (president of the National City Bank), Piatt Andrew (assistant secretary of the Treasury), and Arthur Shelton (Aldrich's personal secretary). For a week at one of the richest and most exclusive clubs in the world, these six men worked through the night devising a new system of banking for the United States. They were impressed by the European nations' use of central banks but knew that something that appeared too centralized would raise suspicion in a country still distrustful of Washington and Wall Street. The system they designed instead would have a series of regional banks, their members and governors democratically appointed, that would together make monetary policy for the country.

It would take another three years before their plan (mostly unchanged) was enshrined into law as the Federal Reserve Act. And while most economists have since agreed that it was a strong solution to the seemingly intractable problem of America's fractured economy, the six men at Jekyll Island never claimed credit. Aside from rumors and a single article in 1916, it wouldn't be until 1930, with an authorized biography of Aldrich, that actual details started to emerge of the meeting. It was not like such men to duck public acclaim for their philanthropic work. As Roger Lowenstein writes in his history of the Federal Reserve, "the bankers spoke with bitterness at having to steal about as though they were criminals. In their own minds, and in any fair rendering, they were attempting to achieve a worthy public reform. They were conspirators, but patriotic conspirators."

Patriotic or not, it was the charge of conspiracy that would ultimately stick. Perhaps this was unavoidable. There was little Aldrich—or anyone on Wall Street—could have done at that late date to stave off accusations of conspiracy. The dysfunctional system of American monetary policy, which had been unworkable since the end of the second Bank of the United States, laid the groundwork for future conspiracy theories decades before the Federal Reserve was even conceived of. By comingling private interests with governmental solvency, the government made itself vulnerable to all manner of charges of collusion, corruption, and conspiracy. Further, by employing a laissez-faire approach for decades, the United States all but encouraged its citizens to develop ad hoc explanations for the wild economic swings that buffeted their lives on an almost daily basis.

So by the time the government finally took action, it was likely already too late to quell the conspiracy theories. But it would be the *manner* in which Aldrich chose to go about solving the problem that would ultimately be responsible for a whole new generation of conspiratorial paranoia.

Why did Aldrich insist on shrouding the meeting in secrecy? He guessed, no doubt correctly, that if the plan could be traced back to Wall Street, the American public would never accept it. Further, he himself was hated as an enemy of the very plan he now found himself advocating—as an apostate, he was untrustworthy, and his imprimatur was as good as a death warrant. As Lowenstein notes, "For gold bugs, anti-Federal Reserve zealots, and flat-out cranks, the 1910 escapade would come to assume mythic significance. . . . For such writers, Jekyll became a metaphor for central banking, supposedly an international plot to bury civilization in debts. Since central bank notes are a form of obligation, each dollar issued by the Federal Reserve, each pound minted by the Bank of England, was, it was alleged, an added enslavement."

It didn't matter; when the plan was finally unveiled, it was assailed by the very populists who, it would have seemed, were most likely to support it.

Aldrich had been right in one sense: the names behind the bill would ultimately matter more than its actual contents. Because it was associated with Aldrich, it was denounced as conservatism rather than populism; those who could not be bothered to read or understand the bill took Aldrich's participation as a kiss of death, proof that it was more Wall Street shenanigans. In the three years it took to get the bill through Congress, the coin had been cast.

The first news of the Jekyll Island meeting was published in 1916, in an article by B. C. Forbes (a year before he founded the financial magazine that bears his name) that described the meeting in a breathless tone filled with conspiratorial insinuation. "Picture a party of the nation's greatest bankers stealing out of New York on a private railroad car under cover of darkness," Forbes's article began, "stealthily hieing hundreds of miles South, embarking on a mysterious launch, sneaking on to an island deserted by all but a few servants, living there a full week under such rigid secrecy that the name of not one of them was once mentioned lest the servitors learn their identity and disclose to the world this strangest, most secret episode in the history of American finance." While Forbes himself recognized both the expertise of these men and the ultimate purpose of the Federal Reserve, others took his article as proof of a far darker conspiracy.

Chief among them was Charles August Lindbergh Sr., Minnesota congressman and father to the famous aviator. In 1917, Lindbergh formally accused the five governors of the Federal Reserve of high crimes and misdemeanors, citing Forbes's article as evidence that they'd engaged in "a conspiracy to violate the Constitution and the laws of the

United States and the just and equitable policies of the Government." Lindbergh alleged that the entire creation of the Federal Reserve had been a massive conspiracy, and that J. P. Morgan and others had conspired "with each other to devise means through social, political, and other ways of strategy and by general chicanery, to deceive the people of the United States," all with the object of paving the way for a central banking system.

Lindbergh had long been afraid of any such financial system, and in 1912 had successfully campaigned to have Congress investigate what he called the "money trust." The subsequent congressional committee, named after its chair, Arsène Paulin Pujo, discovered a number of predatory practices among Wall Street bankers and lenders, but uncovered no proof of conspiracy. Now, with news of this secret meeting, Lindbergh felt he had the goods.

His accusations went nowhere in Congress, and the following year, Lindbergh ran for governor of Minnesota. An ardent isolationist, he published an anti-war pamphlet entitled "Why Is Your Country at War?" Almost immediately, federal agents operating under Comstock laws descended on Lindbergh's publisher, ordering them to destroy the printing plates of the seditious text, along with his earlier critique of the Federal Reserve: *Banking and Currency and the Money Trust*.

Meanwhile, William Jennings Bryan called it "absolute commercial and industrial slavery." Alfred Owen Crozier's tract, *U. S. Money vs. Corporation Currency*, further assailed the plan, hinting that something was rotten in Manhattan. "Why should not Wall Street have panics once in a while?" Crozier offered rhetorically. "And if Providence won't send a panic, why not make one, when it is so easy and will be so useful and profitable." Crozier suggested that the Panic of 1907 had been simply part of the setup: that it had been engineered by Aldrich and Morgan so that the public, in chaos and afraid, would come running to the arms of a "huge private money trust to monopolize and forever control the entire public currency" of the country. It had all been planned, it was all part of the conspiracy. The goal may have been to create a system that would lessen the near-daily economic crises of America's old system, but everyone outside of New York City or Washington, D.C. assumed that hidden somewhere in Aldrich's plan was the means by which the ordinary working man would be further fleeced.

B ecause of its origin and the confusion surrounding the creation of the Federal Reserve, conspiracy theories have been constant. Was there a conspiracy behind the creation of the Federal Reserve? Not likely. As Lowenstein notes, "It is a truism of capitalism that if money is injected into the system, no matter the intent, some of it will end up benefiting well-connected financiers." No matter what system America adopted, men like J. P. Morgan were going to profit. Beyond that, though, we must again distinguish between the conspiratorial and the criminal. Wall Street is full of criminals, as with any industry—though the crimes in the financial sector tend to involve larger sums and do more damage to society as a whole (no one holding up a liquor store for loose cash ever triggered a global recession). Certainly, criminal actors have conspired to defraud their customers and the government—some have been caught, some got away with it. The conspiracist, however, does not merely accept criminality and its fallout; the conspiracist posits a malevolence that goes beyond personal enrichment, whose stakes are the battle of good and evil itself. Further, the conspiracist posits not just skill but omnipotence; everything that's happened has been engineered by design. Most of us could see that a global recession like the housing meltdown in 2008 is proof that many bankers had no idea what they were doing and couldn't foresee the long-term consequences of their short-term avarice. Conspiracy theory posits the opposite of this, that all of this was simply part of a larger plan.

But a lack of evidence and logic could not stop the poet and anti-Semite Ezra Pound, who continued to insist that the Fed was a conspiracy, and ended up doing more than anyone else to keep the canard alive. While institutionalized at St. Elizabeths Hospital in Washington, D.C., claiming to be mentally unfit to stand trial for his treasonous actions during World War II, Pound would discuss history and politics with his famous poet friends and a coterie of young burgeoning fascists, including the neo-Nazi Eustace Mullins. One day, with Mullins, the elder poet produced a ten-dollar bill, pointing to the words "Federal Reserve Note" on the front and the image of the US Treasury Building on the reverse. Explaining to Mullins that this was all proof of a conspiracy hiding in plain sight, Pound paid him to research the Federal Reserve, and the latter ultimately publishing his findings in 1952 as *The Secrets of the Federal Reserve*, which leaned heavily on the Jekyll Island meeting's mythic status as proof of conspiracy.

After all, a group of powerful men meeting in secret could only add fuel to the belief that there are nefarious plans afoot. It's easy to cast suspicion on such actions, as G. Edward Griffin did in his perennially popular 1994 book *The Creature from Jekyll Island*, which essentially recycled Mullins's arguments without the overt anti-Semitism (beyond various dog whistles and references to the "Rothschilds"), and argued for a return to the gold standard, an argument seized upon by former senator Ron Paul in his 2009 book, *End the Fed*.

Meanwhile, a popular (but false) quote that continues to roam the Internet purports to be from Woodrow Wilson, supposedly from 1919, in which he laments: "I am a most unhappy man. I have unwittingly ruined my country. A great industrial nation is controlled by its system of credit. Our system of credit is concentrated. The growth of the nation, therefore, and all our activities are in the hands of a few men. We have come to be one of the worst ruled, one of the most completely controlled and dominated Governments in the civilized world—no longer a Government by free opinion, no longer a Government by conviction and the vote of the majority, but a Government by the opinion and duress of a small group of dominant men."

And to this day, one can still find floating around the Internet, lurking like a dark iceberg of nonsense, theories that argue that the *Titanic* was deliberately sunk in order to make way for the Federal Reserve. Three of the most prominent critics of the Federal Reserve plan, one such website claims, were Benjamin Guggenheim; Isidor Straus, the co-owner of Macy's department stores; and John Jacob Astor—all of whom died on the *Titanic*, a ship that J. P. Morgan had "funded and built," and on which Morgan had a ticket that he canceled at the last minute.

Morgan did indeed bankroll International Mercantile Marine, which financed the White Star Line and the building of the *Titanic*, but beyond that, there's no *there* there. But none of that truly matters; what matters is that a hopelessly complicated system—one with a myriad of stakeholders, many of whom are corrupt or at the very least greedy—be reduced to a simple plan, a simple morality tale. Increasingly, it seems, we respond to complexity by a demand for simplicity, the Devil taking the place of the details.

FOURTEEN

The World's Enigma

You have to track down an early edition of John Buchan's spy novel *The 39 Steps* to find the passage; it's been cut—with good reason—from most modern editions. The protagonist, Richard Hannay, meets a strange, paranoid man, Franklin P. Scudder, who prophecies assassinations and conspiracy. "He told me some queer things," Hannay tells the reader, "that explained a lot that had puzzled me—things that happened in the Balkan War, how one state suddenly came out on top, why alliances were made and broken, why certain men disappeared, and where the sinews of war came from." The point, Scudder explains to Hannay, is to draw Germany and Russia into war, which would make a great deal of people rich ("Capital, he said, had no conscience and no fatherland."). But aside from that, such a war would be disastrous to Russia, and, Scudder explains, "the Jew was behind it, and the Jew hated Russia worse than hell."

Buchan's *The 39 Steps*, a classic bestseller and the template for the modern spy novel, also contains in it the logic of modern anti-Semitism, boiled down to a tight 190 words:

"Do you wonder?" he cried. "For three hundred years they have been persecuted, and this is the return match for the *pogroms*. The Jew is everywhere, but you have to go far down the backstairs to find him.

"Take any big Teutonic business concern. If you have dealings with it the first man you meet is Prince *von und zu* Something, an elegant young man who talks Eton-and-Harrow English. But he cuts no ice. If your business is big, you get behind him and find a prognathous Westphalian with a retreating brow and the manners of a hog.

"He is the German business man that gives your English papers the shakes. But if you're on the biggest kind of job and are bound to get to the real boss, ten to one you are brought up against a little white-faced Jew in a bath-chair with an eye like a rattlesnake. Yes, sir, he is the man who is ruling the world just now, and he has his knife in the Empire of the Tsar, because his aunt was outraged and his father flogged in some one-horse location on the Volga."

That Buchan's novel opens with such naked anti-Semitism, and yet this passage can be cut from the book without changing really anything else about it, says a great deal about how anti-Semitism works. It is everything and it is nothing, it is everywhere and nowhere. Anti-Semitism is fundamentally built on contradictions: as with Buchan's formulation, the anti-Semite sees global instability as caused by the Jews, motivated both by an amoral greed and out of a passionate revenge for the pogroms. Jews are simultaneously described as sexually rapacious and physically weak; they are a small, tiny minority but capable of massive power; they are hyper-capitalists but also Communists bent on destroying capitalism.

This paradox of anti-Semitism may explain what happened to Rosika Schwimmer. A Hungarian Jew, Schwimmer had become a globally known advocate for peace once World War I broke out. On a tour through the

United States in the fall of 1915, she was approached by the industrialist Henry Ford, who shared her pacificist views and had vowed that summer to do everything in his power to "prevent murderous, wasteful war in America and in the whole world." Schwimmer saw in Ford a powerful ally and when she met him at his offices on November 17, she found no need to convert him to her mission.

At some point during their conversation, however, Ford unloaded a bombshell: "I know who caused the war," he told her, "German-Jewish bankers." Slapping his breast pocket, he continued, "I have the evidence here. Facts! The German-Jewish bankers caused the war. I can't give out the facts now, because I haven't got them all yet, but I'll have them soon." Horrified, Schwimmer said nothing, and even agreed to an invitation to meet his wife at his home the following week. Ford, meanwhile, despite his overt anti-Semitism, responded warmly to Schwimmer, ultimately bankrolling her plan to send a mission of peace activists to Europe to broker an end to the war. The mission failed, reducing Ford to a laughingstock, and later Schwimmer would find herself blamed in the press for the industrialist's increasingly visible anti-Semitism.

Having subsequently talked to so many conspiracists during the past few years—a time that has once again seen unprecedented upheaval—it's hard not to see in Ford's statements here the secret *relief* in the face of a conspiracy theory. Here he was, an ardent pacificist and also one of the most powerful, successful entrepreneurs of the United States, unable to stop a war he despised and increasingly afraid that his own country would get drawn into it. Entertaining a belief that this is all happening because of an unstoppable, hidden cabal, whose evilness is matched only by their omnipotence, means there's nothing you can do. He could embrace ugliness because it was easy, because it let him off the hook, and because it simplified things.

Ford's ability to casually espouse anti-Semitic talking points even in the presence of Jews he ostensibly liked reflected a prevailing American attitude. Like most Christians in America, Ford had been raised with a standard amount of background noise anti-Semitism that he had more or less internalized. As a child, he'd learned literacy from the enormously popular McGuffey Reader Series, which included excerpts from *The Merchant of Venice* and advised that "Jewish authors were incapable of the diction and strangers to the morality contained in the gospel." (Ford was so fond of the McGuffey Readers that as an adult he had them reprinted and distributed to libraries across the country, and eventually relocated the cabin McGuffey was raised in to his museum in Greenfield Village, Michigan.)

Most enmity toward the Jews in America ran along religious lines: the slur that Jews were heretics and "Christ killers." Odious and noxious, such beliefs were also centuries-old and slowly becoming anachronistic in a modernizing, secularizing world. The Jewish population in the United States, after all, was small, and largely made up of prosperous, assimilated, middle-class families of German immigrants. In Europe, meanwhile, Jews continued to be—as they had been for centuries—convenient scapegoats for repressive governments and Christian reactionaries. Persecutions and accusations of "blood libel"—the belief that Jews abducted and ritually sacrificed Christian children to use their blood in religious ceremonies—were common.

The last true blood libel case in Europe happened in Kiev in 1913, when Russian officials conspired to frame an innocent man named Mendel Beilis for the murder of a young boy named Andrei Yushchinsky. Yuschinsky had gone missing on March 12, 1911, playing hooky from school; his body was found eight days later, half-dressed; he'd been stabbed forty-seven times and lost most of his blood. Beilis, a brick factory superintendent was quickly singled out as a scapegoat, and in the ensuing hysteria, leaflets appeared throughout the city, claiming that every year before Passover, Jews "torture to death several dozens of Christian children to get their blood to mix with their *matzos*. They do this in commemoration of our Saviour, whom they tortured to death on the cross."

Beilis's trial was about more than just a murder; the prosecution's goal was not just to show that he had killed the boy, but that his motive was ritual sacrifice—it was vital, in other words, not just to convict Beilis, but the Jews as a faith. The Russian government was leaning heavily on anti-Semitism to deflect internal tensions. In 1902, the interior minister, Vyacheslav von Plehve, put this plainly when he said: "There is no revolutionary movement in Russia, there are only Jews who are the true enemies of the government." Establishing the Jews as the enemies of both Christianity *and* the government did wonders in scapegoating any legitimate protest. But despite immense pressure from the highest echelons of the Russian government, the prosecution failed to secure a conviction, and Samuel Beilis was released, a free man. (The Beilis case didn't make much news in the United States at the time, and no blood libel accusations were leveled against American Jews, but it would be less than a century before the accusation of blood libel arose once more from American conspiracists, this time a vaguely secularized form that accused Democrats, Hollywood celebrities, and members of the LGBTQi community of conspiring to use children in blood sacrifice rituals.)

In the last two decades of the nineteenth century, 675,000 Jews had immigrated to the United States, more than double the number previously living there. Such mass numbers were driven by European pogroms in Russia and Eastern Europe, where autocratic rulers increasingly tried to scapegoat political and cultural instability on Jewish minorities. Now, in addition to prosperous, assimilated Jewish families mainly from Germany, the United States had scores of poorer, working-class Jews clustered in cities (New York City's Jewish population exploded from 80,000 people in the 1870s to 1.5 million by 1915), many not speaking English and many Orthodox, and thus more overtly visible as non-Christians.

Hotels, resorts, and other cultural establishments began restricting access to Jews, even in places that had once been welcoming. And no more were Jews simply treated as a religious Other; now, American bigots began conceiving of them as inimical to America itself. As with Catholics, American Protestants saw Jews as unable to participate fully in democracy: an 1845 pamphlet from the American Sunday School Union advised that the resemblance "between Judaism and Popery is clear and remarkable," among other reasons, because both supposedly set "aside the right of private judgment for the interpretations of commentators."

By the end of the nineteenth century, religious animosity had shifted to a more race-based anti-Semitism, most notably with the publication of Telemachus Thomas Timayenis's 1888 books *The Original Mr. Jacobs* and *The American Jew*. Timayenis argued a fundamental difference between the "Aryan" and the Jew: "The one is the child of light, the other of darkness. See how the Aryan raises his head and looks toward the sky; while the Jew constantly looks on the ground, always thinking, always meditating, always contriving, always plotting, plotting, plotting." This was a marked shift from religious differences toward identity; Timayenis strove to offer a typology of character.

This increasing turn to a racialized form of anti-Semitism coincided with two other rising forms of paranoia: fears of socialists and anarchists on the one hand, and a distrust of bankers and the financial system on the other. Both of these involved fears of internationalism. International anarchists and international banking both invoke a series of subterranean networks (one nominally subversive, the other nominally legal) that run through the United States (and other countries, for that matter), ignoring boundaries. And for American anti-Semites, increasingly it became the Jews, and not the Catholics, who best exemplified this. Which is why when the country's most prominent anti-Semite turned his massive propaganda machine against America's Jewish population, he did so through a series of articles entitled "The International Jew: The World's Foremost Problem."

Henry Ford had bought *The Dearborn Independent*—a small, ailing

newspaper—with the hope of using it as a bullhorn to rehabilitate his image as well as shape his vision of America. Despite his success with cutting-edge technology, Ford remained keenly nostalgic for the simpler, agrarian America of his childhood, and he used his newspaper to push a version of America that favored small-town farming, abstemious lifestyles, and church dances. Starting in 1920, he also used it to push his anti-Semitic view of the world. With a reach of 700,000, it was by far the most influential organ for such bigotry, and it drove such conspiratorial musings out of backrooms and into the mainstream public, institutionalizing it and seeking to legitimize it in the press and American culture.

The "International Jew" series, launched on May 22, 1920, totaled ninety articles that appeared weekly for almost two years, in which Ford's mouthpiece hammered on strange contradictions: "The Jew is the world's enigma. Poor in his masses, he yet controls the world's finances. . . . Living under legal disabilities in almost every land, he has become the power behind many a throne." It singled out prominent Jews in culture and finance by name, including Federal Reserve vice-chair Paul Warburg and co-owner of Sears, Roebuck and Company Julius Rosenwald. Most of all, it translated virulent hate into an avuncular, folksy idiom that it connected to "wholesome" American values and a nostalgia for an agrarian past.

Behind the *Dearborn Independent*'s articles was another far stranger and more odious document, which laid the groundwork for connecting the internationalism of socialism, the internationalism of banking, and the Jews together. It was a cheap, slapdash, and confused muddle of a book, a patent forgery, nearly a joke—and yet, it became the most important book of the twentieth century, and it was the book that Ford relied on for his anti-Semitic attacks. Much of the *Dearborn Independent* articles were translations, paraphrases, and exegeses of it. And if Lincoln was right that *Uncle Tom's Cabin* started the Civil War, then the same can be said of World War II and *The Protocols of the Elders of Zion*.

The book emerged somewhere out of Russia at the beginning of the twentieth century. The French aristocrat Alexandre du Chayla first reported hearing of it in a monastery in 1909, when a man named Sergei Nilus showed it to him and translated excerpts during his stay. Nilus (who was so paranoid he didn't keep the manuscript with him for fear of it being stolen) told du Chayla he'd received it from Pyotr Ivanovich Rachkovsky, head of the Okhrana, the Russian secret police—a man with a talent for forging documents and a penchant for blaming the Jews for Russia's ills. Described by one acquaintance as "Fat, restless, always with a smile on his lips," Rachkovsky is the person who was most likely responsible for the *Protocols*.

From almost the very beginning, it was evident the book was a forgery. In August 1921, the *Times* of London was among the first to trace material in the *Protocols* back to a satire by Maurice Joly, titled *Dialogue aux Enfers entre Machiavel et Montesquieu* (*The Dialogue in Hell Between Machiavelli and Montesquieu*). Joly was a lawyer who conceived of the book as an allegory of Napoleon III's repressive policies—since open dissent was not possible, he reasoned he could put Napoleon III's ideas and politics into the mouth of Machiavelli, while Montesquieu could be the voice of liberalism and reason. There is in Joly's *Dialogue* a kind of bitter sarcasm, an awareness that no matter how carefully and beautifully designed a political system might be, it will be forever undone by the worst elements in humanity. Additionally, as with John Milton's *Paradise Lost*, Joly (perhaps inadvertently) made the villain the far more engaging and charismatic figure—Machiavelli is throughout more eloquent and more persuasive than Montesquieu the straight man.

At some point, the Russian secret police reworked Joly's satire into the anti-Semitic drivel it became. As with the Bavarian Illuminati, the *Protocols* emerged from a country undergoing significant cultural and political change, and the specificity of its original politics are more or

less meaningless, bordering on incoherent, from our modern vantage point. Almost without fail, our fear of and obsession with specific secret societies can be traced back to specific political revolutions, and the hodgepodge of conspiracy theories that now exist around them testify to the sustained echo those revolutions can have on modern life. In the fog of upheaval and the confusion surrounding rapid, unprecedented change, people look for simple answers and some are more than happy to latch on to conspiracy theories as they arise. That the Learned Elders of Zion were in fact not all that different from Barruel's conception of the Illuminati reveals how all of these conspiracies can be traced back, in some way, to the French and American Revolutions: from the very foundations of democracy, it turns out, people looked to whispers of secret societies to make sense of the events of the day.

The *Protocols* appeared at a time when the age-old slur against the Jews—that they were behind the monetary system—had begun to evolve. The charges of blood libel weren't as effective as they used to be, but whispers of coordinated Jewish networks seemed to resonate altogether differently. As proponents for liberalism and democracy, they began to be seen as the hidden actors fomenting such changes. In Christian Europe, where there was a tight connection between religious and governmental authorities, non-Christians were naturally disenfranchised. It stood to reason, then, that of course Jews would benefit from the kind of liberal democratic movements that began to sweep the world in the wake of the American Revolution.

But there were plenty of those who rejected these democratic reforms, and some of those looked and saw the Jewish community as a synecdoche for this new world. As America moved away from its reliance on Protestantism as the default religion, Jews could be lumped in with this secularizing trend. Attempting to paint secularization and modernity as not the natural expression and evolution of the country but rather a sinister plan of a hidden cabal of Jews allowed for a means to push back against these changes, one that would become increasingly durable for the next century. Anti-Semitism, in other words, became political at the end of the nineteenth century: it was not just a racist impulse, but a rejection of one mode of politics in favor of another.

In a 1999 radio broadcast, American anti-Semite William Luther Pierce, author of *The Turner Diaries* (a notorious novel that white terrorists like Timothy McVeigh have singled out as an inspiration), asked rhetorically, "Did you ever wonder why the Jews are such great proponents of democracy?" He went on to claim that any time democracy was under attack, the "Jews are ready to send the US armed forces in, and bomb and kill until everyone is permitted to vote," because, he concluded most people aren't smart, and those unable to think for themselves "have their thinking done for them by the people who control the mass media. Which is to say, democracy is the preferred system because it gives the political power to those who own or control the mass media and at the same time it allows them to remain behind the scenes and evade responsibility for the way in which they use that power." By tarring all aspects of modernity and progress—from the right to vote to international finance—with the smear of conspiracy, the anti-Semite hopes to turn back the clock. As political scientist Stephen Eric Bronner explains, "Antisemitism was never simply an independent impulse. It was always part of a broader project directed against the civilizing impulse of reason and the dominant forces of modernity." Thus it was an easy export out of Russia to the rest of the world. Russia may have been undergoing the transition to modernity in a particularly painful and acute fashion, but this tension between the old world and the new was being felt everywhere, from Paris, France, to Dearborn, Michigan.

Anachronistic, poorly written, an obvious forgery, libelous—understanding the *Protocols'* reach means abandoning how we normally think of texts and their impact, particularly on the conspiratorial mind. From the very beginning, the utter transparency of the *Protocols'* forgery has been an asset, not a liability. In one of Ezra Pound's infamous radio broadcasts from Italy, delivered on Hitler's birthday in 1943, he addressed the *Protocols*, beginning with a circular logic that would seem to defy all sense: "If or when one mentions the Protocols alleged to be of the Elders of Zion, one is frequently met with the reply: Oh, but they are a forgery," he begins, then goes on to argue, "certainly they are a forgery, and that is the one proof we have of their authenticity." (In this, Pound was echoing another book he was fond of during this period: Hitler's *Mein Kampf.* "They are based on a forgery, the *Frankfurter Zeitung* moans and screams once every week: the best proof that they are authentic.")

The problem, in essence, is that one side of the dialogue is busy proving the book is a forgery, and that, on a basic level, words mean something and facts can be proven. On the other side, however, anti-Semites like Pound and Hitler sidestep this entirely: they take its contents seriously but not literally. The point is to get their audience to base their opinions not on what is objectively provable, but what is "in their hearts."

As the Existentialist philosopher Jean-Paul Sartre would later explain, anti-Semites are not interested in a serious debate. For Sartre, anti-Semitism is a venue for escaping the pain of existence, with hate becoming the vector by which one avoids the difficulties bound up in a more authentic existence. "How can one choose to reason falsely?" he asks. "It is because of a longing for impenetrability. The rational man groans as he gropes for the truth; he knows that his reasoning is no more than tentative, that other considerations may supervene to cast doubt on it." There are others, by contrast, "who are attracted by the durability of a stone. They wish to be massive and impenetrable; they wish not to change." Such a longing for ignorance finds refuge in racism, Sartre continues. "The anti-Semite has chosen hate because hate is a faith; at the outset he has chosen to devalue words and reasons. How entirely at ease he feels as a result. How futile and frivolous discussions about the rights of the Jew appear to him. He has placed himself on other ground from the beginning." To "read" the *Protocols* as an anti-Semite, then, is to disregard much of its actual content, because the goal here is to seize upon it as evidence of a "truth" behind its own words.

Much of its actual content, after all, is focused on the specific political climates of mid-nineteenth century France and fin de siècle Russia. The actual *Protocols* focuses on three different main topics: first, a critique of liberalism; second, an analysis of how the Jews will achieve domination; and third, a description of the world-state to come. Written for an audience of Russian aristocrats who benefited under the Russian imperial government, the *Protocols* is pro-aristocracy, and pro-monarchy; it attempts to not only identify Judaism with democracy, but also argue that there are worse things than authoritarianism. If we allow democracy to take its course, the *Protocols* suggests, it will degenerate into a perverse autocracy. We're better off, paradoxically, by putting our faith in the repressive authoritarian governments that are fighting against democracy. (For this reason, as many have noted, the *Protocols* served as the blueprint not for Jewish domination but for those repressive regimes most likely to target Jews, including the Nazis.)

And yet, at the same time, the *Protocols* suggest that if the Jews were to achieve their plans of world domination, life would actually not be that bad. Among the various precepts of this sinister rule, society will be made to function efficiently, and taxation will be proportionate to wealth. Unemployment will be abolished, with everyone assigned an employment that matches their skills and interests. The insidious plan of the Elders of Zion, it turns out, is to ensure compliance of the masses by attending to their needs and ensuring their happiness.

It is, in other words, a confused and incoherent document, one that is all but impossible to take seriously once one has actually read it. Its terrible power comes more from its mere existence; its biggest adherents either don't read it at all or willfully read *through* it to adapt it to their own needs. The message of the *Protocols* is not that Jews are evil so much as it is *what is false is true*. The *Protocols* is an invitation to disregard any shared consensus of meaning in favor of a privately held truth, one that supersedes any factual correction. This is what the *Protocols* has gifted modern fascism: an awareness that violence is best furthered by ambiguous texts and utterances. The book offers a seduction into the world of knowing nonsense. By proffering itself as both a transparently shoddy pile of contradictions and the most meaningful document ever uncovered, it offers a reassurance that nothing means anything.

The fundamental configuration of anti-Semitism is that only the end goal of the Jewish community is known: total domination and the destruction of any Gentile way of life. The means to such an end are deliberately under-theorized, left vague and abstract, and often configured as explicitly contradictory. That way, *anything* can be recognized as a sign of Jewish malevolence. Any sign, symbol, or action is further proof of a secret, obscure design of the Elders of Zion, part of a plan that is so byzantine and cryptic that it can never be fully understood by anyone except the conspirators themselves. This is the formulation that the *Protocols* offers, and which will drive anti-Semitism (and, increasingly, other conspiracy theories) throughout the modern world. Literally the only belief required for anti-Semitism is that the Jewish people are bent on world domination and must be stopped; once this belief is accepted, any and all evidence will support that.

Without this contradictory conception of the Elders of Zion, it would be much harder for anti-Semitism to spread. If there was a clear articulation of the strategy for world domination, then one could point to counterexamples. Jewish men and women who were explicitly anti-capitalist and advocating socialist or anarchist reforms could be offered as evidence that not all Jews were hoarding hyper-capitalists. Successful Jewish businessmen and -women could be offered as evidence that the Jews were not in fact bent on destroying free markets.

But by openly embracing contradiction in their formulation of the Jewish community, anti-Semites are able to effectively rebut any and all logical argument against anti-Semitism. There is no logic capable of understanding Jewish motive, they assert, because the true stratagems of the Elders of Zion are so deeply buried that no arguments of plausibility can account for them. All that matters is that they are Jewish; surface actions are irrelevant.

Connecting Communism with Judaism also has the side benefit of avoiding any legitimate questions about capitalism, socialism, or democracy. Once you have branded any and all political reformers as subversive Jews, you can defuse any and all political critiques. The specter of anti-Semitism haunting America could be deployed, effectively and repeatedly, against any claim that America was not the land of the free and home of the brave that it aspired to be. As with anti-Catholic sentiment in the nineteenth century, internal contradictions in American democracy could be effectively displaced by projecting them on to an external, subversive foe.

Anti-Semitism, then, is a philosophical construction theorized as a series of contradictions, but its purpose is to resolve a series of contradictions inherent to the American project. It allows discussions on inequality and injustice to be minimized, and it provides a counterexample to the usurious Christian, allowing the latter to engage in rapacious hyper-capitalism with a clear conscience.

If the two caricatures—Jew-as-anarchist and Jew-as-banker—have one thing in common, it is their multinational flavor. In both cases, the Jew is seen as a threat to the territorial borders of the nation. What connects both is not a policy or aim or ideology so much as an inherent globalism that seems to threaten the bodily integrity of the nation itself.

This has other ramifications, as well. From the beginning of modern capitalism, there has been a tension between capitalism and Christianity. Christianity, at least on paper, sets itself up as opposed to the kind of wealth accumulation that is a core aspect of markets. Increasingly, though, Christians wanted to participate in this economy, creating a cognitive dissonance that is still with us.

It's not just that the Jew, according to the anti-Semite, wants wealth or accumulates capital. It's that the Jew does it, in this racist formulation, without a Christian soul. Christians could talk themselves into believing that hoarding wealth, buying nice things instead of giving all of one's money away to charity, and helping themselves before the poor could all be reconciled with their religious beliefs through personal salvation and other religious performances. Jews became a necessary counterpoint to this: because they did not participate in Christian rituals of salvation, and because they didn't seem to have the same kind of internal contradiction about poverty and wealth, they could be held up as examples of a kind of pure, debased capitalism. Caricaturing them as "money-grubbing" offered not only proof of their soullessness but, by contrast, proof of Christian holiness, even when those Christians were engaged in the same practices.

So long as there is a tension between capitalism and Christianity, religious bigotry like anti-Semitism remains vital. The *Protocols*, after all, lists a series of programs by the Jews, many of which are, from a twenty-first century vantage point at least, very obviously just how capitalism functions. But what the document accomplishes is to project all of those supposedly negative aspects of capitalism onto an insidious force who is doing these things for devious ends, including world domination. The *Protocols*, finally, demonstrates how the concept of parasitism became an increasingly vital way of explaining away the internal contradictions of capitalism itself.

A ttempts to blunt the *Protocols*' impact have been legion, and almost always unsuccessful. A 1933 trial in Switzerland accusing disseminators of the *Protocols* of distributing "indecent" material floundered on appeal, despite the judiciary's universal condemnation of the work itself.

But the problem with the *Protocols* isn't that the document is "indecent"; it's that it's libelous. Which is the tack Jewish lawyers took in the United States. Prominent Jewish lawyer Louis Marshall wrote to Ford and urged him to recognize this fact, that the *Protocols* "constitute a libel upon an entire people who had hoped that at least in America they might be spared the insult, the humiliation, and the obloquy which these articles are scattering throughout the land." Ford wrote back unimpressed, telling Marshall: "Your rhetoric is that of a Bolshevik orator." Apoplectic, Marshall published a subsequent article, "The 'Protocols,' Bolshevism, and the Jews," in which he excoriated Ford, who, "in the fulness of his knowledge, unqualifiedly declares The Protocols to be genuine, and argues that practically every Jew is a Bolshevist." Dismissing these charges out of hand, Marshall concluded that Ford derived his libelous content from "the concoctions of professional agitators," and that he himself was "merely a dupe." And so another Jewish activist, Aaron Sapiro, sued the *Dearborn Independent* in civil court, claiming it had made false accusations about him because he was Jewish.

The trial had been underway for only two weeks when, on March 27, 1927, the day before he was slated to testify, Ford was driving on State Route 12 (also known as Michigan Avenue) between Detroit and Dearborn. Just after crossing the bridge over the River Rouge, his car was hit from behind and forced off the road. His car plunged down an embankment and was saved from going into the river only when it hit a tree and came to rest. Ford was hospitalized with a concussion and minor injuries, but as word leaked out, the story became a national sensation.

"Mystery in Ford Death Plot," screamed the headline of the *Detroit Times*. The *Chicago Tribune* echoed this ("Ford Hurt in Death Plot") as did the *New York Times*, which proclaimed "Plot to Kill Ford Suspected." Newspapers universally reported about two suspicious men who had been responsible for trying to kill Ford, and speculated that it had something to do with the libel trial. His testimony was postponed as sympathy mounted and suspicion swirled of a plot by secret conspirators.

Meanwhile, before Ford was well enough to return to the courtroom, a juror injudiciously expressed her opinions about the case to a local paper, prompting a mistrial. Wanting to avoid the bad press of another trial, Ford reached out to Louis Marshall, who helped him engineer a plan for a public apology for his anti-Semitic views. With that, the libel suit evaporated.

The allegations of conspiracy and a plot to assassinate Ford were also never discussed again. Which seemed odd. The accusation, plastered across the nation's papers only months earlier, somehow just vanished into thin air. It had spread just long enough to buy Ford some time to escape his embarrassing predicament, and then ceased being news almost immediately afterward. It was as if the accusations of a Jewish conspiracy were everything, and, at the same time, nothing at all.

FIFTEEN

The (In)Visible Empire

T here is very little of the occult about his appearance," the *New York Times* reported of the man called before Congress in October 1921. A redhead with a ruddy complexion, he arrived in a Prince Albert coat stuffed with fountain pens and a large spectacles case, and as he spoke, he frequently adjusted his glasses as they slipped down his nose. "If anything," noted the *Times,* "he has the manner of a commercial man who might be selling books or stocks that have not yet been registered in the Stock Exchange." But this was no ordinary door-to-door salesman. This was William Joseph Simmons, the imperial wizard of the Ku Klux Klan.

Populist nativism had been building for decades, coalescing around various conspiracy theories involving Catholics and Jews, as well as international finance and foreign Bolsheviks. Nativists saw the world as riven with secret societies that conspired to control the day-to-day activities of a world that these nativists saw as increasingly out of control. But Simmons, a veteran and failed preacher, had conceived of a secret group of his own—one that could engage in its own conspiracies, and marshal the anomie and paranoia of white Protestants.

The more I delved into the history of the second Ku Klux Klan, the more I started to hear echoes of QAnon: it was, in many ways, an exercise in branding above all else. It harbored, encouraged, and covered for real violence, hatred, and bigotry—while also allowing for disinterested nonpartisans seeking community. Its strengths depended on its perceived reach as much as its actual reach, and it both exploited those violent individuals that acted in its name while simultaneously, as needed, distancing itself from them. And it thrived on negative press, which both magnified its appearance and drew new recruits.

Above all, as a multilevel marketing scam, the Klan wanted to grow, and to thrive. While many in the second Klan endorsed and embraced violence, and many committed horrific, racist acts, this was not the original Klan—this was not the same kind of ideologically motivated, rearguard terrorist group that sought to undo Reconstruction. It was an organization that wanted to make money. And in the 1920s, it found revenue in hatred, xenophobia, and nativism.

The original organization had been founded by some Confederate veterans in the immediate aftermath of the Civil War, and had largely died out due to the Enforcement Acts—three bills passed by Congress in 1870 and 1871 meant to suppress the Klan's terrorism in the South. But under Simmons it had been reborn in 1915 and had risen to national prominence in a few short years, a creature that in many ways bore little resemblance to its earlier incarnation. By 1921, it claimed a membership roll of somewhere between 100,000 and 700,000 Americans, with lodges all across the country. Rumors of lawlessness, violence, and tax fraud finally persuaded Congress to investigate Simmons and his organization in 1921.

The second Klan called itself the "Invisible Empire," and advertised itself in newspapers as "The World's Greatest Secret, Social, Patriotic, Fraternal, Beneficiary Order." But what invisible, secret society advertises openly in newspapers? Unlike the Reconstruction-era Klan or the Klan of the Civil Rights era, which were terrorist organizations, the Klan of the 1920s regularly held picnics, parades, and other public functions, unmasked as often as not. In the history of American secret societies, its lack of secrecy remains among the most vexing questions.

The second Klan was an organization devoted to spectacle, and it's fitting that its rebirth was inspired by a film. Simmons was a non-combat veteran of the Spanish–American War, and he'd been a sometimes-Methodist preacher, recently fired for "inefficiency," when he'd first seen D. W. Griffith's *The Birth of a Nation* in 1915. The film—then as now—was a pioneering achievement in cinematic history, introducing such techniques as close-ups, tracking shots, and other elements filmgoers have come to take for granted. But for all its technical innovations, the narrative of *The Birth of a Nation* is a vile attack on Black Americans, a Lost Cause apology for the South that functions as nothing more than racist agitprop. Reconstruction Republicans and their Black allies are shown stuffing ballot boxes and denying white Southerners the right to vote. The Black figures are nearly all shown as caricatures: rude brutes drinking and feasting on fried chicken, culminating in the sexually rapacious Gus, who is lynched for outraging a white woman. The Klan, meanwhile, are portrayed as semi-mythical heroes, bedecked in fine regalia (it is from Griffith's film, and not history itself, that the Klan first began to be associated with robes and conical hoods). Its narrative turns are a dreary recitation of white grievance and justifications for violence against Black Americans. The film's white audience ate it up.

By reducing lynching to melodrama, *The Birth of a Nation* attempted to make good versus evil a simple matter of Black and white. The lynching in the film is offered not as the work of a frenzied mob engaging in brutal violence, but stoic, reluctant heroes doing a distasteful job to ensure order and harmony. It was powerfully effective; NAACP lawyer Moorfield Storey concluded that any white person who saw the film would come out of it wanting "to kill every colored man in the United States."

Moved by Griffith's film, Simmons spent Thanksgiving 1915 making a spectacle of himself, carrying a sixteen-foot cross on his back up to Stone Mountain, Georgia. Springboarding from this obnoxious pageantry, he recruited a handful of other veterans to join his refurbished Klan, based less on the original Reconstruction-era terrorists and more on a combination of Freemason rites and Griffith's stagecraft. He got a copy of the original Klan's "pre-script," then infused it heavily with Masonic rites and symbolism. "Its ritualism is vastly different from anything in the whole universe of fraternal ritualism," he explained in his advertisements. "It is altogether original, weird, mystical, and of a high class. . . . It unfolds a spiritual philosophy that has to do with the very fundamentals of life and living, here and hereafter."

Simmons was doing free publicity for Griffith's film as much as for his own organization; he ensured that his mountain climb took place before *Birth of a Nation* had premiered in Georgia, so that the Klan would already have a footing there in time for the film. The night of the film's premiere, Simmons outfitted his recruits in bedsheets and had them ride on horseback through the town. The cosplay stunt worked, and he would repeat it in other cities as the film moved throughout the country, stirring up a poisonous nostalgia and gathering new recruits.

But with Simmons at the helm, the organization only got so far. It wasn't until he partnered with the PR firm Southern Publicity Association, run by Mary Elizabeth Tyler and Edward Young Clarke, that the Klan transformed from a group of bitter veterans into a nationwide movement. Tyler and Clarke used straightforward multilevel marketing tactics to push the Klan into every corner of America, with a simple plan: every new recruit into the Klan paid a "kleetoken" fee of ten dollars; the recruiter kept four dollars and sent the remainder to the district king kleagle (local supervisor), who kept a dollar for himself and passed five dollars on to the goblin (the regional director), who took fifty cents before sending the remaining four dollars and fifty cents to Tyler and Clarke, who took two-fifty for themselves and put the last two dollars in the imperial treasury. The iconic robes and regalia were sold through retail catalogs, further boosting the national organization's bottom line. For all its zeal and hatred, the second Klan was fundamentally a money-making operation, and the goal was to broaden its appeal as far as possible.

Accordingly, a key difference between the first Klan and this new version emerged. The Reconstruction Klan had quickly assumed a role as a paramilitary organization, bent on terrorizing freed Blacks and Northern whites with the temerity to want to rebuild the South. Their focus was entirely as rearguard saboteurs trying to undo as much of the Civil War as possible, and their violence was directed exclusively at Black Americans and their white allies.

The second Klan had no such single-minded purpose. As late as 1921, Simmons was telling members that the "Ku Klux Klan has not yet started to work and may not do so for a year. We are merely organizing at the present time and we do not intend to start any definite activity until we have sufficiently organized to make sure success." Indeed, it became clear that the main work of the second Klan was gathering membership dues and selling robes.

Looking at the photos from the era, of smiling picnickers and proud marchers, it's impossible not to be reminded that Americans remain, essentially, joiners. Many of these people were driven by an ideological hatred and a mission of violence. Others were taken in by a feeling of community. But the story of the Klan of the 1920s is also one of how a dangerous ideology grew by the simple act of offering a sense of belonging to those seeking kinship in a time of upheaval.

Focused on marketing and franchising, it seemed almost at times that the second Klan didn't have any time left over for violence. Indeed, various klaverns stressed the importance of nonviolence, urging their members to not antagonize minorities. An exasperated missive from an Ohio klavern in 1923 sternly warned members, "DON'T ABUSE THE ENEMY. Nothing is to be gained by raving hysterically about Catholics, Jews, Negroes, Bootleggers, Foreigners, and the like. A scientific, sympathetic, sportsmanlike presentation of facts will win more people and leave you under the necessity of making no apologies to anybody."

But this was never the whole story. Almost as soon as Simmons had resurrected the Klan, agitators arose who saw it as a new vehicle for racist terrorism. Nathan Bedford Forrest III (grandson of the ex–Civil War general and original grand wizard of the Reconstruction-era Klan) was invited to serve as cyclops of Atlanta's Klavern Number One, but almost immediately began to complain that he was getting a constant barrage of calls (an average of twenty a week, he estimated) asking the Klan to address petty grievances with threats and violence, as well as people asking him to arrange lynchings.

Racist violence, after all, continued to be a pervasive and unrelenting feature of early twentieth-century America; in the two decades leading up to the Klan's rebirth, over 2,500 Black people were lynched in America. These murders were rarely secret, and were often accompanied by crowds of spectators, many of whom would take pictures of the event to sell as souvenirs. Southern white elites saw lynchings as essential mechanisms to maintain racial norms, necessary to preserve the kind of social order they preferred. The resurgent Klan just gave this a new and easy to recognize shape.

Increasingly, members of the Klan saw themselves as independent arbiters of morality and segregation, empowering themselves to carry out rough justice wherever and whenever they saw fit. Masked Klansmen had stripped, tarred, and feathered people in Texas, Missouri, and elsewhere over perceived moral transgressions. The white archdeacon of Miami's English Episcopal Church, accused by the Klan of preaching social equality to Florida's Black population, was kidnapped by eight masked Klansmen who tied him to a tree, stripped him naked, flogged him, and then tarred and feathered him, finally telling him that if he didn't leave Miami within forty-eight hours he would be lynched. Meanwhile, lynchings of Black Americans continued; over fifty in that year alone.

The Klan of public picnics and pageantry, of multilevel marketing schemes and mail-order catalogs, is at once a distinct entity from the freelance vigilante mobs that donned robes and wreaked mayhem on America, as well as being indissociable from it. Simmons's organization offered a public face and "respectable" veneer for all sorts of beliefs, rendering them palatable and mainstream. The violent mobs operated through this public face, but only so far as they kept enough distance to provide the main organization with plausible deniability.

The visible organization of the Klan and its genteel public appearance also helped clarify everything that had led up to it, the pro-slavery, anti-Catholic, anti-immigrant riots that had become commonplace in nineteenth-century America. These were not a series of spontaneous upswellings of emotions, driven by wild paranoia and irrational exuberance. Nor, ultimately, were anti-Catholic sentiments all that different from anti-Semitism or fear of subversive anarchists. Rather, it was the same technique, one whose effectiveness relied on forgetting and surface rebranding. But the Klan showed such actions were not regrettable outliers; they were as American as could be. And they weren't about hiding this fact anymore.

When Congress brought Simmons to Washington, D.C., to testify, it was already unclear who was really in charge of the Klan—Simmons, or Tyler and Clarke. Confusions only deepened once the hearings got underway. Massachusetts representative Peter Francis Tague alternately attacked the Klan for how it worked to "enter the homes of innocent people, take them out and tar and feather them, and commit other brutal acts in defiance of the law," as well as its seeming flouting of American tax law (Tague estimated the organization had 300,000 members, each of whom paid between ten and forty dollars each, and yet there were no IRS returns for the more than thirty million dollars the Klan had supposedly grossed). The committee seemed as interested in the fact that the Klan had stated as their goal the removal of Catholics and Jews from all political office in favor of Klansmen as the rumor that the Klan was selling water from the Chattahoochee River at ten dollars a bottle for "anointing purposes."

Simmons spoke in his own defense the second day of the hearings, offering a careful mix of misdirection, ignorance, and question-begging. After multiple Black Americans testified to the reign of terror by the Klan and called for an investigation, Simmons responded only by noting that their recruitment numbers were "greater in the North and the East than in the South." He blamed the press for manufacturing outrages. "My information," he claimed without evidence, "is that the Hearst papers paid this man $5,000 cash and $100 a week as long as he worked on the stories, and also agreed to protect him from any damage suits and other legal action resulting from his libelous stories, those stories being false from start to finish."

Simmons repeatedly maintained that he knew nothing of the violence that had been attributed to the Klan. He hid behind the ambiguity inherent in such organizations; according to the testimony he offered Congress, it was impossible to tell who was actually committing the violence supposedly attributed to the Klan. Perhaps it was actual Klansmen in rogue klaverns, but perhaps it was imposters impersonating them? Using secrecy to push plausible deniability, Simmons's Klan was able to evade federal law enforcement in a way the original movement—wholly devoted to terrorism—had not. Simmons's testimony affirmed an elastic, resilient secret society whose true motives could not be known, whose dark underbelly could be easily glossed over with platitudes, and who could resist entirely the workings of law and democratic society. What fearmongers had warned about with regard to the Masons, the abolitionists, the Catholics, and the Jews had finally come to pass with the Klan, who could hide literally in plain sight.

And then, on the fourth day of the proceedings, Simmons collapsed on the stand and was subsequently diagnosed with bronchitis. He was able to postpone the hearings for a few days, and they wrapped up shortly thereafter. The whole proceeding, he'd later claim, was an absolute success. "It wasn't until newspapers began to attack the Klan that it really grew," he later crowed. "Certain newspapers also aided us by inducing Congress to investigate us. The result was that Congress gave us the best advertising we ever got. Congress *made* us."

Subsequent historians have tended to agree with Simmons. The Klan was a national organization, to be sure, but it was also vague and diffuse. It depended on national news coverage, linking disparate acts of violence and public displays of robe-wearing Klansmen, in order to make it into the mythical hydra Simmons envisioned, its tentacles spread through every corner of American society.

This lack of a specific mission was in fact a strength: the secret to their explosive success was their adaptability. In the South, the new Klan picked up its old ways of anti-Black racism, but in the North, where there was less explicit tension between Black and white populations, the Klan focused its enmity on Jews, Catholics, or immigrants. They attacked socialism and anarchism, railing against "the hair claw of Bolshevism, Socialism, Syndicalism, I.W.W.ism, and other isms," which, Edward Young Clarke, imperial wizard pro tempore, claimed in 1922 were "seeking in an insidious and powerful manner to undermine the very fundamentals of the Nation." They allied themselves with Temperance advocates, targeting bootleggers during Prohibition (which, not coincidentally, were often Irish, Jewish, and Italian immigrants). They embraced standard anti-Semitic tropes about international banking. Any hate or grievance you could dream up, the Klan was for, so long as it got them new membership dues.

While it didn't have a specific target, the second Klan nonetheless had a specific mission: establishing white, Anglo-Saxon Protestants as the template for "American-ness," to the detriment of all other Americans and foreigners. It followed a well-worn playbook of accusing immigrants of "stealing jobs" as a means of deflecting attention away from the powerful toward the powerless. It invoked tropes of traditional masculinity, urging men to protect and revere women, whom it held up as passive symbols of femininity (hard-charging and shrewd Mary Tyler notwithstanding, apparently).

An anonymous form letter used by Simmons sums up many of the attitudes they were trying to sculpt into being: it called for "REAL MEN whose oaths are inviolate," listing as attributes of such men Christianity, white supremacy, "Protection of our Pure American Womanhood," states' rights, and the "Promotion of Pure Americanism." In seeking to create a hierarchy of Americans—an upper, genteel group composed of white Protestants who embodied a "true" America, and a series of underclasses, from Blacks in the South to immigrant Catholics and Jews in the North—the second Klan ended up having less in common with the Reconstruction Klan than it did the Freemasons of the eighteenth century. Like Benjamin Franklin and his peers, this new Klan took to the streets in lavish parades, decked out in fancy regalia, and set out to occupy public space with their picnics and ceremonies. They embraced pageantry and spectacle to distinguish themselves, to set themselves as a racial and religious upper class. They were not interested in being secretive because their goal was not guerilla terrorism as much as it was to dominate the public sphere and demonstrate their vision of Americanness.

The second Klan, in its own perverse way, was an attempt to update this model of class without class. The goal of the public, conspicuous displays was to make clear to immigrants, Catholics, and Jews that they were not welcome in America, and to affirm to Black Americans that their only place in this country was as second-class citizens. They also thought of themselves as modeling "true" Americanism, displaying the proper way for Americans to act and presenting the positive vision of how they viewed the country. The convoluted hypocrisy of this mix of gentility and violence is where it broke from the eighteenth-century Free-masons, of course, and it shows how far America had come since the Revolutionary War. The exclusivity of this kind of public modeling of proper citizenship could no longer be accomplished just with parades; now burning crosses, violence, and lynchings were needed.

Reactionaries like the Know Nothings and the second Klan relied on visible secret societies as well as paranoia about invisible ones, the two narratives deployed in complementary ways. The visible secret so-ciety announced class difference, and specifically who was above re-proach. Whispers of unknown and unknowable secret groups, be they Catholics or Jews, worked to identify who could never be safe, who would never be above suspicion, and who was vulnerable to mob justice or kangaroo courts at any moment.

That both the Klan and the *Protocols* borrowed Masonic rituals and their conception of fraternity suggests how important the original Ma-sonic experiment had been in shaping the United States. Franklin and his brothers envisioned a class of gentlemen that were defined not by their ancestry but by membership in a fraternity that both allowed so-cial mobility and maintained class distinctions. It was a paradox, an open contradiction, but one which encapsulated the American project: class without class, difference without rigid barriers. The racists loved it.

I t was the towns around Buffalo, New York, where the Masons were nearly destroyed in 1826. And in 1924, it seemed like it might be the place where the second Klan was destroyed as well. The Klan's arrival in Buffalo coincided with a hard-fought mayoral race between the son of German Catholic immigrants, Francis X. Schwab, and a Yale-educated

WASP, George S. Buck. Under a burning cross in a vacant field, the Buffalo Klan had its first initiation ceremony on October 25, 1922, swearing in 800 new masked, anonymous members.

Such ceremonies took place all across America, but what happened in Buffalo is a reminder that, even at its height, the second Klan's rise to power did not go uncontested. Various organizations, both visible and invisible, attempted to drive them out. Among the stranger attempts was an obscure secret society, called variously The Invisible Knights of the Jungle of the Tiger's Eye, or The Invisible Jungle Knights of the Tiger Eye, or words to that effect. Their robes were black, not white, and their mission seemed at first blush to mirror that of the Klan's. The meaning of the group's name was "not announced," ran the widely syndicated newspaper report of the group from 1922, "but presumably it is eccentric and 'fierce,' after the fashion of the Ku Klux, and with the same purpose: to attract the immature and 'adventurous,' and strike terror to the 'timid and superstitious.'" But they were not out to advance the Klan's racist vision of Americanness; rather, here the purpose was "to fight the devil with fire. Mask is set against mask. A hooded figure is to catch, and if possible destroy, another hooded figure." A subsequent proclamation announcing the group's intents stated their purpose was "to band together in this fraternity all men who believe in law and order, supremacy of these United States of America, and the betterment of mankind in general. Our aim to is to sweep away the discording passions which are caused by religious, political, and racial hatred, thereby getting a true fraternal brotherly love between the citizens of our country, regardless of their racial, religious, or social standing in the community. To leave to the individual the manner in which he shall worship God, govern his politics, and conduct his business."

It is difficult to get a sense of how widespread or powerful it was; there mainly exists one staged photograph that was reprinted in a number of newspapers, along with a few smattering references to it here and there. There are records of chapters being active in Alabama, and a notice announcing the group's arrival in New York City, but very little record of what they actually did. The group's mobilization in Buffalo to combat the Klan insurgency there is the most documented activity of the group, but, once again, there is no indication they ever accomplished anything. Perhaps they were too effective as a secret society.

More likely, the Klan's real undoing came from more traditional means, primarily an undercover cop named Edward Obertean, who was tasked with acquiring the secret membership rolls of the Klan and who reported directly to Mayor Schwab. On July 3, 1924, the Klan's offices were ransacked and its member lists stolen, likely through the work of Obertean. The lists were posted outside the police's headquarters for all to see, and the good citizens of Buffalo seemed genuinely unnerved to discover who had been secretly donning the robe. That August, the Klan sent its agent Thomas Austin, of Atlanta, Georgia, to investigate the break-in; Austin apparently guessed Obertean's role, and on August 31, the two met outside of an office on Durham Street. Shots were fired, and both men were killed.

It is difficult to prove a negative, so it's hard to say for certain if anyone claiming involvement in the Invisible Knights of the Jungle of the Tiger's Eye helped Obertean with the break-in or otherwise worked to bring down the Buffalo Klan, beyond just donning some black robes and sending out press releases. The story does reflect the bizarre fluidity that characterized the public's understanding of the Klan in the 1920s. While Buffalo's citizens were horrified to learn who among them were secret Klansmen, in other parts of the country, the Klan was open and public without fear of reprisal. But what happened in Buffalo also suggests that it was not a rival secret society so much as that perpetual disinfectant, sunlight, that was most effective.

An unsigned article announcing the arrival of the Tiger's Eye lamented such a development, arguing that the group was "all wrong": "Instead of multiplying them, let us do away with all masks. Let us not adopt fire as a weapon even in fighting the devil. . . . We are facing a serious situation in this country. But it is not beyond remedy by open means frankly employed. Let us stick to American methods. They have served us well in the past, and their usefulness is far from being exhausted." The reference to "American methods" seems an odd one, though, given how "American" all secret societies had become by that point.

Journalist Randolph Bedford, writing in 1923, was closer to the mark in his own lament of the Tiger's Eye, writing how it is a "queer condition that happens most successfully in America, where most people treat the law cynically or contemptuously, and agree that if any crisis arrives—business organisation must handle it. That belief makes things easy for the grafters; and organisations formed to fight the Klan will soon copy the grafting methods of the Klan itself." Secret societies, for good and for ill, erupted constantly in the United States as people lost faith with government—or when they wished to subvert it. The goal of all of these groups, from the Underground Railroad to the Molly Maguires to the Klan (albeit in radically different ways and to radically different aims), was to violate the law in secrecy to achieve political aims that could not be got through legal means. And each could claim, in various ways, the country's founders as their inspiration. What could be more American than that?

But bringing down the national organization would take more than just a few good undercover cops like Obertean, and it would take much more than whoever the Invisible Knights of the Jungle of the Tiger's Eye thought they were. It finally took a young woman named Madge Oberholtzer, whose tragic story would have far more ramifications than any group of masked men. A native of Indianapolis, Oberholtzer was the manager of the Young People's Reading Circle, part of the Indianan Department of Public Instruction. She was twenty-eight years old when she met D. C. Stephenson, the grand dragon of the Indiana Klan. He pursued her repeatedly in the weeks that followed until she relented and agreed to go out with him on a date. She soon began acting as his aide during the 1925 session of the Indiana General Assembly (she also, apparently, helped him write a book on nutrition). But she broke it off with him shortly thereafter.

On March 15, at about 10:00 in the evening, Stephenson called Oberholtzer and told her he was leaving that night for Chicago, and asked to see her, offering to protect her reading program from impending budget cuts if she came over. Once she arrived, Stephenson forced her to drink whiskey until she became sick, then threatened her with a gun before abducting her and, on a private train to Chicago, raping her repeatedly, leaving deep bite wounds all over her body.

The next morning Oberholtzer, having recovered, told Stephenson the law would get him, to which he replied only "I *am* the law in Indiana." He checked them into the Indiana Hotel in Hammond, Indiana, on the border of Illinois, forcing her to write a telegram to her mother explaining that she'd gone to Chicago with Stephenson on a trip. At some point, Madge Oberholtzer convinced Stephenson's chauffeur to take her to a drugstore, where she procured enough mercuric chloride tablets to kill herself.

Still in a weakened state, she could only manage to swallow three of the tablets, not enough for instant death. At first Stephenson said he would only take her to a doctor if she married him first, but then panicked and returned her to her parents in Indianapolis. By then she was still conscious enough to be able to relate the terrible ordeal she had been through. Unable to recover, she died on April 14.

Ultimately, Stephenson was convicted of second-degree murder. His crimes were abhorrent enough on their own, but they struck a significant blow to an organization that had marketed itself as the great savior of white women's purity. The rank hypocrisy of his barbaric actions made clear that the rhetoric around the cult of womanhood that the Klan pushed was lip service at best.

But as we've seen in more recent times, such figures can often get away with such hypocrisy; a sex scandal is often no longer enough to bring down a prominent politician, even one who's supposedly an advocate of traditional family values. What actually brought the Klan down is less satisfying, from a moral position, since it hinged less on the Klan being punished for its hypocrisy than it did Stephenson—terrified of his own legal jeopardy—singing like a canary about his organization. From jail, Stephenson cooperated in a criminal trial against Klan-backed candidates. He also supplied information on the inner workings of the Klan and detailed the methods used by local chapters to fleece their members as part of a civil suit between rival Klan organizations in Pennsylvania. Knowing he was going down, he adopted a scorched-earth policy toward the society that had abandoned him, bringing down the Klan from the inside. By 1930, the Klan, whose member rolls had exceeded four million in 1924, was down to about 45,000 people nationwide. The *Washington Post* described it as "once the world's most high powered 'racket,' today a crumbling shell."

Writing in the wake of the Klan's demise, the sociologist John M. Mecklin argued that the organization's downfall could be traced to a lack of a positive agenda; they were merely reactionary and had nothing real to contribute to American culture. It succeeded, he noted, by "creating false issues, by magnifying hates and prejudices. . . . It can not point to a single great constructive movement which it has set on foot. Men do not gather grapes of thorns nor figs of thistles." This position has some merit, but it is not the whole story, either.

The Klan didn't need longevity to be successful. Such organizations that seem to rise spontaneously at moments of cultural change and crisis do not seek longevity; they seek to brutally enforce the status quo. They emerge as needed and dissipate under certain conditions, but not without causing the intended damage. And by treating them as isolated groups—the second Klan as a failed organization without a constructive platform to build on—rather than as part of the same, extended reactionary impetus, we're likely to underestimate their purpose and efficacy. After all, the Klan, even though vastly diminished, didn't die off entirely; it continued in its weakened state like the *Magicicada cassini*, the seventeen-year cicada—unseen, feeding off the roots of American culture, until it emerged once again in the 1950s to launch another terrorist campaign.

PART FOUR

Wonders of the Invisible World

It is important to remember that people do not act on
reality but rather their perceptions of reality.

—SHERRI J. BROYLES, *"Subliminal Advertising and the Perpetual
Popularity of Playing to People's Paranoia"*

I don't believe in fucking conspiracy theories.
I'm talking about a fucking conspiracy.

—GARY WEBB, *as quoted in* Kill the Messenger *by Nick Schou*

SIXTEEN

Subliminals

I n the post–World War II landscape, the topography of conspiracy theories takes on an oddly banal cast. The focal points for fear and paranoia, for secret cults and hidden groups, are no longer to be found in grand marbled lodges or gothic convents. Suburban homes, movie theaters, public parks—these are the places where rumor and conspiracy start to gather. Anything and everything can be suspect.

On September 12, 1957, the advertising executive James Vicary held a press conference announcing the formation of his new company, the Subliminal Projection Company—founded on a revolutionary principle of advertising whose efficacy he had recently proven. Recent innovations in motion pictures had allowed for the projection of images so quickly that the conscious mind wouldn't notice them. Nevertheless, Vicary announced, the subconscious brain could still register such images, and act on them accordingly.

Vicary claimed to have proven this over a six-week experiment in Fort Lee, New Jersey, during a run of the film *Picnic*, starring William Holden and Kim Novak. Vicary claimed to have installed a machine that inserted subliminal messages that had flashed across the screen at

1/3000th of a second, urging viewers to buy refreshments. Over the six weeks, he alternated one night with subliminal messages followed by one night without as a control group. Vicary claimed Coke sales increased 58 percent and popcorn sales rose 18 percent.

This subconscious manipulation seemed to herald a revolution both awesome and terrifying. Writing for *Life* magazine, Herbert Brean summed up the question on the mind of everyone from advertiser to consumer to governmental operative: Could such messages "sneak into your brain without your knowledge and make you do or feel something you did not consciously desire?"

It seems likely that none of this happened, or, if it did, Vicary's results were grossly inflated. For one, to get the kind of numbers he claimed for his experiment (50,000 test subjects in all), Fort Lee was woefully inadequate; the Lee Theater (never named outright by Vicary, but the only theater in the town showing movies that year) was too small. By the 1960 census, there were less than 22,000 people living in Fort Lee, which would mean that during the six-week run of his experiment, every single night close to 10 percent of the town would have to be out watching *Picnic*. More importantly, no one has ever been able to replicate anything close to Vicary's results.

None of that mattered, though. The idea of subliminal messaging, of mind control, had become an article of faith, and it quickly became the way people understood advertising to work. Vance Packard, in his 1957 bestseller *The Hidden Persuaders*, describes how the subliminal effects of advertising had advanced to such a state as to render consumers in a grocery store into a trance of sorts: "Their eye-blink rate, instead of going up to indicate mounting tension, went down and down, to a very subnormal fourteen blinks a minute. The ladies fell into what Mr. Vicary calls a hypnoidal trance, a kind of light trance that, he explains, is the first stage of hypnosis." The net effect was to reduce these shoppers into a kind of zombie: "Many of these women were in such a trance that they passed by neighbors and old friends without noticing or greeting them. Some had a sort of glassy stare. They were so entranced as they wandered about the store plucking things off shelves at random that they would bump into boxes without seeing them."

This fear—that somehow hidden persuaders were able to cause us to lose control over our minds and actions—was not just about shopping or popcorn. The consumer aspect of this new kind of mind control was only a pop reflection of a much deeper fear, one involving Communists and a new, terrifying procedure: "brainwashing."

Americans had long feared international groups that disregarded national sovereignty, that utilized underground networks, that could move under and through borders. Fears of Catholics and Jews in the United States had always been in no small part motivated by this idea—that members of such groups owed allegiance to controllers outside of the United States and thus couldn't be fully trusted as American citizens. Fears of anarchists worked along similar lines.

Postwar paranoia involved these same fears, most explicitly in terms of Communist infiltration, to be sure. But it also increasingly moved to fears surrounding bodily autonomy. Fears of mind control involved an analogy of the same kind of fear of sovereignty that drove anti-Semitism or anti-Catholicism: What if the borders of even the self were permeable?

The fear of subversive Communists infiltrating the country would in turn enable two organizations that would—far more than anything else this country has seen—embody our fear of secret societies. These two groups were well funded, extremely powerful, and possessed vast secret networks that covered every square mile of the country. They operated with near impunity, they broke laws and attempted to manipulate the consciousnesses of law-abiding Americans. They sought techniques of mind control and saw the human mind as a battlefield to be dominated. And these two organizations, each in their own way, sought to undermine the basic principles and values of America, in pursuit of ends that were kept obscured from the American public.

And while they used code names, dummy corporations, and front organizations, neither went by any names as baroque as "The Illuminati" or "Freemasons." They were known simply as the Central Intelligence Agency and the Federal Bureau of Investigation.

SEVENTEEN

Truth Drugs

The real estate listing for the house on Telegraph Hill in San Francisco boasts five bedrooms (including a "sumptuous" main suite), an office, a playroom, and a three- to four-car garage. Each floor features panoramic windows to make the best use of the sweeping view of the San Francisco Bay, which spreads out in all its splendor. Directly below are Piers 33 and 35, and off to the right is Treasure Island.

The street is a quiet dead end, and it feels far from the bustle of city life. But it's only a few blocks from the Marina District and North Beach, where there are plenty of bars and clubs for those looking for a good time. Despite the rapid gentrification of San Francisco and the massive influx of tech money over the course of the past few decades, North Beach still manages to maintain a hint of its former "seedy" edge: strip clubs like the Garden of Eden, the Condor Club, and Larry Flynt's Hustler Club still line Columbus Avenue alongside City Lights bookstore and a flurry of Italian eateries. Steps away from the nightlife, the house on Chestnut Street feels a world away. When it was listed on the real estate market in 2015, it sold for just under $10.7 million—which feels like a lot, even in the inflated prices of San Francisco. But getting a look at these views, you can see why someone might be willing to pay for them.

It didn't always look like this. In the 1960s it lacked the bay windows, and its main architectural feature was the iron fire escape that dominated the front façade. Back then, it hardly called attention to itself, though its location—secluded and yet close to the city's nightlife—made it ideal for the Central Intelligence Agency's purposes. For once upon a time, this "sumptuous" Telegraph Hill stunner was home to one of the strangest projects ever funded by the American taxpayer.

Around 1954, the CIA started using an apartment in the Chestnut Street building as a hub for experimenting with LSD on unwitting subjects. Sex workers on the CIA payroll would pick up johns in nearby North Beach bars and clubs, and then bring them back here. The apartment—always referred to as the "pad"—was modeled after a *Playboy* magazine photo shoot and decorated with framed photographs of women in bondage. It was also outfitted with two-way mirrors and various listening and monitoring devices; one CIA agent later commented that the place "was so wired that if you spilled a glass of water, you'd probably electrocute yourself." The sex workers would slip their oblivious clients massive doses of LSD, and then CIA agents would watch these men have sex while tripping on acid. "We were very interested in the combination of certain drugs with sex acts," one CIA agent later testified. "We looked at the various pleasure positions used by prostitutes and others. . . . This was well before the *Kama Sutra* had become widely popular. Some of the women—the professionals—we used were very adept at these practices." This was not the only CIA experiment involving LSD and other illegal drugs, but it featured some of the furthest excesses of the agency and the limits of its cavalier attitude toward drugging unwitting subjects with untried, sometimes dangerous substances. The CIA was constantly on the hunt for new and more exotic drugs, and, as another agent commented, "If we were scared enough of a drug not to try it out on ourselves, we sent it to San Francisco."

The man in charge of the San Francisco safe house was George White, who hardly fit the profile for a CIA operative in charge of a high-level, top-secret program. As a friend described him, White was more of a "rock-em, sock-em cop not overly carried away with playing spook." White worked in the Federal Bureau of Narcotics but was recruited by the head of the CIA's Technical Services Staff, Sidney Gottlieb, to be an agency consultant in 1952. Operating first out of an apartment in Greenwich Village, White multitasked for the two agencies by busting drug dealers and users in various undercover stings while also surreptitiously dosing targets with LSD supplied by the CIA. After being transferred to San Francisco as regional head of the Bureau of Narcotics, White, in collaboration with the CIA, established the much more technologically sophisticated pad at Chestnut Street, running a clandestine and patently illegal operation for years. As he later wrote to Gottlieb, "I was a very minor missionary, actually a heretic, but I toiled wholeheartedly in the vineyards because it was fun, fun, fun. Where else could a red-blooded American boy lie, kill, cheat, steal, rape, and pillage with the sanction and blessing of the All-Highest?"

What was known as Operation Midnight Climax was just one of many different experiments that the CIA conducted under the direction of Gottlieb, the officer in charge of MKUltra, a covert program designed to investigate whether or not LSD and other substances could be used as mind-control drugs. Unlike most government projects, no records were preserved, and so the actual scope and purpose of the program and many of its operations were deliberately kept out of the public eye, even after stories came to light and Congress held hearings. At this point, it's safe to say that much of what took place is still unknown, and likely to remain that way.

According to those inside the agency itself, much of their inspiration came from the Hungarian show trial of Cardinal József Mindszenty in 1949. The news footage of Mindszenty's confession felt like nothing anyone had ever seen before. During the 1930s, Mindszenty had been

an outspoken critic of both fascism and communism; fiercely independent and unyielding, he had become an immediate target of the
postwar Hungarian Communist Party. Arrested the day after Christmas 1948, he claimed that he had not been involved in any kind of illegal activities, and that any confession he might make to the contrary
would be the result of torture. The Hungarian government obliged and
tortured him, and then subjected him to a public trial. Before television
cameras, the formerly implacable anti-Communist delivered a vacant-
eyed, haunting confession where he claimed to have been orchestrating
the overthrow of the Hungarian People's Republic and the beginning of
a third World War, with the goal of assisting the Americans and then
assuming supreme political power.

The trial shocked American intelligence officials, who watched in
disbelief, convinced that Mindszenty was under some kind of new and
terrifying mind-control drug. A CIA report from the time concluded
that it was "a reasonable certainty (though unproven) that 'confessions'
in high-level trials of political or propaganda significance in Russian-
dominated areas are prepared by hypnosis." These fears only intensified
during the Korean War, as Americans watched while captured GIs repudiated capitalism and embraced Communism. Through the work of
journalist and propagandist Edward Hunter, the West soon had a name
for this process: brainwashing.

The growing obsession with brainwashing in the West reflected a fundamental, unanswerable question: Why would blue-blooded American
soldiers turn their back on American capitalism and embrace Communism? That this question was literally unthinkable to Western intelligence and military officials primarily reveals their own blind spots, but it
was the very unthinkable nature of such a question that led to increasingly
bizarre attempts at an explanation. "The basic problem that brainwashing is designed to address is the question 'why would anybody become a
Communist?'" writer Timothy Melley told *Smithsonian* magazine in 2017.
Because there could be no possible logical, rational answer to that ques-

tion, Americans needed something that defied logic or rationality. Brain-washing became a conspiracy theory to demystify the inexplicable; as Melley notes, it became "a story that we tell to explain something we can't otherwise explain."

I n his classic book *The Structure of Scientific Revolutions*, Thomas S. Kuhn argued that scientific progress does not always happen through a gradual accumulation of facts and vetted hypotheses. Sometimes, he argues, anomalous data will build up, at first ignored or dismissed, un-til it suddenly triggers a massive realignment in thinking—what Kuhn called a paradigm shift. Such paradigm shifts are cataclysmic and change everything about how we approach a given topic.

Something like that happened in the 1950s: an entire paradigm shift. Mental conditioning, acts of persuasion, deprivation methods—for centuries humans have attempted to influence each other. But now the question was being approached from a whole different angle. It wasn't just the Mindszenty trial. Prisoners of war in Korea gave bizarre performances. All of this stacked up to a sense that something had shifted, that we were in new territory, that the Communists had access to some kind of secret mind-control drugs, something that they could use to influence people's thoughts and behaviors.

Americans had come to fear international networks of subversive Catholics, anarchists, and Jews—secret groups whose allegiance re-spected no borders, whose networks violated national sovereignty at will. With the postwar era, this fear coalesced around Communism, and the increasing recognition that the government itself was already infiltrated and despoiled.

"The United States is in the sorry plight it is today," activist Louis Francis Budenz warned in 1954, "because of the Red infiltration of the federal government which led us to agree to our own defeats." Budenz had been raised a Catholic but left the church to marry a divorcee;

through the 1920s and '30s he became heavily involved in the labor movement, and, subsequently, the Communist Party. In the years after the war, he renounced his former views, citing "the Communist conspiracy against America and Catholicism" and returning to the church. His 1947 autobiography, *This Is My Story*, details episodes from his life and both how he did act as a Communist and how he should have acted as a Catholic. A paid FBI informant, he testified against numerous Communists (including Alger Hiss). As an apostate, his testimony carried significant weight among the American public and anti-Communist crusaders in the government. But his story also demonstrates how seamlessly anti-Catholicism had been exchanged for anti-Communism—both, essentially, were the same fear: a foreign group of subversives who took orders from abroad and sought to undermine American democracy.

It wasn't just the fear of another political faction, another group of foreign intruders. What was new was a sense that the human body itself was now violable, that the mind's borders could also be crossed with impunity. Such fears tapped into anxieties around national security or personal identity, and increasingly, were also tied together with the basic cultural assumptions about American families. Richard Condon's 1959 runaway bestseller, *The Manchurian Candidate*, equated mind control and Communist infiltration with weak men, strong women, and deviant sexuality (the incest theme is hit much harder in the original novel than it is in John Frankenheimer's 1962 adaptation), echoed a common theme that resonated not just during the Red Scare but also within the larger history of conspiracy theories, which are often intertwined with questions of sexuality, patriarchy, and family roles. And often, when those roles are undergoing change or refinement, conspiracy theories erupt to attempt to manage and restrict those changes, arguing for a "normal" version of sexuality and family life, one that has been improperly perverted by a conspiracy.

With so much seemingly at stake, the sense that America was falling behind in technologies of mind control set off a panicked race within the intelligence agencies, coalescing around the CIA's Project BLUE-BIRD. The American government believed that the Soviets had achieved "amazing results" with so-called truth drugs, and were eager to catch up. Research began in 1950 as part of the CIA's Project BLUEBIRD, focusing on finding drugs that could both prevent captured soldiers from revealing American secrets and induce captured enemies to give up their own secrets. Mescaline, sodium pentothal, scopolamine (an anti-nausea drug), and a host of other chemical cocktails were tried, but increasingly interest focused on LSD, a newly synthesized drug that seemed to have limitless potential. A year into the project, the program was renamed Project ARTICHOKE, with the specific goal of determining whether or not an individual could be made to involuntarily commit an assassination.

In 1953, the project's designation was changed again, now being formally known as MKUltra. Once again, though, the mandate was broad: develop tools to prevent American agents from divulging secrets, while simultaneously developing "truth serums" to get foreign agents to talk. As laid out in a memorandum to the director of intelligence, Allen Dulles, "we intend to investigate the development of a chemical material which causes a reversible non-toxic aberrant mental state, the specific nature of which can be reasonably well predicted for each individual. This material could potentially aid in discrediting individuals, eliciting information, and implanting suggestions and other forms of mental control."

The head of MKUltra, Sidney Gottlieb, deemed the project to be highly sensitive and requiring a special funding mechanism to avoid any oversight or public knowledge. Not only was the program kept secret through its entire existence, but in January 1973, Gottlieb had nearly all of the records of MKUltra destroyed.

For conspiracists, a secret society is any hidden, networked group that is working behind the scenes to suppress democracy, restrict freedom, or subvert the rule of law. By that definition, there is no clearer exemplar in our nation's history than the CIA and the FBI, two networks that worked in secret to violate civil liberties, commit blatantly illegal actions, and suppress American democracy. For all the fearmongering associated with the Freemasons or the Illuminati or the Jews, with MKUltra the CIA embodied our deepest paranoia: working in secret and without oversight, they made test subjects out of everyday American citizens—including Frank Olson.

The idyllic cabins surrounding Deep Creek Lake suggest nothing but rest and relaxation. Like the house on Telegraph Hill, their very innocuousness makes the story behind one cabin in particular seem particularly insidious. On November 18, 1953, a group of men, including several from Gottlieb's Technical Services and some from the Defense Department's Special Operations Division, spent the weekend here as part of an official retreat. Their second night together, Gottlieb poured everyone present a glass of Cointreau; about twenty minutes afterward, he revealed to them that they'd all been unwittingly dosed with LSD.

Among the CIA employees present was Frank Olson, a bacteriologist and biological weapons specialist. Olson returned home to his family, unable to eat and distant, muttering to his wife, "I've made a terrible mistake." Returning to work, Olson was still disoriented and confused; he tried to resign and was instead advised to undergo psychiatric treatment. On November 24, he agreed to fly to New York City with his supervisor and Robert Lashbrook, Gottlieb's deputy. What transpired over the next few days is not entirely known. But around 2:00 a.m. on the morning of November 28, Olson went through the window of room 1018A at the Statler Hotel next to Penn Station, falling ten floors to his death.

The family was told initially that Olson had "fell or jumped" to his death, and then the CIA had done their best to bury the story. Not until 1975 did a congressional report reveal that Olson had been dosed without his knowledge ten days earlier; when the news became public, the government paid Olson's family a settlement in exchange for broad immunity from liability.

Meanwhile, suspicions continued to grow in Frank's son Eric, who would turn his crusade into understanding what had happened to his father a lifelong pursuit. In 1994, Olson's body was exhumed and an independent autopsy was performed by George Washington University forensic science professor James E. Starrs. Eric and others alleged that Olson had neither jumped nor fell, but that he had instead been pushed.

Eric Olson believes that what happened to his father was not the result of a terrible reaction to LSD, but a crisis of conscience. When his CIA coworkers realized he might leak information regarding their top-secret projects, they murdered him, staging his death to look like a suicide.

The evidence that Frank Olson was murdered is strong: there is his comment to his wife the night he returned from Deep Creek Lake, "I've made a terrible mistake," hinting that perhaps he'd had second thoughts about his involvement in MKUltra. His nephew, Paul Vidich, who later wrote a novel about the alleged murder plot, later recalled how Olson had spent time with his brother (Vidich's father) months before his death: "My father saw a man who was in a deep moral crisis. He wasn't suicidal. He was a man who had begun reading the Bible to find answers to disturbing questions."

In addition to these suggestions of a moral crisis, Starrs's forensic report raised more questions. The autopsy found a hematoma on Olson's left temple, a wound inconsistent with a fall from a hotel room but consistent with blunt force trauma from a hammer or other weapon. Eric Olson would later uncover a classified CIA assassination manual from the early 1950s that advised that the "most efficient accident, in simple assassination, is a fall of 75 feet or more onto a hard surface."

But nearly all of this, upon further review, is entirely circumstantial.

Almost none of it is in any way objective evidence of foul play. The lone exception is the hematoma wound on the side of the head—and yet, even Starrs could not come to a firm conclusion, and his findings explicitly avoid a final decision on the matter. "We didn't find any smoking gun," Starrs acknowledged in his 1994 press conference regarding his final findings. The evidence, he further cautioned, "gives not strong comfort either to those who maintain that Dr. Olson committed suicide, nor does it give strong support to those convinced that his death resulted from a homicide."

And particularly in the early days of psychedelics research, psychosis induced by LSD was not entirely uncommon. As psychiatrist and psychopharmacologist Julie Holland explains, psychedelics work primarily by amplifying in your brain whatever is already going, so "how you're feeling ahead of time, and what the setting is for what you're about to do" both have a dramatic impact on your experience while on LSD. "And so if you don't know what's happening, and then your perceptions are changing, unfortunately most people will think, 'Oh no I'm going crazy, I'm turning into someone who is crazy and I will never be sane again.'" That sense of a sudden onset of psychosis, she explains, is a far more common reaction than thinking you've been drugged—especially, she says, "early on when nobody even knew that these drugs existed."

In a subsequent report on Olson's death, the Senate concluded that his death "could be viewed, as some argued at the time, as a tragic accident, one of the risks inherent in the testing of new substances." But if his death was not an explicit goal, then still it must be seen, in the context of what Gottlieb and his peers were after, as a success. After all, the whole purpose of ARTICHOKE and MKUltra was to answer the question posed in a January 1952 memo: "Can we get control of an individual to the point where he will do our bidding against his will and even against fundamental laws of nature, such as self-preservation?" It seems plausible that Olson was murdered by the American government, but it also seems plausible that he was not—and if he wasn't, his defenestration must be viewed as a success.

W hen Sidney Gottlieb died in 1999, the *Independent*'s obituary described him as having been the "living vindication for conspiracy theorists that there is nothing, however evil, pointless or even lunatic, that unaccountable intelligence agencies will not get up to in the pursuit of their secret wars." The long-term legacy of MKUltra was not just the illegal violations of American citizens' rights and the damage done to its research subjects. It also contributed to the destruction of any public faith in the government. At the time Eisenhower left office in 1960, warning of a "military-industrial complex" corrupting democracy from within, public trust in government was still high, peaking at 77 percent in the weeks before the 1964 election. By the time Nixon left office, public trust had fallen to just 36 percent, and after MKUltra was made public in 1975, trust fell even further, cratering to just 27 percent during the Carter years. Revelations about MKUltra made clear to Americans that Watergate was not just a one-off crime by a paranoid president, but part of a whole system of government that seemed to have turned on its own citizens.

In the CIA's 1963 survey of MKUltra, the inspector general's office warned that the research was considered "professional unethical" and would raise questions of legality, since "the testing of MKUltra products places the rights and interests of U.S. citizens in jeopardy." As such, they concluded, "Public disclosure of some aspects of MKUltra activity could induce serious adverse reaction in U.S. public opinion, as well as stimulate offensive and defensive action in this field on the part of foreign intelligence services." As it happened, the fallout would spread even further, opening up a paranoid rift that would never again be healed. The CIA, by its own reckoning at least, ultimately concluded that mind-control drugs were implausible, even as they conceded that films like *The Manchurian Candidate* made it all-but-impossible to convince the public that such drugs were fiction. Having invested in the belief of such things, the CIA now found it impossible to stop the public from believing it as well.

Jonathan Vankin and John Whalen's *The 80 Greatest Conspiracies of All Time: History's Biggest Mysteries, Coverups, and Cabals* offers just one example of a widespread, generally agreed-upon attitude regarding the CIA and LSD. "The CIA's experiments with LSD are the most famous MK-ULTRA undertakings, but acid was not even the most potent drug investigated by intelligence and military agencies," they write. The acid story, they suggests, may have just been a sideshow to whatever more nefarious projects—still classified and unknown—the government might have been engaged in. The public revelations of a failed mind-control project can't possibly be the whole story, especially when actual cults seemed to have accomplished what the CIA claimed it could not. Only the stupidly credulous could believe "that the U.S. government failed where all-too-many far less sophisticated operations—from the Moonies to Scientology to EST—have scored resounding triumphs. Brainwashing is commonplace among 'cults,' but not with the multimillion-dollar resources of the United States government's military and intelligence operations?"

Others have taken this line of reasoning even further—what if the cults themselves are the work of the CIA? In a 2019 book, journalist Tom O'Neill alleged that the Manson murders were themselves an offshoot of MKUltra's attempts to use LSD to turn ordinary Americans into assassins. Even as Gottlieb and others would claim that they could never achieve their goals of creating a truth serum, skeptics have basically averred that there will never be any reason to believe them. The gaps in the historical record have further eliminated any sense that we'll ever know for sure what really happened to Frank Olson.

Fears about secret societies that boil over into moral panics, as we've already seen, often create an epistemological rift where it becomes impossible to trust evidence or reconstruct a historical certainty after the fact. But with the case of the Molly Maguires or the Denmark Vesey trial, these are generally acute crises in response to a specific set of events, and the historical rift is often limited to a specific panic that passes eventually. In a postwar landscape, the American government, fueled by fears of subversive Communists, created an open-ended moral panic *about itself,* one where we have become so conditioned to fear and distrust the government that we can no longer accept or interpret historical evidence.

Meanwhile, belief that the CIA killed Frank Olson remains something of an article of faith, something that we all assume as a matter of course, because naturally the CIA is capable of such things. But what really drove Frank Olson out the window of the Statler Hotel remains frustratingly lost in a labyrinth of deception and incomplete information—there are no definitive answers here, only an affirmation of your previously held beliefs, whatever they may be.

And perhaps this is the real point. Writer Malcolm Harris has suggested that the entire project of the CIA "exists in part to taint evidence, especially of its own activity." For as long as the agency has been in operation, he notes, "the US government has used outlandish accusations against the agency as evidence that this country's enemies are delusional liars. At the same time, the agency has undeniably engaged in activities that are indistinguishable from the wildest conspiracy theories." Rhetorically, Harris suggests, the CIA allows for a sort of international gaslighting—a laboratory for attempting the strangest and most implausible illegalities, which then bring about accusations that are so outlandish that no one can take them seriously. To truly contemplate the range of activities the CIA has been involved in through the years is to admit that history itself is mad; isn't it easier to decide instead that you're the mad one for thinking your government is capable of such things?

EIGHTEEN

Purity of Essence

There is a sinister network of subversive agents," the 1952 article in *The Catholic Mirror* explained, one composed of "Godless 'intellectual' parasites, working in our country today whose ramifications grow more extensive, more successful and more alarming each new year and whose true objective is to demoralize, paralyze, and destroy our great Republic—from within if they can, according to their plan—for their own possession." With what insidious device did these saboteurs plan to bring down America? Sodium fluoride. "Fluoridation of our community water systems can well become their most subtle weapon for our *physical* and *mental deterioration*. When 'the hour' marked on their program strikes, it can be their most potent weapon for our *quick 'liquidation'*—if we continue to prepare it for them."

The author signed his warning "Einstein's nephew, your Chemist Dr. Bronner." The good doctor had originally been Emanuel Theodore Heilbronner before emigrating from Germany in 1929; he dropped the "heil" due to its association with the Nazis (who murdered his parents in the camps), and he soon dropped the unsubstantiated connection to Einstein. In time, he would also drop his fluoride conspiracies, going on to great fame as the name behind the eighteen-in-one castile soap beloved by campers, poor college students, and hipsters everywhere.

Though Dr. Bronner's belief that fluoride was a Communist plot was not widely shared within the anti-fluoridation movement, he was by no means alone. Charles Betts, a dentist from Ohio, warned that for foreign agents, fluoridation was "better THAN USING THE ATOM BOMB *because* the atom bomb has to be made, has to be transported to the place it is to be set off while POISONOUS FLUORINE has been placed right beside the water supplies by the Americans themselves ready to be dumped into the water mains whenever a Communist desires!"

But many in the anti-fluoridation movement warned against this kind of rhetoric. Frederick B. Exner, a prominent anti-fluoridationist, warned that if you described fluoride as a Communist plot, "you are successfully ridiculed by the promoters," and that such anti-Communists had become themselves a "fifth column" in the movement. In her book *Fluoridation and Truth Decay*, Gladys Caldwell stated, "No, I don't think fluoridation is a Communist plot; it is Industry's scheme to camouflage their deadliest pollutant, with government officials and Madison Avenue advertisers beating the drums." In a strange way devoid of actual political ideology, anti-Communism paranoia and anti-industrial capitalism paranoia dovetailed. Both, after all, were fears of large, inchoate, but far-reaching networked systems in which corporate and bureaucratic bodies connected together in byzantine and often indecipherable ways. If the Enlightenment had posited man as the measure of all things, in the twentieth century it was clear that individual humans had been displaced by the networked body—be it political or corporate—and increasingly individuals saw themselves as merely cells of this networked body. Conspiracy theories surrounding secret societies—Communists, Jews, whomever—were the most obvious and id-driven version of an unsettling feeling that had settled over everyone. Fluoride—omnipresent but invisible, diffused through city infrastructure, unstoppable, permeating our bodies—was just one more manifestation of a growing feeling.

These days, the Communist fluoride conspiracy exists in our cultural memory primarily as a scene in Stanley Kubrick's 1964 satire *Dr.*

Strangelove Or: How I Learned to Stop Worrying and Love the Bomb. "Do you realize that fluoridation is the most monstrously conceived and dangerous Communist plot we have ever had to face?" rogue general Jack D. Ripper asks Peter Sellers's Captain Mandrake, after revealing that he only drinks grain alcohol and rainwater. "It's incredibly obvious, isn't it? A foreign substance is introduced into our precious bodily fluids without the knowledge of the individual, certainly without any choice. That's the way your hardcore Commie works."

Where did Ripper first become aware of this? "During the physical act of love. Yes, a profound sense of fatigue, and a feeling of emptiness followed. Luckily I was able to interpret these feelings correctly: a loss of essence." In Kubrick's film, this fear of a "loss of essence" is played out as a satire of masculine insecurity: everywhere aging men are terrified of their own oncoming impotence and covering for it with phallic fantasies and warmongering. Ripper, unable to get it up anymore, fixates on a Commie plot to sap "our precious bodily fluids" rather than face this fact, setting off a chain of events leading to humanity's destruction.

When I first saw *Dr. Strangelove*, I was probably ten or eleven years old and watched it with my father, who weaned me on Kubrick's films. The line about fluoridation made me laugh, seemingly the most absurd thing in a comedy where much of the Cold War humor went over my head. But my father stopped me short: "You know," he told me, "that wasn't a joke. People really believed that."

He should have known. His own father was a member of the John Birch Society, the most vocal proponents of the conspiracy theory that fluoridation was the work of Communists.

The John Birch Society emerged in 1959 in a hotel in Indiana, the brainchild of a former candy maker Robert W. Welch Jr. A child prodigy and later Harvard Law dropout, Welch was involved in a string of failed business ventures until he joined his brother's candy-making company and found financial success through such enduring American staples such as Junior Mints. An ardent anti-Communist from his teenage years, by 1950 he was warning of a "vast conspiracy" of socialism. After running unsuccessfully for lieutenant governor in Massachusetts in 1952, he ultimately moved away from direct engagement in politics, preferring to comment from the sidelines. Throughout the 1950s, Welch watched with dismay as the country grew tired of the antics of Joseph McCarthy. He believed McCarthy was onto something, and America ignored him at its peril. Because if there was one thing Welch embraced as much as anti-Communism, it was conspiracy theories.

He published a book in 1954 on John Birch, an OSS agent who was killed in a confrontation with Chinese Communist soldiers ten days after the end of World War II (as such, Welch argued, Birch was the first casualty of the Cold War). The fact that almost no one had ever heard of this man was proof, for Welch, of how thoroughly the conspiracy against America had permeated all social strata. Around the same time, he began work on a manuscript, originally a letter, then a tract, then a book, eventually called *The Politician*.

Over two days in December 1958, Welch gathered eleven men together in Indianapolis to discuss the founding of a new organization dedicated to repulsing the Communist threat. They included a number of wealthy industrialists, such as Fred C. Koch, founder of Koch Industries and father to David and Charles Koch. Also present was University of Illinois classics scholar Revilo P. Oliver (according to Oliver, for six generations of his family the firstborn son was given this curiously palindromic name), an ardent anti-Semite and white nationalist.

Welch envisioned the JBS to be a "monolithic body" that operated under complete authoritative control from the top. It was also to be a largely secret organization. In what would become the organization's bible, *The Blue Book*, Welch talks about the need to erect dummy organizations and fake groups—"little fronts, big fronts, temporary fronts, permanent fronts, all kinds of fronts"—to hide the true nature of the

JBS and to ensure its motives were left obscure until the time was right. Bankrolled by wealthy men like Koch and Welch himself, operating below the surface in secret meetings, and with its purpose generally obscured, its influence rapidly began to spread throughout the country.

My father was living in Downey, a sleepy suburb of Los Angeles, when the Birchers found his father. The area south of Los Angeles—and in particular Orange County—was a fertile ground for the John Birch Society at the end of the 1950s and early 1960s. Defense money had gushed into Southern California throughout the 1950s, leading to a new affluence that was based not just on direct military contracts, but on second-tier private businesses (housing construction, professional services, entertainment, and so forth), which created, paradoxically, an increasing hostility toward government. Californians saw their prosperity markedly improved, but the cause (defense spending) was either removed enough that they didn't credit the government outright, or, if they did deal directly with the government, they experienced with regulation and bureaucracy. The nouveau riche in Orange County came to embrace a contradiction: flourishing as a result of government spending, they nonetheless saw their wealth as independent of the federal government, which existed primarily for them as a source of red tape.

In such fertile soil, the John Birch Society took root. By the end of 1962, there were thirty-eight different active chapters of the JBS in Orange County alone, and a membership of more than eight hundred. Within three years, there were more than five thousand Birchers in Orange County.

By the time my grandfather joined the Birchers, my father had turned eighteen and moved out, so he couldn't recall much about his own father's involvement with them. But he would have fit the profile of an ideal Southern California Bircher: a professional who worked in the defense industry; educated but afraid of a culture changing before his eyes; a racist, middle-aged man realizing that his prime was ebbing away. Precisely the kind of person primed to accept whatever conspiracy theories Welch might have offered to explain this loss of vitality and cultural influence.

As with other secret societies, the John Birch Society got an unexpected PR boost by muckrakers attempting to infiltrate it and expose it. Highlighting its mystery and its secrecy, such critics only deepened the mystique and exaggerated the potential power of such a place. The first exposé appeared in July 1960 in the *Chicago Daily News*; others soon followed. Mostly, such exposés focused on Welch's authoritarian tendencies. *The Blue Book* had recorded his belief that "democracy is merely a deceptive phrase, a weapon of demagoguery, and a perennial fraud," said Jack Mabley, in his *Chicago Daily News* piece, warning that those attracted to the JBS "should know the thinking of the man to whom they are pledging their energies and loyalty." This attitude toward democracy dovetailed neatly with a variety of conspiracy theories that Welch and his followers began to espouse: if you distrusted democracy itself, then any kind of popular movement could be dismissed.

Writing for the *New York Times*, Tom Buckley infiltrated a Bircher meeting and recorded a speech by an organizer who lamented how "it's all tied together . . . Civilian review boards, gun laws—they want to disarm the American people!—the civil-rights business . . ." At this point the Bircher interrupted himself, before lowering his voice a bit and continuing. "Don't get me wrong. I'm all in favor of Negroes getting what they're entitled to, but the fact remains that as early as 1928 the Communists drew up a blueprint for a Negro soviet nation here, and they haven't wavered one iota since then. It's those people who are misleading a lot of good, patriotic Negroes today."

The supposition that Black Americans did not want democracy, equality, or civil rights themselves, and that they were just being manipulated by Communists (or, in darker rationales, by the Jews), is a common way racist resistance to equality finds comfort in paranoid musings. Conspiracists thus allow themselves the freedom to disregard the political aspirations of those they disagree with.

In 1960s America, however, it was Welch's attacks on democracy it-self, rather than the racist views it enabled, that raised the most suspi-cion. That, combined with the secrecy of the John Birch Society, helped create a climate of hysteria around the society itself. New York City Police Commissioner Howard Leary had barely been appointed in Feb-ruary 1966, Buckley reported, before "reporters were asking him what he planned to do about members of the department who belonged to the John Birch Society." The sense that Birchers were everywhere, and that they had infiltrated further and further into institutions and con-verted figures of power to their cause was not entirely inaccurate (two California congressmen, Edgar Hiestand and John Rousselot, were re-vealed as members), but the fear of the Birchers had started to look a little bit like the Birchers' own fear of Communists. The anti-Birch hys-teria continued in the run-up to the 1964 presidential election, with the appearance of an anonymous book titled *Birch Putsch Plans for 1964*, which purported to reveal secret plans by the JBS to install a totalitar-ian leader in the presidency that would turn America into a fully fascist state.

This was an extreme over-reading of the Society's powers and inten-tions (the California attorney general, Stanley Mosk, prepared a thor-ough investigative report on the JBS that concluded that they consisted "primarily of wealthy businessmen, retired military officers and little old ladies in tennis shoes," bound together by a fear of "communism" which they defined primarily as "any ideas differing from their own," and that the Society was, in a word, "pathetic"), but it was not that much more far-fetched than the kinds of things the JBS itself was theo-rizing. A semi-secret society dedicated to rooting out secret Commu-nists, cleansing the body politic of foreign, polluting influences and restoring the nation's purity of essence, the John Birch Society became an incubator for conspiracy theories on the right.

When the college-age son of a prominent Bircher, Newton Arm-strong, hanged himself in his San Diego bedroom in 1962, Armstrong claimed that his son was actually the victim of a "ritualistic murder by the Communists." After a six-week investigation by San Diego District Attorney James Don Keller upheld the coroner's initial verdict of suicide, Keller and other officials, along with journalists across the nation, began receiving anonymous postcards reading: "Dear Comrades—did your Communist friends murder Newton Armstrong Jr.?" Keller himself would later confess, "This is the most pressure I have ever had on an investigation"—though he declined to reopen the case, even after Birchers began to regularly picket his public appearances.

In addition to using small family tragedies to spur coordinated harassment campaigns, there was anti-fluoridation and the belief that the war in Vietnam was itself a plot, a carefully stage-managed program by Lyndon Johnson to project his anti-Communist bona fides, even as a secret military conspiracy kept the United States from ever winning the war. The Society, naturally, viewed Martin Luther King Jr.'s assassination as a Communist plot, and among its more insidious actions was its attempt to blame the Civil Rights movement on Communist agitators. In 1967, Welch published his "To the Negroes of America," in which he warned Black Americans, "you are being deceived and inflamed today by Communist lies in the hope that you will actually help the Communist-led agitators to achieve those results. Wake up, my friends, Stop listening to the voices of Satan, which preach the Communist theme of *hatred* as the very core of their strategy."

Nevertheless, when Alan F. Westin investigated the Society for the then-liberal magazine *Commentary* in 1961, he failed to find a strong anti-Black sentiment among the Birchers. Within the framework they established, they welcomed Black members, and open anti-Black racism never made up a strong part of the JBS's platform. Rather, they were explicitly and avowedly anti-Communist, and viewed any kind of agitation, conflict, or disharmony within the United States as the result of foreign subversives. But this is not to excuse such attitudes; rather it illustrates the way in which systematic racism benefits from conspiracy theories such as those advocated by the Birchers. After all, one does not need to be actively and vocally racist to maintain systems of repression. One needs only to express discomfort and sow suspicion on any activist movement that seeks to end such repression. It is imprecise to say, as former president Harry Truman did, that the Birchers were simply "Ku Kluxers out of nightshirts"; instead it seems important to recognize that one of the fundamental jobs of conspiracy theories is the flattening of specific historical problems and the dismissal of their remedies, creating an all-purpose mechanism for explaining the world's evils without regard to history or fact.

All this, then, was complementary to the American right wing at the time, if a little extreme. What was genuinely shocking to the right was Welch's idea that President Eisenhower was himself a Communist spy. As outlined in his book *The Politician*, Welch maintained that Eisenhower's policies and ideology were so antithetical to the American project that the only way they could be explained was through subversion, that the Communist infiltration McCarthy worried about went far further than anyone could imagine, all the way to the top. It was this heresy that would create an ongoing headache for the right during the 1960s. Presidential candidate Barry Goldwater was hand-delivered a copy of Welch's *The Politician*, but fully and completely repudiated its argument, and when asked about it replied bluntly, "I want no part of this. I won't even have it around."

The rising visibility and success of the John Birch Society made the establishment begin to feel fretful. William F. Buckley was among the most conscientious in trying to blunt the spread and impact of the Society. Buckley, an increasingly prominent voice on the intellectual right, had spoken glowingly of Welch's *May God Forgive Us* and *The Life of John Birch*, but, like Goldwater, he was aghast at *The Politician*.

"I for one disavow your hypotheses," he wrote to Welch after reading his magnum opus. "I do not even find them plausible. I find them—curiously—almost pathetically optimistic." Buckley, like few others, correctly perceived the perverse optimism in conspiracy theories—if the problem lies with one extremely well-placed Soviet spy, then the remedy is simple.

"If Eisenhower were what you think he is," he continued, "then the elimination of Eisenhower would be a critical step in setting things aright. In my view things will not get better but very possibly worse when Eisenhower leaves the White House and the reason for this is that virtually the entire nation is diseased as a result of the collapse of our faith. We suffer, as Richard Weaver so persuasively concludes, from anomie, from which we are not likely to emerge with our whole skins, barring a miracle." Unlike Welch, Buckley saw in America a moral decline that happened on all levels, one that had to be rectified by articulating a new kind of American morality rooted in conservatism and its values.

But crucially, Buckley did not want the John Birch Society eliminated; he also correctly understood that they provided a great deal of fire and energy for conservatism at a time when New Deal politics were the norm and the Democrats were in ascendancy. He may have disagreed with Welch, but he understood that Welch was selling something that the base wanted, and he wanted their continued enthusiasm and their devotion. The question then became, how to segment the strange fever swamp of paranoia from respectable GOP politics.

The action Buckley ultimately settled on has since become an important chapter in the establishment of modern conservatism. In his 2017 book, *A Man and His Presidents: The Political Odyssey of William F. Buckley Jr.*, Alvin Felzenberg writes that of all the crusades Buckley undertook in his career, "none did more to cement his reputation as a gatekeeper of the conservative movement—or consumed more of his time—than that which he launched against the John Birch Society, an organization Robert Welch founded in 1958 and used as his personal vehicle to influence public policy."

But this line, while it has become a commonly accepted narrative, is inaccurate. Specifically, Buckley finally resolved himself to Welch personally while at the same time endorsing the membership of the John Birch Society itself. Buckley's February 13, 1962, article in the *National Review*, "The Question of Robert Welch," attempted to have it both ways, castigating the man who founded the JBS while somehow praising the organization itself. "How can the John Birch Society be an effective political instrument while it is led by a man whose views on current affairs are, at so many critical points, so critically different from their own, and, for that matter, so far removed from common sense?" Such a statement makes very little sense in light of the simple fact that Welch's ideas *were* the JBS's ideas, and there was little to no daylight between the rank and file and their leader. Nonetheless, Buckley ended his piece: "I hope the Society thrives, provided, of course, it resists such false assumptions as that a man's subjective motives can automatically be deduced from the objective consequences of his acts."

For all his attempt to thread this needle, Buckley's ploy failed: he succeeded in alienating a good number of Birchers, loyal to their man, while doing nothing to stem the association between conservatism and Welch's conspiratorial fringe. After Barry Goldwater won the 1964 Republican nomination, it was clear that it was the Birchers—not the *National Review*—who had captured the heart and soul of the Republican Party.

In retrospect, the Cold War was a crazy time: by its very definition it was a paranoid, unstable, and conspiratorial age. The problem with the Birchers was that they responded to the irrationality of the time irrationally rather than trying to pretend that everything was fine and normal. Having been told repeatedly by their own government that Communists were everywhere, they found themselves increasingly isolated for proclaiming that Communists were everywhere. They had to be banished because to admit that the John Birch Society might be nothing other than one more manifestation of the age would be to admit how paranoid and unsettled that age was. Better to push them out of the establishment consensus, and then point to them as an object lesson of what *crazy* truly was.

The best way to marginalize them was to seize on their obsession with internal saboteurs. This became the easiest distinction between the John Birch Society—and by extension, the entire lunatic fringe—and the mainstream. The mainstream, including everyone from the Democrats of the Kennedy administration to Buckley's *National Review*, feared the Communists, but as a foreign adversary, one to be met in the summit room and, if necessary, on the battlefield. The Birchers, on the other hand, saw Communists hiding everywhere. This was, in the final analysis, a rather slight distinction, but it was enough of one to draw a line.

Buckley would renew his attacks against Welch after Goldwater's failed campaign, calling him out again in a 1965 article. But by then, Welch's single-minded obsession with Communism had fallen far from favor, even among the Right, and he had begun to broaden his approach. After the failure of Barry Goldwater's campaign and the subsequent reckoning from within the Right, ardent anti-Communism no longer had the same heat. Welch, rather than back down from his paranoia, shifted rhetorical tactics instead. Taking a cue from the writings of Revilo P. Oliver, Welch came to see Soviet Russia and China as only the latest iteration of a much older foe: the Illuminati. "Whether or not this increasingly all-powerful hidden command was due to an unbroken continuation of Weishaupt's Illuminati, or was a distillation from their leadership of this and other groups, we do not know," he wrote in 1966. "Some of them may never have been Communists, while others were. To avoid as much dispute as possible, therefore, let's call this ruling clique simply the INSIDERS."

As Welch's biographer Edward Griffin notes, "the term 'Communist' no longer was able to satisfy the available facts." The world was shifting, new facts had come to light that had strained Welch's belief that foreign infiltration lay behind all of America's ills. Rather than abandon the theory wholesale, he folded it into a new one, where Communists now were only "the lower, activist part of the Conspiracy," distinguishable from the "small, controlling group of wealthy, urbane, elegantly tailored power-lusters at the top." The term "Insiders" was simultaneously vague and all-encompassing, and allowed Welch to maintain a worldview largely unthreatened by facts, even as it was no longer falsifiable.

E ven as the John Birch Society became more and more associated with the fringe right wing, it had other long-term effects on American politics. Chiefly, it became one of the main targets in Richard Hofstadter's analysis of the "paranoid style" in American politics. Using the Goldwater campaign as the spur to reevaluate what had happened in America, Hofstadter retold the story of American conspiracists from the Illuminati scare to Robert Welch, whom he noted had inherited the "mantle of McCarthy," and, in doing so, was able to create an enduring narrative of how paranoia worked in the country's history.

Hofstadter began his essay explicitly calling out the Goldwater campaign, noting that it revealed "how much political leverage can be got out of the animosities and passions of a small minority." Behind such movements, he went on, is a "style of mind, not always right-wing in its affiliations, that has a long and varied history," which he termed the "paranoid style" because, as he put it, "no other word adequately evokes the qualities of heated exaggeration, suspiciousness, and conspiratorial fantasy that I have in mind."

By lumping such discredited and rejected political movements under the monolithic banner of "paranoid," Hofstadter was working to bolster his idea of a "sensible middle": a consensus, moderate ideology that resisted fringe excesses on both the right and the left, a kind of stable middle ground that kept the ship of American democracy pointed in the right direction. Hofstadter was looking for a way to valorize what he saw as the essential business of American politics: compromise and coalition building. He wanted to explain why members of the two major parties often acted in ways that conflicted with their established ideologies—this contradiction, he reasoned, could only be explained through the mechanism of compromise, which he increasingly came to see as the best expression of democracy.

The sin of Robert Welch and those who'd come before him, Hofstadter argued, was their ideological rigidity, which kept them from doing the people's business. He saw the paranoid style as emerging from this rigidity—unable to work with nuance and ambiguity, the dogmatic mind looks not just for simplicity in policy, but simplicity in the cause of the problem. Like Buckley, he saw in Welch an almost optimistic belief in the simple, direct solution, one which denied the messy reality of how democracy actually works.

The creation, via Hofstadter and others, of the category of the "unacceptable conspiracist" reflected the final move in a shift from a world where human agency was at the heart of world affairs to one where the assumption of such a mechanism was inherently disqualifying. But, at the same time, it also created a place where critiques—legitimate or not—could be shoved to remove them from polite political discourse. Having established a landscape of a "sensible middle" and "fringe conspiracists," now everything from the John Birchers to the Black Panthers could be labeled "conspiracists."

But in retrospect, this all seems a misdiagnosis of the problem. After all, Richard Nixon and Ronald Reagan—supposedly the centrist correction of the far-right Goldwater—both embraced vile conspiracy theories. On the left, too, there was overwhelming agreement that JFK had not been assassinated by a lone gunman. Conspiracy theories suffuse the supposedly sensible middle as they do the fringes of American politics, and they do not determine or reflect one's ability to work together in coalitions.

Hofstadter was looking for a mechanism that would explain the seemingly irrational behavior of political actors without losing a belief that humans are fundamentally rational actors. Ultimately, it seems the better question is to ask whether conspiracy theories are rational or not. If we decide that political behavior is rational, and that conspiracy theories are irrational, then it is easy to exclude them from the sensible middle. But it is as easy to say that political behavior is not rational as it is to say that, in their own ways, conspiracy theories are rationally motivated irrational behavior.

How we narrate our own history is integral to how we define what will be allowed to be part of it. History is never an objective recounting of facts; it is a shaping of a story, and its ultimate goal is to act as a road map for the future and the possibilities of what can and can't be thought. In the same way that Robert Welch gathered up moments in the past and strung them together to tell one unified picture, so, too, did mainstream historians, in their own way, gather together the ephemera of the past and try to make sense of it by singling out lines of thought, telling specific stories that do their best to make authentic sense of the past while guiding us where to go from here.

NINETEEN

Beware the Siberian Beetle

I n 1968, American tax dollars were hard at work creating the mystique of the Siberian Beetle. A deliberately crude depiction, just a watermelon seed-shaped bug with six stick legs and two antennae, accompanied by the words: BEWARE! THE SIBERIAN BEETLE.

This cryptic warning might appear in the mailboxes of members of what had become known as the New Left—anti-war college students, hippies, and peaceniks, and especially those organizing: members of the Students for a Democratic Society (SDS), the Weathermen, and other anti-war groups. It might also be sent to Black activist groups such as the Black Panthers. In time, perhaps, that same image would be followed with further cryptic warnings: THE SIBERIAN BEETLE IS BLACK or THE SIBERIAN BEETLE CAN TALK.

What, exactly, was this crap? The Siberian Beetle idea was one of several psyops projects proposed by the Philadelphia field office of the FBI, who, by the late 1960s, was regularly engaged in attempting to disrupt the anti-war movement and instill fear and paranoia in leftist groups. It's not clear how much impact the operation had, but there were many others, some of which had devastating consequences.

All of these operations fell under the heading of what was known as

COINTELPRO, or Counter Intelligence Program, a secret FBI operation that ran in various incarnations from 1956 to 1971, when it was exposed and subsequently shut down. Operating at first with congressional blessing, and then increasingly on its own, the FBI infiltrated and harassed dozens of American citizens. Some of these activities seem in retrospect not much more than petty pranks. In Princeton, bureau agents altered mugshots of SDS members to make them look dirty and unkempt, and then sent them to the university's conservative club. They also sent fake postcards to the homes of SDS members congratulating them on their "anti-establishment and anti-military/industrial complex activities," hoping that their parents would find them and raise alarm. But some actions were far more serious, including the FBI's role in the assassination of Fred Hampton, a rising leader of the Black Panther Party, who was murdered on the night of December 4, 1969, while he lay sleeping.

The CIA's MKUltra program involved conducting unethical, illegal operations on American citizens, dosing them with drugs and subjecting them to horrific experiments, but with MKUltra there was rarely any actual animus directed toward such individuals—they were just the unwitting test subjects at hand. COINTELPRO, on the other hand, directly targeted Americans for their political beliefs and actions, and sought to shape and control American democracy through subterranean means.

What becomes evident—perhaps too self-evident—is that what the FBI created with COINTELPRO was precisely the kind of secret, subversive group that Americans had long feared. It was a secret program, it was well-financed and well-coordinated. Agents moved together— they conspired—to achieve goals that were not publicly announced. They set about to achieve these goals through duplicity, sabotage, and misdirection. And these goals were patently un-American: the stifling of free speech, the interruption of due process, and, in extreme cases, the extrajudicial murder of American citizens. The Student Left movement and Civil Rights organizations of the 1960s saw themselves as working toward a more perfect union, employing constitutionally protected democratic ideals to strive for a fairer, more equitable nation. The FBI responded with illegal and coordinated secrecy to frustrate those goals. COINTELPRO is perhaps the clearest example of what Americans fear when they imagine the Freemasons or the Illuminati: a hidden organization with nefarious goals that operates behind the scenes to change the direction of American history.

How did the FBI get involved in such openly anti-American activities? Through its long history, there have been periods when the FBI has operated under strict supervision and has been largely focused on universally popular goals: primarily the national coordination of law enforcement activities. But there have been other periods when the FBI has seemed to operate as a sort of secret police, focused not just on day-to-day police activity but the collection of counterintelligence and the monitoring of "subversive" elements in America. Such activities tend to arise during times of political instability, such as the second half of the 1960s, when officials and politicians in Washington begin to fear a potential political crisis. In the presence of such fears, the FBI has traditionally been given increasing freedom from oversight in order to diffuse these possible crises, and they are even encouraged to go after perceived instigators.

This counterintelligence overreach, then, goes hand in hand with a sense of political instability. As perhaps the most notorious, most wide-reaching, and most clearly illegal example of FBI malfeasance (at least that we're aware of), COINTELPRO was, as one might expect of a program from the time, born initially from a fear of Communism. In the late 1940s and early 1950s, the FBI had regularly made use of the Smith Act, a World War II–era law which allowed for the prosecution of anyone advocating the violent overthrow of the government (or anyone belonging to a group with such goals). But starting in 1957, the Supreme Court held that numerous provisions of the Smith Act were unconstitutional infringements on free speech, and it mandated a higher burden of proof. Hoover responded by forming a new program within the FBI, COINTELPRO Communist Party, in August 1956, with the goal of keeping tabs on the American Communist Party and, where possible, disrupting it. Chiefly, Hoover understood that it was far less effective to target the Communist Party from the outside, which would build a sense of persecution and solidarity. Rather, the FBI would target it from the inside, sowing confusion, mistrust, and infighting.

The program had broad support within Congress for a number of reasons. For one, even if COINTELPRO Communist Party involved spying on Americans, it was largely believed that anyone allying themselves with Communism was making common cause with foreign powers, and thus could be treated as a foreign subversive. Second, the covert spying on American Communists was seen by many anti-Communist liberals as preferable to the public circus of the McCarthy hearings. Hoover was thus able to carry out his subversion of the American Communist Party almost entirely free from any political opposition.

Lawlessness spread subtly at first. Having received the green light to attack the Communist Party, Hoover soon broadened the FBI's CO-INTELPRO mandate, opening a counterintelligence operation on the Socialist Workers Party as well. Though initially focused on foreign subversives, the bureau gradually widened its focus. How it did so, however, was in its own way quite novel. Hoover and his boys rationalized their new list of targets by insisting that even if such groups were not actively working with foreign Communists, they were ripe for exploitation by such foreign actors, and their susceptibility to infiltration made them fair game.

Hoover's personal racism was well known and well documented, and it spread through the culture of the FBI. But it was this belief that Black activists were somehow uniquely vulnerable to Communist co-optation that provided cover for the FBI's increasing focus on Black activism. As Hoover's biographer Richard Gid Powers wrote, the bureau chief's "condescending attitude toward black intelligence and judgment made him inclined to see these organizations as easy prey for the skilled propagandists and agitators of the Communist party." From this it followed that the more effective the black organizations were, therefore, the more tempting they were to the Communists, thus Hoover's *reductio ad absurdum* conclusion that "the country would be better off without an organized black civil rights movement—and, by implication, without effective black leadership." As long as such groups existed, Powers concludes, "Hoover saw only the potential for disloyalty, and whatever information he received seemed to confirm his belief in the insincerity and illegitimacy of black protest." By the late 1960s, every major civil rights organization and leader was regularly being monitored by the Feds, including the NAACP and Martin Luther King Jr., himself.

The fear of Communism wasn't the only thing emboldening Hoover's decision to reach deep into the lives of American citizens. An even more important vector for this overreach came from an unexpected place: the KKK. While the second Klan had flamed out following D. C. Stephenson's conviction and betrayal, embers had stayed lit in the darkness, and a new breed of Klansman had resurfaced in the 1950s and '60s. Like the original Reconstruction Klan, the third era of the Klan was primarily based in the South, and almost entirely devoted to anti-Black terrorist violence. No longer a national, visible organization, now Klan activities took the form of disparate, individual groups that sprung up as a terrorist resistance to the Civil Rights movement. At the same time that the FBI was infiltrating and disrupting Civil Rights organizations, it also began monitoring and attempting to disrupt the Ku Klux Klan.

To be clear, the FBI did not have a problem with the racist attitudes of the Klan. The bureau itself was rife with racist agents. But Hoover saw the Klan as a group of poor, white terrorists, and as much as he supported their general aim, he recognized their means—unchecked violence—as something that the bureau could not let stand.

As with groups on the left, the FBI's surveillance of the Klan went well beyond legal law enforcement tactics. But Hoover was given cover by liberal politicians who wanted the Klan stopped but knew full well that local law enforcement could not be relied upon, and were willing to look the other way on any potential civil liberties violations. And so, with the blessing of Congress, the FBI was given free rein to spy on, infiltrate, and harass American citizens, citizens who had nothing to do with Communism or foreign subversion. COINTELPRO White Hate Groups was opened on September 2, 1964, and would continue on for the rest of the 1960s. The Klan, of all people, were as anti-Communist as Americans could be—and yet, as FBI Assistant Director William C. Sullivan would explain, "organizations like the KKK and supporting groups are essentially subversive in that they hold principles and recommend courses of action that are inimical to the Constitution as are the viewpoints of the Communist Party." Which is to say, the FBI had found a way to transfer their focus: now Communism was not the single target, but rather the model for a generalized kind of subversion, one that could apply equally to actual Communists and anti-Communist nativists.

By the end of the 1960s, the FBI was running COINTELPRO operations on a series of different types of groups, in ways that seemed at times contradictory, attempting to infiltrate and disrupt both Civil Rights organizations and the Klan. But in a way, it saved its greatest hostility for the New Left. According to Assistant Director Sullivan, the entire nation was itself "undergoing an era of disruption and violence caused to a large extent by various individuals generally connected with the New Left," a group he defined broadly, in a memo beginning COINTELPRO New Left in May 1968, as activists urging "revolution in America and call for the defeat of the United States in Vietnam." The FBI's mandate for the New Left was far broader than it had been for the Klan, since in the case of the latter, what bothered the bureau was the Klan's tactics. The Feds hoped to temper and restrict the Klan mainly in terms of its violent activities. But they saw the New Left as a threat to an entire way of life, an ideology that imperiled the American status quo to its very core. They didn't just want to disrupt protest activities or other behavior by the New Left; they wanted the very nature of the movement to be stamped out entirely, to destroy it altogether. (Among other things, the bureau saw the New Left as antithetical to the very work of law enforcement—including the FBI itself; as Sullivan explained, "They continually and falsely allege police brutality and do not hesitate to utilize unlawful acts to further their so-called causes. The New Left has on many occasions viciously and scurrilously attacked the Director of the Bureau in an attempt to hamper our investigation of it and to drive us off the college campuses.")

The FBI's COINTELPRO New Left program accordingly focused not on tactics, as they had with the Klan, but on members' lifestyles instead. And because such groups were spread out across the country (rather than in a specific region, as was the case with Civil Rights groups and the Klan in the South), Hoover notified *all* regional FBI offices that they had to involve themselves in the disruption of the New Left. As he wrote to the Oklahoma City office in 1968, "It is to be noted that you have previously reported that an SDS chapter has existed at Oklahoma University since the latter part of 1963 and that there was a plan being considered by SDS to interest high school students in that organization. *The above information, in itself, is sufficient grounds for the Agent to whom this matter is assigned to develop a hard-hitting program designed to neutralize the SDS in your territory.*" At the same time, he also admonished the director of the Knoxville office, who had concluded that, since campus officials were themselves working to prevent New Left groups from organizing on campus, the FBI could close its counterintelligence file. Not so, Hoover responded. "*In view of the serious [acts of] violence which occurred on campus during the last academic year, many of which were spontaneous, and in view of the fact that there has been no evidence whatsoever to substantiate the conclusion that the New Left's efforts on the Nation's campuses are abating, you should not close out this Program in your office,"* he admonished. "During this period of abated activity by the New Left, you should prepare for and seek new ways of arresting the attacks by the New Left which will, in all probability, develop during the coming academic year."

What emerges in these letters is the fact that Hoover was less interested in disrupting the SDS or similar groups in terms of the organizations themselves, but rather in rooting out the *idea* that such groups represented, an idea he loathed and wanted to suppress at all costs. Radical leftism had become like fluoride: an insidious, uncontrollable foreign substance, seeping into the bloodstreams of otherwise upstanding Americans, poisoning and corrupting them from within.

Afraid no longer of a single group but of a nebulous and attractive idea, the FBI, as it became further involved in attempting to sabotage the New Left, became increasingly creative in its tactics. The Feds believed that the New Left in particular was susceptible to weird magic, superstition, and other conspiracy theories, and sought to influence them through these means. Straitlaced G-men sought to fathom why young people were increasingly turning to radical ideas, unable to understand why those young people might imagine a better, less racist, and more equitable America, and finally came up with mumbo-jumbo. The Philadelphia field office explained in a memo that the emergence of the New Left had "produced a new phenomenon—a yen for magic. Some leaders of the New Left, its followers, the Hippies and the Yippies, wear beads and amulets. New Left youth involved in anti-Vietnam activity have adopted the Greek letter 'Omega' as their symbol. Self-proclaimed yogis have established a following in the New Left movement. Their incantations are a reminder of the chant of the witch doctor. Publicity has been given to the yogis and their mutterings. The news media has referred to it as a 'mystical renaissance' and has attributed its growth to the increasing use of LSD and similar drugs." This, the bureau further reasoned, might provide an opportunity, a means of attacking "an apparent weakness of some of [the] leaders" of the New Left by capitalizing on this supposed superstition by sending them "a series of anonymous messages with a mystical connotation."

Thus, the Siberian Beetle was born, initially proposed in 1968 as a plan to disrupt Student Left movements at Temple University. "The recipient is left to make his own interpretation as to the significance of the symbol and the message and as to the identity of the sender," the plan, as articulated by the Philadelphia office, suggested. "The symbol utilized does not have to have any real significance but must be subject to interpretation as having a mystical, sinister meaning. The mathematical symbol for 'infinity' with an appropriate message would certainly qualify as having a mystical, sinister meaning." Such gnomic and obscure missives, the bureau hoped, would "cause concern and mental anguish on the part of the 'hand-picked' recipient or recipients. Suspicion, distrust, and disruption could follow." Bizarre as it was, the program was explicitly intended as a "harassment technique. Its ultimate aim is to cause disruption of the New Left by attacking an apparent weakness of some of its leaders. It is felt there is a reasonable chance for success."

Hoover wrote back two days later, applauding the idea, suggesting only that they needed to be sure they had the proper target. "The significance of the symbols," he advised, "should be slanted so as to be interpreted as relating to something that is currently going on in the New Left," suggesting that the Siberian Beetle be deployed to heighten factional disputes and be sent to leaders already in contact with FBI informants, who could help shape the interpretation as need be and heighten paranoia. But while Siberian Beetle mailings were indeed sent out, there is no record that they caused anything close to the "mental anguish" the bureau was hoping for.

Their attacks on the Black Panthers, meanwhile, became increasingly blunt. Among these were attempts to sow discord between rival Black power groups, including the Blackstone Rangers out of Chicago.

The Rangers' leader, Jeff Fort, received an anonymous note at one point claiming that the Panthers had put a hit out on him—the note had come from the bureau, of course, the goal being (according to a memorandum to headquarters) to "intensify the degree of animosity between these two black extremist organizations"; similar tactics were used to foster a war between the Panthers and Ron Karenga's US ("United Slaves") Organization in Southern California.

There violence did ultimately break out, leading to the deaths of several Panthers, including Los Angeles chapter leader John Huggins in 1969. The bureau, which had been using anonymous notes and other tactics to inflame tensions between the Panthers and US, were eager to claim credit for this to Hoover; a report issued to the director in September stated that violence and a "a high degree of unrest continues to prevail in the ghetto area of southeast San Diego." Although "no specific counterintelligence action can be credited with contributing to this overall situation," the report continued, nevertheless "it is felt that a substantial amount of the unrest is directly attributable to this program."

Nothing, however, was as brazen as the murder of Fred Hampton in Chicago on December 4, 1969. Hampton was a rising star within the Black Panthers, chairman of the Illinois chapter and deputy chairman of the national organization. His chief success had been in forging a multiracial coalition between the Panthers, the Young Lords (a predominantly Hispanic group), the Young Patriots (composed of poor whites), and various street gangs in an effort to end infighting and coordinate social justice movements.

The FBI opened a file on Hampton in 1967, and shortly thereafter recruited William O'Neal to infiltrate the Panthers and work as an informant. O'Neal quickly rose in the ranks and was appointed Hampton's bodyguard. The FBI continued to employ its usual tricks to sow infighting and suspicion, but after two Chicago police officers were killed in an armed confrontation with the Panthers, the bureau, in coordination with the Chicago police and the state attorney's office, decided to move.

Ostensibly, the December raid was authorized to search for a cache of weapons O'Neal had told them was located at Hampton's apartment. After providing the police with a detailed layout of the premises, O'Neal drugged Hampton and then left. At four in the morning, over a dozen armed officers entered the premises; Panther Mark Clark had been sitting in the front room with a shotgun on his lap as security, and the police shot him instantly upon entering. They then reached the bedroom where the drugged Hampton was sleeping with his girlfriend, and they shot him repeatedly—first in the shoulder and then twice in the head.

The concerted and viciously racist acts of the FBI during this period makes it harder to understand why they were still, at this time, actively targeting the Klan, attempting to disrupt (or at least monitor) the activities of a group that ostensibly shared some of their same goals. The Klan continued to be worthy targets of suppression only because they didn't use the proper channels, but this strategy, when it was finally unmasked, resulted in an acute kind of cognitive dissonance among Klansmen.

The Left, after all, had no illusions about what was happening— they *knew* they were being targeted by the government, and they acted accordingly. It was awful, illegal, nerve-racking, and demoralizing, of course, but it was something they expected. And, in a perverse way, it affirmed their devotion to their cause. They were, on some level, trying to effect a change in America, and it didn't surprise any of them that they were encountering resistance (even if some were not prepared for the level of coordinated resistance—and violence—from their own government). This sense that there was an "FBI agent behind every mailbox" became a crucial aspect of uniting and focusing the New Left, even as they had to deal with near-daily illegal harassment. An early SDS leader, Dick Flacks, spoke explicitly to this concern long before the FBI's spying was widely known. He advocated against a great deal of "self-protective behavior," he later explained, "because I thought that was the purpose of surveillance more than anything else, to make people feel intimidated, secretive, turn them into a conspiratorial, paranoid people. And so I would rather practice a kind of bravado and say, 'well, of course they're watching us—so what?'"

The Klan, meanwhile, was flummoxed. Given their understanding that they saw themselves as engaged in the same work of "protecting" America from subversion as the FBI itself, they had an increasingly difficult time understanding *why* the bureau was targeting them. Unable to square that circle, they turned increasingly to conspiracy theories. In 1971, the Klan publication *The Fiery Cross* ran a five-part exposé of the FBI and the CIA, in which they depicted Hoover as nothing more than a bureaucrat forced to "swallow his pride and obey orders." Rather than the mastermind behind the suppression of the Klan, Hoover himself was just a flunky; the real figure in charge of the FBI was a figure *The Fiery Cross* identified as David Liberman, a "Jew from Hong Kong" who had become the de facto head of the bureau in 1953. No such person existed, but the newsletter portrayed him as a high-level Communist who'd infiltrated the American government at the highest levels, and who now had power over even hardworking anti-Communists and white supremacists like Hoover.

Continuing to seek out some kind of rationale for this betrayal by the bureau, *The Fiery Cross* offered up multiple, contradictory characterizations of Hoover. At times he was depicted as a tool of "fanatical Zionists," whose personal failing allowed him to be manipulated into ordering "the FBI to harass any American citizen who opposed the State of Israel." Other times, he was an "honorable man," but unable to stand up to his own deputy, William Sullivan, who was the true tool of the Jews. This narrative was itself subsequently tossed in favor of one that portrayed *Sullivan* now as the "honorable" figure in the bureau, stymied by his overlord, philo-Semite, and coward J. Edgar Hoover.

The specificities of the Klan's accusations, and its changing story about who was actually pulling the strings at the FBI, are less significant than its constant recourse to anti-Semitism as the overarching conspiracy explaining events. In the confused reaction of the Klan to COINTEL-PRO, it's possible to better understand the persistence of anti-Semitism in the American Right, and why, of all the various conspiracy theories and racist ideas, it maintains a singular, stubbornly dubious honor. The Klan—and more broadly, figures on the Far Right—did not see themselves as challenging America and its government; they saw themselves as upholding it. Then as now, such individuals see themselves as the bearers of a fundamental "Americanness," inheritors of its true culture, one that's being attacked from the outside.

The Left is imagining a new country that they're attempting to bring into existence; every achievement is proof that they're slowly making progress, and the arc of history is bending slowly toward justice. The Right is more prone to seeing each evolution as a falling away. In evangelical communities, of course, this falling away is phrased in terms of morality, and often in terms of Godlessness and Satan. But another explanation (and one that overlaps constantly) is the notion that there are inside infiltrators—in the government, in Hollywood, in the schools—who are responsible for this sense that America is giving up on its own Americanness.

Anti-Semitism on the Right acts as a means of accounting for this cognitive dissonance. The reason that it persists, both in the far extreme fringes of violent actors like the Klan and its more contemporary incarnations, as well as in mainstream, "respectable" conservatism (including among figures like Richard Nixon and Ronald Reagan), is because it exists always to massage the anxiety and trauma such individuals feel when they see the "center" of America slipping away from them.

The Klan's obsession with secret Jews in the FBI also reveals to what extent the way that the very idea of secret conspiracies—real or imagined—had infiltrated American society by this point. One government-sanctioned secret society launches a war against another, extralegal secret society, who in turn, in order to make sense of the resulting cognitive dissonance, fixates on a third, imaginary secret society.

The legacy of those years is the certainty many Americans feel that any and all conspiracies and secret plots by hidden groups *involve* the government, rather than being plots *against* the government. Even legitimate attacks against the government are now presumed, by most, to be inside jobs, as with the case of JFK's assassination in 1963. (Most Americans believe that Lee Harvey Oswald did not act alone, and a 2013 survey of believers found that a plurality blamed the CIA, FBI, Lyndon Johnson, or other governmental actors.) Connections to the military-industrial complex or the intelligence community are now the default assumptions when it comes to American conspiracy theories. Thus, when contract hitman Charles Harrelson (actor Woody Harrelson's father) was arrested for the murder of District Judge John H. Wood in 1979, he was found high on cocaine, raving that he not only killed Wood but also Kennedy. Conspiracists have not only taken this rather dubious confession as proof of Harrelson's involvement in the assassination, but have also subsequently connected him to "intelligence agencies and even the military."

And so the shadow of those years still looms over us. Decades after these abuses came to light, decades after the congressional hearings, decades after laws and reforms were passed meant to prohibit this kind of behavior from ever happening again. Mistrust of American government by its own citizens, and the default assumption that the government is constantly engaged in an active war against its own citizens, has driven public opinion on both the right and the left.

By 2006, polls were finding that as many as 36 percent of Americans believed that the government had something to do with the World Trade Center attacks of September 11, 2001. Since then, those numbers have decreased, but as of 2020 polls suggest as many as one in six Americans still believe some version of the various conspiracy theories floating around concerning that day. Mostly, conspiracy theorists group themselves into two camps: Let It Happen On Purpose (LIHOP) or Made It Happen On Purpose (MIHOP). But it wasn't just the active conspiracy theorists; average Americans, by and large, assumed (or at least were willing to entertain) the idea that the Bush administration had known something was going to happen, and had exploited world events for its own policy goals, even at the expense of 2,977 lives.

I was talking to one 9/11 truther who was patiently explaining to me how the Twin Towers were not hit by planes but were destroyed by internal demolitions placed inside them, how there had been planes in the sky that day but they had not hit the towers (this, despite the fact that United Airlines Flight 175's crash into the South Tower was one of the most filmed events in history).

As we talked, trying to contain my own exasperation, I asked him finally what he wanted. What he repeatedly stressed was that while there had been a report by the 9/11 Commission, there had never been a trial by jury. "I have confidence," he told me, that if the evidence was presented in a courtroom, that "a jury would refute the official story." Much of the evidence had been lost, he conceded, but he still believed that a jury of twelve ordinary, unbiased Americans, if presented with what we know about the September 11 attacks and asked to render a verdict, would not agree that the hijacking was the work of al-Qaeda, and would instead conclude that it was an inside job of some kind.

What would happen, I asked, if such a trial took place, and this jury *did* accept the official story? "If that happened," he answered quickly, "my mind would be blown." If this hypothetical jury accepted the official story, I wondered, would it change his mind about what really happened? No, he told me, not in the least. "I don't have a lot of confidence in the integrity of the American government or the media."

Naively, one may think of courtroom trials as a means of determining what did or didn't happen—the evidence is presented, the arguments are made, and a reasonable group of citizens is asked to make a call, and that judgment is usually accepted. But this was not what this conspiracist was asking for—he did not want the truth of 9/11 to be discovered, since he already knew the truth. He wanted his own truth to be validated in an open court of law. And if the jury reached a different truth, that only meant that the trial was corrupt.

A paradigm shift has happened in the American consciousness, one that has exchanged our naive belief in the benevolence of government with a radical, unshakable suspicion. And the more I listened to him talk, the more I realized that what he was most interested in was giving the American legal system a chance *to prove itself to him*. If this mythical trial would come to the "correct" verdict, it would mean that the justice system had worked, and he could once again have faith in it. Behind all the paranoia, suspicion, and faulty reasoning, I couldn't help but detect a sense of longing, a nostalgia for a belief that one could have faith in America once more.

PART FIVE

Behind the Hieroglyphic Streets

In an odd way, the conspiracy theorist's view is both frightening and reassuring. It is frightening because it magnifies the power of evil, leading in some cases to an outright dualism in which light and darkness struggle for cosmic supremacy. At the same time, however, it is reassuring, for it promises a world that is meaningful rather than arbitrary. Not only are events nonrandom, but the clear identification of the evil gives the conspiracist a definable enemy against which to struggle, endowing life with purpose.

—MICHAEL BARKUN, *A Culture of Conspiracy*

Behind the hieroglyphic streets there would either be a transcendent meaning, or only the earth.

—THOMAS PYNCHON, *The Crying of Lot 49*

TWENTY

Networks

E*ither way, they'll call it paranoia.* In the last few decades, many of us have come to find ourselves in the same situation as Oedipa Maas, the protagonist of Thomas Pynchon's 1965 novel *The Crying of Lot 49.* Through the mysterious bequest of a deceased ex-lover, Oedipa gradually becomes aware of a secret, centuries-old conspiracy, a hidden society called Trystero that uses an alternative postal system and communicates via cryptic symbols, including a muted trumpet ("Either you have stumbled indeed," she tells herself, "onto a secret richness and concealed density of dream," something so rich and complex it may even open "onto a real alternative to the exitlessness, to the absence of surprise to life, that harrows the head of everybody American you know"). Or at least, that's what she thinks she's found. For Oedipa can never quite escape the suspicion that there is no conspiracy, that either she's the victim of a massive prank, or that she is "fantasying some such plot, in which case you are a nut, Oedipa, out of your skull." But either way, paranoia.

In the years since Watergate, MKUltra, the Tuskegee experiments, Iran–Contra, and countless other government scandals, we've entered a period of epistemological crisis, where it's increasingly difficult to know for sure what is real and what is too outlandish to believe. Paranoia and skepticism have seeped into the foundations of the country, and it's impossible to know any longer where to draw the line. As such, it's become increasingly impossible to talk about conspiracy theories in any kind of rational sense at all. If you believe them, you're crazy; if you don't, you're an idiot.

Increasingly, it has become necessary to distinguish between conspiracy theories and conspiracies themselves. The term "conspiracy theory" does not refer simply to a theory about a conspiracy. After all, by the end of the 1970s, Americans had learned of multiple conspiracies—Watergate, Tuskegee, COINTELPRO, etc.—and one could reasonably have theories about any number of them.

The term "conspiracy theory" itself first came into usage in 1945, in Karl Popper's *The Open Society and Its Enemies*. Popper understood that human history is "man-made," that is, "its institutions and traditions are neither the work of God nor of nature, but the results of human actions and decisions, and alterable by human actions and decisions." But, he stressed, this did *not* mean the events of history "are all consciously designed, and explicable in terms of needs, hopes, or motives." On the contrary, even conscious intentions lead, as a rule, to *the indirect, the unintended, and often the unwanted by-products of such actions.*

It is this fundamental contradiction—intentional acts can have unintentional results—that, Popper understood, give rise to the need for conspiracy theories. The modern conspiracy theory, he argued, is not dissimilar in structure from earlier forms of polytheism like the model found in Homer's epics, such as *The Iliad*. "Homer conceived the power of the gods in such a way that whatever happened on the plain before Troy was only a reflection of the various conspiracies on Olympus," Popper argues. "The conspiracy theory of society is just a version of this theism, of a belief in gods whose whims and wills rule everything. It comes from abandoning God and then asking: 'Who is in his place?'

His place is then filled by various powerful men and groups—sinister pressure groups, who are to be blamed for having planned the great depression and all the evils from which we suffer."

The contemporary conspiracy theory, then, is a secularized version of religion; after the gods are "abandoned," Popper goes on to argue, "their place is filled by powerful men or groups—sinister pressure groups whose wickedness is responsible for all the evils we suffer from—such as the Learned Elders of Zion, or the monopolists, or the capitalists, or the imperialists."

If eighteenth-century conspiracy theories were an accepted part of American belief, simply because it was generally understood that human agency had to be behind all surprising events, by the twentieth century mainstream thought had embraced a belief that much of history happens due to chaos and unintended side effects. The conspiracist is at heart nostalgic for an earlier model of the universe with distinct causality, one where everything can be explained and understood, where randomness is banished evermore. So while conspiracies can be intentionally planned events, they nonetheless lead to unexpected, unpredictable outcomes (even if they're otherwise successful). A conspiracy theory, on the other hand, denies this possibility entirely.

Popper also reminds us of the simple way of differentiating science from metaphysics: falsifiability. A proposition is scientifically valid if it can be theoretically disproved, whereas most metaphysical propositions ("Mercury is in retrograde"), as well as religion ("It's all part of God's plan") fail this falsifiability test because one simply can't propose any kind of scientific test that might disprove such propositions. Conspiracy theories—particularly those about secret, networked groups—also fail this falsifiability test. The story of anti-Semitism, as we've already seen, depends on the belief that *anything*, positive or negative, can be proof of the deviancy of *The Protocols of the Elders of Zion*. Bolshevism, international banking—it's all, if you dig deep enough, the work of the Jews (in the darkest corners of the Internet you'll regularly find assertions that the rise of the Nazis and the Holocaust itself were both the work of the Jews).

The conspiracy theory, in other words, is itself an article of faith. Which is to say, there's a reason that believers are so resistant to facts that would disprove their theses. On a basic level, the conspiracy theory allows the believer to see the world as they want to see it.

The cultural war we're currently fighting is not just whether or not this or that conspiracy theory is true—rather, on a fundamental level, what conspiracists are pushing back against is the entire rise of social sciences and other theories of causality that replace human intention. One way to look at the changes that happened at the beginning of the twentieth century involves a cultural shift in which new theories arose to displace human agency and the centrality of human existence: Darwin, arguing that humans were not the divine reflection of God but a happy, if random, accident of evolution; Marx arguing that socioeconomic forces drive us and our actions; Freud's insistence that we are governed by unconscious forces. What connects the mutual reaffirming hatred of Marxism, of evolution, and of other forms of cultural modernity is this refusal to cede the primacy of human agency and intention. Belief in conspiracy theories is another way this refusal is argued.

In an age when it was common—even enlightened—to believe that all of history was governed and determined by the intentional acts of powerful men, conspiracy theories were not only not aberrant, they were in many ways the accepted understanding of the world. What changed is not the conspiracy theories themselves but rather how the mainstream saw the world; what was once accepted as true (that human actions determine history) became increasingly fringe as we adopted a new mode of seeing: one in which global events are as much governed by chaos, accident, unconscious forces, systematic structures that operate almost without our direct knowledge, and so forth.

It is possible that the idea that our day-to-day lives is determined far more by chaos than by human agency may be too much for many people to process. At this point, the question is less about whether or not one believes in conspiracy theories but *which* conspiracy theories one believes in. A 2019 survey found that nearly a third of Americans believed that search engines like Google discriminate against conservatives and that a secret "Deep State" was working against President Donald Trump and his supporters, while 23 percent still believed the September 11 attacks were "an inside job." Like it or not, we are a nation of conspiracists.

In 2015, political scientists Eric Oliver and Thomas Wood polled people on a series of different conspiracy theories, some of which had a liberal slant to them (the Iraq War was not launched to fight terrorism but was driven instead by oil companies; the 2008 financial crisis was orchestrated by Wall Street and the Federal Reserve; and US government officials planned the attacks of September 11 to provoke a war in the Middle East), some with a conservative slant (President Barack Obama was not born in the United States and billionaire George Soros is behind a hidden plot to destabilize America). They also polled people regarding nonpartisan conspiracy theories (vapor trails left by aircraft are actually chemical agents being sprayed on an unsuspecting populace and compact fluorescent light bulbs are actually part of a secret governmental mind control program).

What Wood and Oliver found was that there was little difference between liberals and conservatives when it came to belief in nonpartisan conspiracy theories like chemtrails. They found a slight ideological tilt: conservatives were a little more likely to believe right-leaning conspiracy theories than liberals were to believe in left-leaning conspiracy theories.

But, as they told the *Washington Post*, "Contrary to popular speculations, conspiracy theorists are *not* the sole domain of conservatives nor are conspiracy theorists all paranoid." They found that conspiracy theories did tend to appear among the less educated, and among people who were less trusting of others and more politically alienated. But mostly, they found, "the biggest predictor of whether someone believes in conspiracy theories is whether they also hold other magical beliefs—conspiracy theorists are much more likely to believe in the supernatural and paranormal or believe in Biblical prophecy."

"We think of conspiracy theories," Wood and Oliver concluded, "as simply another form of magical thinking. And as with all types of magical thinking, people engage in conspiracy theories in order to cope with difficult emotions."

R ising up out of the plains on the far edge of civilization, the white spires of the Denver International Airport draw not just travelers but the dreams of conspiracy theorists. It's not just the airport's remote location, its convoluted and lengthy construction process, or even the blazing-eyed, demonic blue bronco rearing on its hind legs that greets you as you approach, a sculpture that killed its own creator, Luis Jiménez, when a piece fell and severed his femoral artery. It's also the Masonic symbols carved into the building's time capsule (not to be opened until 2094), the labyrinthine underground tunnel network, and the unusual murals throughout the terminals—which, some allege, contain secret occult messages.

What if the airport is not just a hub for Frontier and United airlines but also for a vast, subterranean secret society whose tentacles stretch in all directions? What if its location, inexplicably distant from Denver, is in fact located over precise coordinates whose significance is known only to Satanists and the Illuminati? What if the time capsule's reference to "The New World Airport Commission" is a veiled reference to a coming New World Order? What if all these signs and symbols are really there to taunt weary travelers, subtly indicating the building's true, nefarious purpose?

In addition to the time capsule, the major proof of conspiracy is often traced to two large murals commissioned for the airport. Leo Tanguma's *In Peace and Harmony with Nature* and *Children of the World*

Dream of Peace flank the baggage claim areas with brightly colored figures and bold, expressionistic images. In the former, a scene of environmental destruction (including a forest on fire) is counterpointed by the children of the world coming together to plant new life. In the latter, a storm trooper–esque soldier with machine gun, sword, and gas mask spreads violence, only to be triumphed in the second half of the mural by a scene of peace and hope. If you follow the murals from left to right, they each offer a scene of hope and promise building out of destruction. But if you just crop out the soldier or the forest fire and post them on the Internet, it's easy to proclaim, as one Reddit member summed up, that the whole place is "like some crazy Illuminati Freemason Nazi Airport of Doom."

(It's worth noting in passing, perhaps, that the Denver Airport is *filled* with murals and other art, and yet conspiracists tend to focus almost entirely on the two works by Chicano artists: Tanguma's murals and Jiménez's *Blue Mustang*. That the murals depicting white prospectors and similar art do not elicit paranoid musings is a reflection of how easy it is to construct sinister narratives around uses of symbolism and imagery that aren't immediately familiar.)

Theories about the Denver airport date back to before its opening, when a woman named Alex Christopher flew here in the early 1990s to participate in a conference about the global agenda of extraterrestrials. As people discussed the much-delayed, over-budget new airport, Christopher would later remember, "I started looking at all the murals and floors and weirdness. . . . I got really intrigued." Christopher visited the muralist Tanguma, asking him if he had been given instructions on what to paint and talking about how the United Nations was a conspiracy to take over the United States.

Within a decade, her ideas had spread among the conspiracist community. In his 1998 book, *The Biggest Secret*, conspiracy monger David Icke suggested that Denver was "scheduled to be the Western headquarters of the US New World Order during martial law take over," and reporting that "contacts who have been underground at the Denver Airport claim that there are large numbers of human slaves, many of them children, working there under the control of the reptilians." The late-night talk show *Coast to Coast AM*, a popular clearinghouse for Bigfoot, aliens, and other government cover-ups, devoted an entire episode to it in 2007, where one guest told listeners the airport was "some kind of cathedral" to the New World Order, "a cathedral to the world that they're making." And in 2010, during the season finale of *Conspiracy Theory with Jesse Ventura*, the ex-governor used it as the focal point for his discussion about the impending apocalypse in the year 2012.

Satanists, the Illuminati, Nazis, Freemasons, Reptilian slavers—the Denver Airport is hub for not just one conspiracy theory but a weird, syncretic mix of so many. Here, visions of the Antichrist mingle with UFOs and Freemasons, an increasingly weird hodgepodge of different conspiratorial visions blended together. Throughout much of American history, specific conspiracy theories would arise to address specific historical and cultural anxieties. But in recent decades, there has been an increasing blur between varying theories as separate strands and narratives have collapsed in on one another. And more and more, such conspiracy theories have articulated a fundamental war between good and evil, one in which the lives of all of humanity is at stake.

TWENTY-ONE

The Suburban Uncanny

The artist Mike Kelley had long dreamed of buying his childhood home on Palmer Road in the Detroit suburb of Westland. Born in 1954, Kelley had become an established Los Angeles–based artist when, in the early twenty-first century, he decided to re-create a nearly exact model of it, currently a public art display at the Museum of Contemporary Art, Detroit. From the exterior, it appears identical to the original house, but it's not a perfect copy, because, while the aboveground floor plan is the same, there is an underground level, a maze of labyrinths and hidden corridors. Kelley envisioned the aboveground portion of the home to be used for public gatherings and community events; the basement labyrinth, meanwhile, was "designed for private rites of an aesthetic nature."

This structure of a suburban home, both rooted in banal precision and fantastical speculation, was part of Kelley's long-standing fascination with the Satanic ritual abuse panic that swept America through the 1980s, and his *Mobile Homestead* offers the perfect topographical metaphor for the way the idyllic home gradually became a site of imagined nightmares, and how paranoid delusions turned the suburbs uncanny.

When Sigmund Freud popularized the term "uncanny," he offered a number of examples that might trigger the feeling, including "the factor of the repetition of the same thing," an experience that evokes for him "the sense of helplessness experienced in some dream-states." Freud was writing before the rise of the suburbs, but in their layout and construction they seemed almost purpose-built to evoke the uncanny. Anyone who's ever been lost in a labyrinth of cul-de-sacs knows this sensation: the houses, row after row of them, the streets seemingly straight but also strangely curved and bent, as if to subtly guide you toward a dead end in the subdivision's heart. All the houses structurally the same, but with slight variations—perhaps because of a different car in the driveway, a different conglomeration of yard waste at the curb, a distinct rosebush or hedge—eliciting a simultaneous sense of sameness and difference. At night, driving slowly through such a maze, the orange glow of streetlights brightening and fading along the way, or even in daytime, as you pass by house after house shut up against the world, you are in the landscape of disquiet.

Perhaps it was not a question of if but when the topography of such spaces would become the locus of a nationwide nightmare.

In 1983, in Manhattan Beach, California, the owners of a respected and elite day-care center, the McMartin Pre-School, were arrested under suspicion of child molestation. A woman named Judy Johnson had accused the staff of molesting her son, Matthew, launching a trial that would consume much of the 1980s. The case would become one of the longest and most sensationalized legal battles in American history and would come to stand in for a whole series of occult conspiracies and allegations about day-care workers that swept through the country like a virus.

This series of legal battles came to be known as the Satanic Panic: all over the country, childcare providers were accused of not just molesting children but forcing them to participate in fantastical and elaborate Satanic rituals involving animal and human sacrifice, orgies and sexual abuse, and brainwashing and memory wipes. In addition to day cares, much of the paranoia centered around suburban homes. Before the McMartin case even broke in Southern California, Bakersfield, to the north, had been incubating suspicion and fear. In 1982, a woman named Mary Ann Barbour began to suspect that her two granddaughters were being molested by a relative, Rod Phelps. She filed child endangerment charges against their parents and moved to have her daughter-in-law's day care shut down. Under questioning, the two young girls told authorities they had been abused not only by Phelps, but also by their father. Eventually, they would claim their parents had run a sex trafficking ring, suspended them from hooks while abusing them, and shown them snuff films to warn them what would happen if they ever talked. When police came to search their homes, they found no pornography, or any evidence of hooks, or any other physical evidence to corroborate the children's stories. In what would become a strange hallmark of the child abuse cases to come, children would repeatedly claim they had been subjected to atrocities and abuse for which no forensic evidence could be found, and which often contradicted known facts. The girls' parents were sentenced to over two hundred years each and would spend the next twelve years in prison until their convictions were finally thrown out.

For decades, it was the city that had been seen as a place of crime and danger, where no one was safe, where no self-respecting middle-class person would venture. The suburbs were the answer—they embodied the locus of the ideal family: middle-class respectability, the signal that one had "arrived," financially and socially. Not coincidentally, they are a place of aesthetic control and conformity, of homeowner's associations dictating the color of a house, the height of a tree, the state of a lawn. Aesthetic conformity guarantees property values and ensures a kind of cultural homogeneity as well. In response to that outward uniformity, the nuclear family of the suburbs turns inward: the home becomes a private space, its insides are what makes it unique and give it personality.

You can't drive slowly down an avenue of identical houses without giving some thought to how each might be different on the inside. But as fear of secret Satanic cults overtook the nation, that curiosity about what was going on behind those walls became pathological. The stories children told were of a separate suburban landscape, one that seemed to exist alongside this picture of normality, a nightmare world of hidden suburban depravity, laid like a palimpsest over ordinary America. The low-slung houses lining these cul-de-sacs might look identical, each one home to some happy family going about its days—but behind venetian blinds and locked doors strange rituals were afoot.

Among those swept up in the Bakersfield panics were Mary and Brad Nokes. Their ten-year-old son, Mike, was removed from their custody in 1984 and questioned as to whether he'd been abused. At first Mike denied having been molested, then changed his mind six days later, but then reversed his story once more three weeks after that.

When Mike Nokes was asked why he had accused his parents of molestation if it wasn't true, he responded that he had been coached by the county childcare investigator, Cory Taylor. "When I tell the truth," Mike told a private investigator working on behalf of his parents, "she [Taylor] says, 'C'mon. Better start telling me the truth, or I'il keep you in this room all day.'" Subjected to this kind of intense questioning, in which the only correct answer was one that implicated parents and daycare workers, Mike Nokes became hysterical. Alone and subject to the increasing stress of endless questioning, Mike seemed driven by separation anxiety: when the police told his grandparents they could no longer visit him, he accused his grandparents of molestation. When his first interlocutor, Cory Taylor, was taken off the case, he accused her of molestation, too.

Under the intense questioning of another social worker, Carolyn Heims, Nokes finally began telling a story that would send the child abuse panic into a new level of sensationalism. Nokes told Heims not only that he had been abused, but that he had been forced to witness and participate in the ritual murder of infants. "Michael said that once everybody got there, all of the adults would take their clothes off and stand in a square around the children, who were in a circle," according to reports of his testimony. "Michael said that all during this time the adults were chanting prayers to Satan. Michael said that he (and a little girl) were handed knives." Michael said he and the girl were forced to throw their knives at one of the infants, after which "all of the adults started throwing knives that they had."

Nokes's story was so bizarre it seemed impossible that anyone could believe him. Instead, he was not only believed, but Kern County officials began dragging local lakes, searching for evidence of the disposed baby corpses. None were found, though that didn't stop them from believing that this sexual abuse was in fact the work of a secret ring of Satanists. Nokes and several other children eventually named twenty-seven different victims of this supposed Satanic cult; when it turned out that two people on the list were still alive, and a third had died during surgery, officials were undeterred; they assumed instead that the children had been brainwashed and instructed to recount false memories to throw authorities off the trail of the true story.

What had started as molestation accusations became increasingly baroque, bound up in occult ritual. Judy Johnson, the accuser at the heart of the McMartin case, began leaving increasingly bizarre answering machine messages for the LA County investigators, relating her son Matthew's stories of a "goatman," accusing day-care worker Peggy McMartin of drilling "a child under the arms, armpits." The preschool's atmosphere, she alleged, was one of ritual magic: "Peggy, Babs and Betty were all dressed up as witches. The person who buried Matthew is Miss Betty. There were no holes in the coffin." Bob Currie, a parent of one of the McMartin children who devoted his life to ferreting out Satanic ritual abuse, would later state on *Geraldo*: "The truth about Satanism is they truly do use blood, and they mix it with urine, and then they also use the real meat, the real flesh. This is what makes Satanism true, and this is what 1,200 molested kids in the city of Manhattan Beach have told the sheriff's department."

What's noteworthy about the Satanic ritual abuse panic of the 1980s was how quickly it became about more than just child abuse. History is rife with sexual abuse scandals, including those orchestrated by large conspiracies, be they the Catholic Church or the politicians protecting Jeffrey Epstein. But what happened in the 1980s was that the public—and prosecutors—became far more fixated on the suburban occult aspects than the actual abuse. After the McMartin trial ended in a hung jury, nine of eleven jurors held a press conference in which several jurors stated they felt abuse had occurred but hadn't been proven, and that the focus on bizarre stories of animal mutilation, blood drinking, and other occult behavior had tainted those allegations that seemed substantial. "I am concerned," FBI profiler Kenneth V. Lanning would later write, that in some cases "individuals are getting away with molesting children because we cannot prove they are satanic devil worshipers who engage in brainwashing, human sacrifice, and cannibalism as part of a large conspiracy."

Why did so many families become convinced of these massive cults, their tentacles reaching throughout the country? For some parents, it offered a strange means of assuaging real guilt that their children may have been victims of abuse. As Lanning put it, "If your child's molestation was perpetrated by a sophisticated satanic cult, there is nothing you could have done to prevent it and therefore no reason to feel any guilt." Lanning recalled parents describing day-care centers whose cults "had sensors in the road, lookouts in the air, and informers everywhere," a secret, indefatigable network of malevolence that no parent could match.

But writer Richard Beck also notes that such fantasies could be empowering, and that they "lent a sort of heroic glow to the very idea of parenting." The middle-class suburbs of the 1980s had become a place of selfishness lacking in any kind of moral or ethical center. The Mc-Martin case, Beck notes, "reimagined life there as a battle to preserve that peaceful, comfortable way of life." The Satanic Panic turned the suburbs into a battlefield between good and evil, and allowed ordinary parents starring roles in waging Holy War.

The Satanic ritual abuse panic reconstituted another, earlier panic: the anti-Catholic fears that convents and churches contained secret catacombs wherein all manner of perverse sexual abuse was taking place underground. Aside from the locus having shifted from the Catholic institution to the day care and suburban home, the structure and format was largely the same: a foreign religion with strange rituals scooping up the most vulnerable and subjecting them to vile, depraved practices involving sex and death. But such stories had always involved either adult women or at least pubescent teenagers. Now the victims were young children, a dramatic departure.

Shifting from women to children meant that the animating narrative behind many of these accusations began to look similar to the old anti-Semitic canard of blood libel, repackaged for the daytime talk show age. "Satanists" had taken the place of Jews, and there was very little overt anti-Semitism in the Satanic ritual abuse panic, but the hallmarks were still the same: non-Christians were abducting children and subjecting them to bizarre, lethal ceremonies, much of which involved blood drinking.

But there are other reasons that conspiracists no longer envisioned the most vulnerable as adult women. For one, the legal nature of children themselves had changed. When Boston Protestants were fretting about the women in the Ursuline convent in the 1830s, children had a far different cultural standing. During the nineteenth century (and well into the twentieth), corporal punishment was not only widespread but considered acceptable, if not essential, to proper child-rearing, and children had few if any legal rights of their own. It wasn't until the 1960s that American psychologists began to look seriously into the question of child abuse; in the early 1970s, legal scholars (including a young Yale Law graduate named Hillary Rodham) began to differentiate the rights of a child from that of their parents, and to begin to sketch out under what conditions it might be permissible to remove a child from their parents' custody in order to save them from harm or neglect. In 1974, Congress passed the Child Abuse Prevention and Treatment Act to establish a National Center on Child Abuse and Neglect, a clearinghouse for research and protocols on child abuse prevention.

These questions were then—as they are now—still fraught. What rights do parents have to be free from government intervention? What is "best" for a child? Amidst an already swirling debate happening in churches, school board meetings, and governmental organizations, the threat of Satanists performing rituals on children triggered a sizable portion of the population into the panic that they simply weren't doing enough, and that the children were in dire risk.

At the same time, the status of women had changed as well. No longer were women treated by American society at large as passive objects, things to be protected from violent threats. The feminist movement that had exploded in the 1960s and '70s demanded recognition for adult women as fully fledged actors and agents in their own rights. "The special tie women have with children is recognized by everyone," Shulamith Firestone wrote in *The Dialectic of Sex*, going on to argue that the true nature "of this bond is no more than shared oppression." (Critic Cynthia Enloe would go on to coin the term "womenandchildren" to highlight the way these two groups share a status as "symbols, victims, or dependents.") The shift in focus that had happened from adult women to children was essentially one of convenience: moral panics need a pure victim, an object to protect, and if women were increasingly vocal about not playing that role, then conspiracists were happy enough to switch their focus to children.

In his assessment of the Satanic Panic scare, sociologist Jeffrey S. Victor diagnosed the epidemic as the result of a convergence of forces: when multiple, distinct social groups—each with its own concerns and agendas—begin to fixate on the same topic, the groundswell of concern can grow exponentially as each group echoes and amplifies the others' fears and anxieties. Numerous interest groups also had a stake in fueling the panic, interest groups that had little in common with one another but made common cause against this nebulous network of occultists and abusers.

Fundamentalist Christians saw accounts of these rituals as proof of the literal work of the Devil, as well as validation that the messages they perceived in heavy metal and Dungeons and Dragons were far from benign. Social conservatives, as well, saw in the children's accusations extreme proof of the lax permissiveness of liberals, who'd eschewed traditional morality and now were reaping what they'd sown. Most curiously, however, were feminist groups, who found themselves on opposing sides of the debate. Many feminists saw the whole panic as an attack on working mothers, while others saw it as proof of both the dangers of pornography and the pathological result of a patriarchal culture that failed to take seriously the voices of abused women and children. (When the McMartin Pre-School was finally raised to the ground, it was Gloria Steinem who paid for the excavation in search of hidden tunnels beneath the building.)

But in the case of the Satanic ritual abuse trials, these groups would in turn be aided by the nascent field of recovered memory hypnosis. This new field was popularized by the book *Michelle Remembers*, written by Lawrence Pazder, a psychiatrist who'd used hypnosis on his patient Michelle Smith to recover a series of memories about a group of Satanists who abused her when she was five. In a trance she recalled scenes such as one where Satanists dismembered and then reassembled a corpse, reanimating it with electric shocks ("God help me! He cut off its feet! Oh no, I don't want to hear. I can hear him cutting its legs. I can *hear* him cutting the bones up. . . . Oh, God, that's what they're going to do to me next."). Many of Smith's recovered memories contradicted known and incontrovertible facts, and nothing from the book could be corroborated. But the popular reception of books like *Michelle Remembers* and Flora Rheta Schreiber's *Sybil* gave practitioners of recovered memory therapy a foothold and a means of establishing themselves within the larger psychiatric community.

Little wonder the talk shows ate it up. Oprah Winfrey, Geraldo Rivera, Sally Jessy Raphael, Phil Donahue—the final piece of the puzzle, all of them running breathless testimonials of abuse, terror, ritual, and blood sacrifice. In 1989, long after *Michelle Remembers* had been thoroughly debunked, Oprah invited Smith (who'd since married her psychiatrist, Pazder) on as a guest, along with another supposed abuse survivor (Laurel Rose Willson, who'd later reinvent herself as an ersatz Holocaust survivor). Winfrey gave both hoaxers an uncritical platform to spin their wild, unsubstantiated tales to a rapt audience.

In the daytime talk show, the host offers witness and affirmation while the guest offers her- or himself up, blood and body, for immediate consumption by the studio audience and millions of viewers. It is a format designed to generate a kind of pathos, a response to the human soul in extremis. Particularly for their primary demographic, stay-at-home mothers, they became a means to escape, if only for a few hours, from the drudgery of the suburbs, a kind of emotional adventurism, a journey through someone else's psyche. The talk shows were perfect peddlers of conspiracies, panics, and hoaxes because truth is of secondary importance to emotional impact. It is no surprise that years after Michelle Smith's appearance, Oprah offered a dangerous platform to antivaxxer Jenny McCarthy.

Like repressed memory therapy, the talk show is about recovering a testimony, bringing what was hidden into the light. Neither the talk show guest nor the therapy patient is expected to substantiate her or his story with facts or evidence; it is the act of testimony itself which is sufficient, which substantiates itself. If the repressed therapy session was like the confessional booth, the talk show was the tent revival.

Conservative Christians and talk show hosts, psychotherapists and social workers, feminists and anti-feminists: the heart of the Venn diagram where they all overlapped was a fear of the occult. Anti-Christian, defined by an orgiastic quality that could imperil women and children, and a direct rebuke to the notion of a nuclear family—all governed by a fear of ritual abandonment and a loss of self-control.

Most importantly, the Satanic ritual abuse panic was not a singular moment; it was a bridge. It started as a synthesis of earlier anti-Catholic and anti-Semitic panics, secularized and deployed in a suburban landscape, but it would not end in the 1990s with the McMartin trial. Rather it receded into the background, giving the public just enough space to forget it entirely. So when new conspiracy theories emerged in the run-up to the 2016 election about Hillary Clinton and her associates as blood-drinking Satanists, the accusations could seem new and fresh and not simply an obvious retread of allegations that had happened so recently that most voters were alive to witness them.

The fear of secret rites speaks to something more primal, more terrifying for many people than the threat of actual sexual abuse. Rituals—particularly those foreign, unknown, or unexplained—strike at the very core of how a society constructs itself. Bodies writhing in ecstasy, speaking in tongues, sexual licentiousness, the use of blood and other bodily fluids, all come together in the perfect convergence of threats. An elevated emotional ecstasy offers a kind of dissolution of the self: your boundaries break down, you lose yourself, you become frenzied, bestial, *something not quite human.* In such a state the normal rules that govern a culture are suspended: laws don't apply, shame and guilt no longer limit activities. Familial and communal bonds—the things that normally manage our behavior, the very heart of the suburban world—cease to have an effect. And traditional authority figures—the priest, the police officer, the governmental authority, the head of the household—are replaced with hierarchical figures of unknown provenance. If we fear the specter of such rituals, it's because they offer the chance to dissolve all of the normal restraints that govern middle-class life and replace them with an entirely different set of values that cannot be restrained or controlled in the usual manner.

The Reagan eighties were in every way about selfishness, about asserting oneself and one's own needs over others. Cults offered a most radical rebuke to this individualism: an inverted world where there is no self, where you are not yourself, not in charge of yourself—and afterward, you are not even in control of your own memories, which bear no trace of how much of yourself you've lost. It was the perfect hysteria for the inherently uncanny feeling of living in the suburbs, feeding the fear of what other people were doing in their own homes.

Alone at home with the TV on in the background, dwellers of the suburbs peered through the blinds and wondered if the neighbors were letting themselves go.

TWENTY-TWO

Attack of the Lizard People!

By the time I could get to downtown Nashville in July 2021, I assumed there wouldn't be any lingering traces of the explosion. When I told people why I was going there, most of my friends didn't even remember what had happened on December 25, 2020—or if they did, they had only the vaguest recollection. In a year when so much took place, including a global pandemic and a monumental presidential election, the strange incident involving Anthony Quinn Warner had quickly, it seemed, faded from memory. I assumed downtown Nashville would be back to normal.

My friend Karl and I parked in the six-story garage adjacent to Second Avenue, where the plywood in the stairwell was the first indication that not all was right. The plywood, it turned out, was everywhere—on windows up and down the street, for a full block and beyond, and stretching onto side streets. This had been a bustling artery of Nashville's nightlife, home to a Coyote Ugly and a B.B. King's Blues Club and a strip of local bars and clubs. Now it was a cordoned-off construction zone. There are still garlands wrapped around the light poles from the Christmas decorations—garlands that somehow miraculously survived the fireball. Crews were hard at work trying to salvage the street that Warner had utterly destroyed on Christmas morning at 6:30 a.m. Having parked his RV in front of AT&T's Main Central Office on 185 Second Avenue North earlier that morning, a strange countdown began at 6:00 a.m., in which a recorded voice urged people to stay clear of the area, interspersed with a recording of the 1964 Petula Clark song "Downtown." Thirty minutes later, the bomb in Warner's RV exploded, taking the RV, him, and much of a city block with it.

Warner's broadcast had warned people away, and several police officers worked diligently to clear the area in time, but it still seems something short of a miracle that only Warner was killed in the blast. Now, even six months later, it's easy to get a sense of how massive the damage was. The AT&T building itself is a ruin, three brick walls and not much else.

Just at the edge of the roped-off area is the Original Snuff Shop, a tobacco shop that has just reopened after six months of renovations. I talk to the two employees, who relay a number of theories they've overheard as to what has happened here. Sean tells me he heard one story that some uncounted ballots for Donald Trump were being held here, ballots from Georgia that were deliberately removed to ensure Joe Biden's victory in that state. He's also heard another story, that the bomb was instigated by the business improvement district, which wanted to renovate Second Avenue and paid Warner to commit suicide so that they could destroy the block and start again. Wyatt, meanwhile, tells me a friend is convinced that it wasn't a bomb at all, that it was a missile strike, and that in certain YouTube videos you can see the missile onscreen a split second before the explosion.

Wyatt and Sean are both skeptical of these various theories, though Sean did end up more or less shrugging as to what actually happened. "Nobody will ever really know," he tells me. I understand his hesitation. After all, these theories, as far-fetched as they clearly are, aren't that much more bizarre than the actual story, that Anthony Warner Quinn was targeting the AT&T building because he believed a secret race of reptilian overlords were using 5G technology as a mass mind control device.

He's not alone. In 2022, a documentary titled *Watch the Water* began to circulate amongst conspiracy theorists, claiming that Covid-19 is not a virus; it is a synthetic form of snake venom, and it's being distributed through vaccines and public drinking-water systems. "I think the plan all along was to get the serpent's, the evil one's DNA into your God-created DNA," chiropractor Bryan Ardis explains in the video. "They're using mRNA . . . from, I believe, the king cobra venom. And I think they want to get that venom inside of you and make you a hybrid of Satan."

If this sometimes seems absurd, it can get tragic quickly. In August 2021, the owner of a Christian surf school in Santa Barbara, California, drove his two young children to the Mexican resort town of Rosarito, where he killed both children (ages two years and ten months) and left their bodies by the side of the road. He would later claim that his wife "possessed serpent DNA" and he had killed his children out of fear of "interbreeding" between humans and reptilians—a theory he seems to have adopted through the work of ex-athlete and Green Party politician David Icke.

The idea of lizard people—reptilian aliens with vaguely humanoid shapes, who wear human disguises so as to move undetected in our midst—is a long-standing trope in science fiction, appearing in pulp magazines through the decades. The idea broke through into mainstream consciousness through the movie, and subsequent TV show, *V*. The miniseries' creator, Kenneth Johnson, took Sinclair Lewis's 1935 novel *It Can't Happen Here*, about a fascist takeover of the United States, and adapted it for the science fiction genre, creating a narrative about a seemingly benign visitation by extraterrestrials who look just like us and come in peace. As they insinuate themselves into human government and culture, it slowly becomes apparent that underneath their human masks they are in fact bipedal reptoids who are secretly consuming humans for food. It was meant as a clear allegory for Nazi Germany, down to the Visitors' uniforms and swastika-like insignias ("The Nazis showed us one face for a while and then they took it off and showed us their real faces—metaphorically speaking," Johnson explained.).

V was a ratings hit and a cultural sensation, but while it made for great television, within a decade there were some who had begun to take a version of it as literal truth. The strange transformation of fiction into fact happened primarily through David Icke. Born in Leicester, England, in 1952, Icke became famous as a footballer, enjoying a meteoric rise before injuries ended his career in 1971. He spent the 1970s and '80s as a journalist and broadcaster, with reliably left-wing political views, and in mid-1988, he announced he was running in the upcoming general election as a Green Party candidate—within a year, he had ascended through the ranks of the organization, being elected party spokesman. Embracing far-left environmentalism, Icke also began to adopt a New Age dimension to his public persona, publishing a series of books that moved him further away from mainstream politics and journalism and into strange, conspiratorial musings.

In *The Robots' Rebellion* (1994), Icke explains "a story of a conspiracy to control the human race," one created by "manipulators" who "do not want us to know that we are eternal beings of light and love with limitless potential"; unfolding a cosmology that reads like a synthesis of J. R. R. Tolkien's Middle-earth mythology, the Book of Genesis, and *Star Wars*, Icke prophesied a coming time when the world will be "re-synchronised." He gave a name to these manipulators in *The Robots' Rebellion*: the "Brotherhood," an amalgamation of Freemason motifs and a grab bag of images cobbled together from everyone from the ancient Egyptians to the Nazis. He goes on to explain how the world is controlled by this Brotherhood, indicating that the "swastika, the lamb, the obelisk, the apron . . . and of course the pyramid and eye are still the symbols of the Brotherhood societies."

Freemasons, he goes on to elaborate in 1995's . . . *And the Truth Shall Set You Free*, manipulated the events of the Revolutionary War to gain control of the United States, which is supposedly why one can still find an image of an eye atop a pyramid on the US dollar bill. But even these "Global Elite" are only partially responsible for the widespread negative energy that keeps humans from realizing their limitless potential for light and love. For behind the Global Elite are a group of "negative manipulators on the Fourth Dimension": the Prison Warders. These extraterrestrials "manipulate the Brotherhood network, and the Brotherhood network manipulates the world. Each lower level doesn't know what the level above knows, and none of them knows what the Prison Warders know. It is a manipulators' paradise, with most people within it not knowing what they are part of or what the final goal will be." By *The Biggest Secret* (1998), Icke was ready to describe these Prison Warders in greater detail: known as the Anunnaki, they are reptilian extraterrestrials from the planet Draco—and their existence is the biggest secret lying behind war, inequality, injustice, and your own personal feelings of frustration and unhappiness.

In addition to repeating conspiracy theories about the Freemasons and the Illuminati, Icke has also at times referenced *The Protocols of the Elders of Zion*. They reappear throughout his books and he quotes from them heavily, citing their ability to correctly predict world events— while at the same time attempting to distance himself from charges of anti-Semitism. "I call them the Illuminati Protocols," he writes in . . . *And the Truth Shall Set You Free*. "Some say they were a forgery made public only to discredit Jews, and I use the term 'illuminati Protocols' to get away from the Jewish emphasis." Icke claims that they preexisted their appearance in the late nineteenth century and were originally focused on an elite group called the Priory of Sion, the leadership of the Knights Templar. Thus, Icke argues, they're authentic, but were later altered to be about Judaism. "Whatever the arguments," he concludes, "one fact cannot be denied, given the hindsight of the last 100 years. The Protocols, from wherever they came, were a quite stunning prophecy of what has happened in the twentieth century in terms of wars and the manipulation I am exposing here. Whoever wrote them sure as heck knew what the game plan was."

Icke is not the first writer to offer up *The Protocols* while simultaneously attempting to distance themselves from anti-Semitism. Icke himself claims to have borrowed the Priory of Sion thesis from Michael Baigent, Richard Leigh, and Henry Lincoln's book *Holy Blood, Holy Grail*—a work of speculative nonfiction that heavily influenced Dan Brown's mega-blockbuster *The Da Vinci Code*. Milton William Cooper, a conspiracist who built a long career out of UFO theories that became an increasingly strange and elaborate set of paranoid accusations and musings about world events, also celebrates the *Protocols* in his perennially in-print book *Behold a Pale Horse*. In his book, Cooper reprinted the *Protocols* in its entirety, offering for context a headnote that reads "Every aspect of this plan to subjugate the world has since become reality, validating the authenticity of conspiracy," while also instructing that "reference to 'Jews' should be replaced with the word 'Illuminati'; and the word 'goyim' should be replaced with the word 'cattle.'"

Cooper, along with Icke and Baigent, Leigh, and Lincoln, all appear to be attempting to transform the *Protocols* from a literal slur against the Jewish community into something like a structural narrative that encapsulates a wider conspiracy. It does not excuse the *Protocols*, and whether or not they felt they were being anti-Semitic in doing so is irrelevant; they introduced them to a new generation of readers who were free to discard or embrace their anti-Semitic content. The flourishing of visibly anti-Semitic content that references the *Protocols* on YouTube and other social media sites suggests that the damage has been done regardless of their intentions.

But it also reflects the direction in which conspiracy theories surrounding secret societies began to move by the end of the millennium. What has happened by the 1990s is that there are no longer distinct moral panics. It's become syncretic: everything gets folded into the same morass, without distinction. It is simultaneously anti-Semitic but also welcoming to Jews and others who ignore the anti-Semitic tinge. It can be about aliens, or about the Illuminati, or about lizard people—but it doesn't have to be about any of these things in particular. No longer is a specific article of faith required for membership in this group.

What draws people to such outlandish theories? When David Robertson looked into those who'd gravitated toward David Icke and others who had blurred the line between science fiction and conspiracy, he repeatedly found a yearning for something he called epistemic capital. For most conspiracists, there is a belief that the masses are ignorant, acquiescent, and unable to understand what is happening to them—encapsulated most succinctly in a term popularized by William Cooper: "sheeple." While Cooper, Icke, and others seek to enlighten the masses, there is a persistent pessimism that they'll never be able to receive the true enlightenment concerning the Illuminati, the lizard people, or other malevolent figures.

In a landscape populated by manipulating elites and sheeple, conspiracists emerge as a third category: they are not allied with the controlling elite, but they are enlightened in a way that differentiates them from the sheeple. Robertson suggests that they thus see themselves as a "counter-elite": although they lack the power of the elites, they nonetheless have an exclusive knowledge—their capital is epistemic rather than financial. It is, so to speak, a knowledge-based economy all its own. So while we may think of the conspiracist's world—one in which shadowy, malevolent forces control everything, dominate our every move, and engage in horrific acts of violence and murder to pursue their goals—as a dark, strange, and terrifying outlook, for the conspiracist there is actually a measure of power in thinking this way, because it elevates them above the sheeple who know nothing, and vests them with epistemic capital.

It's like a strange form of cryptocurrency. This form of capital is ultimately worthless, because it's not based on truth (though peddling such nonsense can be quite lucrative for hucksters like Icke). The value of such epistemic capital turns out to be based only on how many other people believe it and buy into it. Conspiracists like Icke work by developing a kind of Ponzi scheme of false knowledge, offering lower tier believers their own epistemic capital: secret clues, hidden riddles, shibboleths, and other insider knowledge. They encourage a kind of mining of new secrets: spend your time on the Web finding new clues—all of which further enhances the value of the secrets and knowledge already held by those at the top of this pyramid scheme.

This mechanism has been greatly aided by the rise of the Internet, which increasingly has put the raw material of such epistemic capital in the hands of ordinary individuals, who can stitch together facts and data from any number of sources to come to whatever conclusion they'd like. This surfeit of information has not created more clarity; rather, it has heightened the question of how we know what we know. As we are increasingly inundated with mediated sources of information— television news, social media, etc.—more and more of our daily work is involved in evaluating the sources of such information, determining who is trustworthy, and adjudicating which news items will be believed or dismissed.

In conspiracy circles, this has given rise to the citizen sleuth, a development that theorist Kathryn Olmsted traces to the *San Jose Mercury News*'s decision in 1996 to publish online a trove of research related to an investigative series of articles by reporter Gary Webb. Webb's series, "Dark Alliance," told the tale of a Los Angeles drug dealer, Ricky Ross, and two Nicaraguan drug smugglers, Oscar Danilo Blandón and Norwin Meneses, who provided Ross with cocaine that he in turn sold as crack on the streets of South Central. Following the lives of these three men, Webb argued that for the previous decade, Ross's drug ring flooded the streets of Los Angeles with "tons of cocaine" while using the proceeds to funnel "millions in drug profits to a Latin American guerrilla army run by the U.S. Central Intelligence Agency." The implication that the crack cocaine epidemic of the 1980s and early '90s was connected—directly or indirectly—to the CIA was a bombshell, and led to congressional investigations and parallel journalistic efforts by rival papers. Many of Webb's claims either could not be substantiated by other journalists or were denounced outright by the CIA, and the *San Jose Mercury News* ultimately retracted some of Webb's claims after not being able to independently verify them. Webb turned the "Dark Alliance" series into a book in 1998, but his professional reputation was never the same; he committed suicide in 2004.

The claims of Webb's articles aside, the decision by the *Mercury News* to upload Webb's original research alongside his writing ushered in a new era of web sleuthing, with readers now able to sift through the same raw material that Webb had. They could spot things that Webb had missed, make connections that might not have been as initially obvious, and could draw their own conclusions about what happened. One of the primary kinds of intellectual activity enabled by the Internet is the cobbling together of disparate facts, events, names, and other errata into ever-more complex webs of nefarious actors and their malevolent deeds. This has given rise to the mantra that has come to define the twenty-first century's version of conspiracism: "Do Your Own Research."

The Internet has provided the tools to form any kind of narrative or theory one wants, and it encourages sifting through a surfeit of information, picking and choosing which facts and events to suture together. The "Do Your Own Research" mantra gained steam primarily through the anti-vaccine movement that was spawned in the wake of Andrew Wakefield's now thoroughly debunked claims linking the MMR vaccine to autism. It was driven by vaccine skeptics like Jenny McCarthy, who appeared on Oprah Winfrey's talk show in 2007 to encourage viewers to distrust science and turn to the Internet for answers, proclaiming, "The University of Google is where I got my degree from."

It's been depressingly effective; American support for vaccines had fallen from 94 percent in 2001 to 84 percent by 2015, with millennials being the age group most likely to subscribe to the belief that vaccines were harmful (20 percent versus 10 percent for the population as a whole). And it's since moved out of the initial resistance to the MMR vaccine to become the dominant mantra of conspiracists everywhere. It appears on Alex Jones's InfoWars site, where he urges his audience to do their own research on everything from the Covid-19 vaccines to the war in Ukraine. YouTube videos by the hundreds encourage viewers to do their own research on hydroxychloroquine, essential oils, and the Second Coming of Jesus Christ. In September 2021, Nicki Minaj tweeted about her resistance to getting a Covid-19 vaccine, stating she'd only do it "once I feel I've done enough research." NBA star Kyrie Irving, asked about his comments about the Earth being flat, responded that it wasn't "about whether the world is flat or whether the world is round. It's really about just everyone just believing what they want to believe and feeling comfortable with it. . . . For me, it's just giving everyone a chance to do their own research and find their own knowledge instead of having knowledge just shoved to you."

The problem with doing your own research is that it doesn't work. As psychologists Nathan Ballantyne and David Dunning explained in the *New York Times*, "when it comes to technical and complex issues like climate change and vaccine efficacy, novices who do their own research often end up becoming more misled than informed—the exact opposite of what D.Y.O.R. is supposed to accomplish." Dunning in particular should know; he helped coin "Dunning–Kruger Effect," the term for the cognitive bias in which people with limited knowledge on a given subject come to greatly overestimate their own expertise. In one study, a third of respondents claimed to know more about the causes of autism than medical professionals—a belief that was correlated with the respondents' own resistance to a public vaccination policy, suggesting that the overconfidence associated with the Dunning–Kruger Effect may be a psychological defense to accommodate previously held beliefs.

Doing your own research then doesn't just feel empowering; it can also feel strangely liberating. Writing about rumor and urban legend in America, sociologists Gary Alan Fine and Patricia A. Turner borrow a phrase from the French anthropologist Claude Lévi-Strauss, who has said that some ideas are simply "good to think." As Fine and Turner note, urban legends and conspiracy theories are good to think because "they connect to a powerful 'cultural logic' that makes sense to narrators and audiences. Plausibility is key. Rumor permits us to project our emotional fantasies on events that we can claim 'really did happen,' protecting ourselves from the implications of our beliefs." By rejecting the dominant narrative without offering a substantive replacement, conspiracy mongers like Icke offer their audiences the freedom to pick and choose among sources and studies and devise a narrative that best fits with their preconceived notions and biases. By encouraging people to "make up their own minds," they encourage listeners to disregard anything that is discomfiting to their worldview.

Ultimately, people are not looking for answers; they're looking for permission.

One last bit of information I was able to learn about the Nashville bomber was that he had apparently spent a great deal of time out in Montgomery Bell State Park, hunting lizard people. It seemed entirely unlike any other version of the lizard people narrative I'd heard, but I wanted to see for myself, so Karl and I drove out to the park. It was a lovely midsummer day, a light drizzle falling intermittently, leaving the leaves and grass glistening and gauzy.

At some point, though, the thought occurred to me: *What on Earth are we doing out here?* Karl and I were not going to see any lizard people. There were no lizard people to be found. For that matter, lizard people were supposed to be highly intelligent extraterrestrial overlords; if they existed, they'd be in a ship floating in space or in some glossy board-room in Manhattan, discussing strategy with Bill Gates and the Clintons. They weren't a random bunch of cryptids like Bigfoot or the Chupaca-bra, roaming the forest waiting to be caught by hikers. Slowly, the ab-surdity of the trip sank in.

Not knowing what else to do, we walked into the ranger station. The rangers at the front desk were initially friendly; one woman got up from her desk and came to the front counter, where she handed us a map and discussed pleasantries. After a few minutes just passing time, I asked about Warner and his lizard people hunting out here, at which point her eyes narrowed. "Do you know anything about that guy?" I asked. She watched me closely, trying, I suppose, to divine my motives for such a question. After a few seconds, she turned to her coworker, seated at her desk twenty feet away.

"Hey, Mary, do you know anything about any *supposed* lizard people and that guy who *supposedly* blew himself up on Second Avenue?"

No, Mary said after a pause, no, she did not.

TWENTY-THREE

The Banality of Evil

C ypress Williams doesn't remember seeing any human sacrifice. When she was eighteen years old, she worked as a server at the Bohemian Grove in Monte Rio, California, about two hours north of San Francisco on the Russian River. Every summer, dozens of powerful men flock here for a retreat under the towering redwoods—an exclusive resort whose elaborate secrecy has earned it a bizarre reputation for nefarious goings-on.

Williams, a native of the nearby town of Cazadero, worked a summer as a server in the resort's restaurant, spending her time catering to wealthy men, and described to me exactly the kind of experience you might expect a young woman would undergo in such a climate. "I basically remember it was a mix of some people being nice," she told me, "and then some people being total dicks, or even purposefully being dicks just to be entertained by torturing these poor staff—these kids, these young kids, who were busting their asses. . . . I guess I would put it with any other job where you're serving people who are more privileged than you."

Founded in 1872, it started as a social club for San Francisco journalists and artists; within a decade, they'd established an outpost on the Russian River an hour north of the city, and in the 1890s, they bought 160 acres of land in a place called Camp Meeker, gradually building a permanent escape amidst the towering redwoods. Once consisting of writers and artists—the kinds of people the term "bohemian" might call to mind—members now consist primarily of incredibly wealthy, mostly white, men. Membership is exclusive and members are held to a strict code of secrecy, but that hasn't stopped journalists and provocateurs from regularly sneaking in: *Mother Jones*, *Time*, and *People* are among the various magazines that have managed to slip reporters in undercover to report on its secret goings-on. Getting a glimpse of this hidden world kept from outsiders, most have come to the same conclusion: it is a social club where rich men come out, put on childish skits, get drunk, and pee on trees. It is, basically, not much more than a summer camp for the 1 percent.

One person who refused to believe this story is Alex Jones, the longtime conspiracy theorist who runs the website and radio channel InfoWars. In 2000, Jones and his cameraman Mike Hanson got in with the help of journalist Jon Ronson and managed to videotape the Grove's marquee ceremony: the Cremation of Care. Before a giant statue of an owl, members are invited to give up their earthly cares and worries to be ritually banished at the beginning of the week. In the subsequent video he produced of the infiltration, *Dark Secrets: Inside Bohemian Grove*, Jones described the Cremation of Care ceremony as involving a procession by a carriage accompanied by men in black and brown robes "burying a bound body." According to Jones, this act was accompanied by "lots of smacking of lips and bizarre enjoyment by the crowd." His narration concludes, "We still haven't made out exactly what was going on, but a real sacrifice may have been developing, according to some occult experts." At the conclusion of the footage, Jones intones: "There you see the funeral pyre burning with the effigy of a human . . . or it could be real, ladies and gentlemen. There's been a lot of strange goings-on in that area of Northern California. This is what the establishment is into, right here in America. These people are deadly serious."

Ronson, who accompanied Jones, saw no such thing, nor has anyone else who's ever infiltrated the Grove. Another interloper in this land of men told me much the same thing. Melanie Gallagher served on the board of the local nonprofit LandPaths, an organization devoted to preserving wilderness in the region, and some time after they acquired land adjacent to the Grove, the club held a luncheon where they invited the neighbors, in order to, as Gallagher put it, "open the kimono a bit." Gallagher recalled a pleasant lunch in a beautiful setting: the Grove's buildings are old and rustic, but the silverware and the food were nice ("They can get pretty fancy in the woods when they want to," she said). Gallagher didn't see any evidence of ritual human sacrifice, either; as a local resident for years, she told me that most of the rumors she hears about the Grove is that locals think "there's a bunch of gay stuff going on," or that they're bringing in sex workers.

Among those who subscribed to Jones's darker theories was a man named Richard McCaslin. McCaslin had grown up obsessed with Marvel Comics, and as an adult had become heavily invested in the world of Real Life Superheroes (or RLSHs)—men and women who dress up in costume (either established Marvel and DC heroes or characters of their own creation) and patrol the streets, looking to prevent crime. McCaslin adopted a number of different personas before he settled on a character he named the Phantom Patriot: a red-white-and-blue themed costume paired with a skull mask. The mission of this new superhero: to fight the New World Order; among his targets was the Bohemian Grove itself.

In January 2002, McCaslin drove four and a half hours from Carson City, Nevada, to the Bohemian Grove. In the darkness, he snuck onto the grounds of the Bohemian Grove, dressed as the Phantom Patriot. His plan? To stop children from being murdered and destroy the Grove's Satanic mascot: the Great Owl. His mission was ill-fated from the start:

His flashlight ran out of batteries and he'd neglected to bring extras, so he spent the night in the dark waiting for sunrise. At daybreak, he found, finally, the Great Owl he'd hoped to set on fire. But the statue was made out of concrete, not wood. Forced to abandon his plan to burn the Owl, he broke into a banquet hall and attempted to set it on fire instead. No sooner had the fire caught then the sprinklers came on and an alarm went off, alerting security. By the time McCaslin got back out on to the main road, a bevy of police cruisers had arrived; after a tense armed standoff, he surrendered.

Released from prison, McCaslin eventually fell further down the conspiracy theory rabbit hole, finding new inspiration in the work of David Icke and connecting with online conspiracy groups pushing darker and darker visions of the United States. In 2011, he set out on a tour of the nation to protest the reptilian elite he believed to be behind the world's ills. He created a new superhero persona for himself—Thoughtcrime—and started his tour in May at the Bohemian Grove's San Francisco offices. Moving east, he made it to New Haven, Connecticut, in early August, where he planned to protest Yale's most famous secret society, Skull and Bones.

Skull and Bones is an elite fraternity for Yale University seniors, the most famous of several such societies, and the one that swirls with the most conspiracy theories. In James Pollock's 2017 book, *Notorious Secret Societies: The Illuminati, Bilderberg Group, Freemasons, Scientology, Skull and Bones, Knights Templar and More*, Skull and Bones members are described as having "already infiltrated just about every major financial policy, media government, and research institution in the United States in its desire to establish—wait for it—a New World Order (again) where individual freedoms are curtailed and the power to rule lies in the hands of the few, ruling elite. Many believe that the group has actually been running the United States for many years now." Pollock further expands on the hidden rituals that go on behind closed doors, fretting about the "Nazi-related items like skulls, coffins, innards, and skeletons" the

Bonesmen employ, while also noting that "newly initiated members are introduced to the tomb's one and only full-time occupant, who is unfortunately called the Bones' Whore, whose responsibilities include ensuring that the new members are more mature as they leave the place."

It's true that some members of Skull and Bones were also Freemasons, or worked with Masons, as Pollock alleges (though his claim that Franklin Delano Roosevelt was a member of the Illuminati is a bit more suspect), and it is also true that the society, as its name implies, relies on skeletal symbolism. But how sinister such motifs are is up for debate. An art conservator who spent years restoring the building's collection of paintings described the atmosphere inside as "spooky, but funny spooky . . . It's sort of like the Addams Family; it is campy in an old British men's smoking club way. The place is musty and old. It's not glamorous by any means. It's just like a funky old house with dark, narrow passageways and little tiny stairwells everywhere."

Few locations in the United States have as many strange stories attached to them these days as the Bohemian Grove and Skull and Bones. And they are stories that even the storytellers understand, on some level, to be nonsense. When Jon Ronson later confronted Jones about his sacrifice narrative, Jones told him, "Oh, Jon, you know that, I know that, but I'm not gonna tell my listeners that."

But why do these places need conspiracy theories attached to them? They are already networks for old boys, rich boys, nepotism and the connected one percent, and what is already visible is more than enough to account for the outsized power and influence these predominantly white men have. What does anyone gain from attaching bizarre, false stories to them?

A s Alexandra Robbins notes in her history of Skull and Bones, the secret societies of Yale are really just part of a larger, long-standing tradition in which undergraduates are assigned a social rank within the hierarchy that is rigidly enforced on multiple levels. In its earliest years, Yale assigned class rank not based on academic achievement but on one's class and family connections. Skull and Bones, the first of Yale's secret societies to be born, was founded in 1832 as this system began to collapse. As class ranking became more mutable, based on academic prowess instead of family connection, and hazing fell from favor, the secret societies (which would come to include the Scroll and Key Society, Wolf's Head, and others) became a substitute way to ensure that there was still an elite at Yale.

At least some of this fascination with Skull and Bones, then, is similar to our fascination with the Freemasons and their reach—all of which can be traced back to this lingering need to create a social caste on which the republic was founded. We are still trying to reconcile this contradiction, that America is a classless society with a strongly entrenched upper class that goes beyond merely money. The belief that there is no aristocracy in America—or that there *should* be no aristocracy in America—in turn helps drive the belief that there is something sinister or manipulated in places like Yale, whose purpose has always been to reproduce and replicate class in America. Secret societies such as Skull and Bones are themselves formed from anxiety—the product of a frightened and insecure class of people who know that their claim to prestige is tenuous. Faced with social mobility and egalitarianism, America's elites have always looked for ways to push back against the possibility of a meritocracy, and in New Haven this took the form of obscure and elaborate rituals, gothic decorations, and secret clubs.

Which is to say, the elite, insecure about their own status, dream up rituals concocted at their remote retreats in order to assure themselves that they're different from us. Meanwhile, conspiracists respond with panic and paranoid musings: *they're different from us.* From there, they attach increasingly outlandish claims, most often involving ritual child abuse and sacrifice—in the twenty-first century, accusations of Satanic murder have shifted from suburban homes and day cares to the hidden retreats of the most powerful. On the conspiracy site *WND*, writer Selena Owens explained that the 2014 Ice Bucket Challenge (in which celebrities and others posted videos in which they dunked themselves with ice water in order to raise awareness and money for ALS research) was actually a Satanic ritual. According to Owens and others, "ALS" refers not to "amyotrophic lateral sclerosis" but to "Antichrist Lucifer Satan." Among the most frequently targeted was ice-bucketer Oprah Winfrey, who was forced at the beginning of the Covid-19 pandemic to respond to wild rumors that she was under house arrest for Satanic sex trafficking. "Just got a phone call that my name is trending," she tweeted. "And being trolled for some awful FAKE thing. It's NOT TRUE. Haven't been raided, or arrested. Just sanitizing and self-distancing with the rest of the world. Stay safe everybody." (That Winfrey has now become a target of those obsessed with Satanic ritual abuse is itself a bit awkward, given that she helped spread the original myth through her talk show in the 1980s.)

The most common target of such accusations remains Hillary Clinton, who supposedly participated in a ritual with her former aide Huma Abedin, wearing masks made from the skin of a young child they had murdered while they drank the victim's fresh adrenochrome (a naturally occurring and easily synthesized hormone that features prominently in many of these conspiracies). Rumors that a video of this fictitious event (nicknamed Frazzledrip) existed became so widespread on social media, pushed out relentlessly by conspiracists, that Google CEO Sundar Pichai was asked about it during a House Judiciary hearing in 2018; what, Democratic representative Jamie Raskin demanded, was Google and its subsidiary YouTube doing about the ubiquitous spread of such obviously nonsensical conspiracy theories that were increasingly clogging up social media channels?

The misreading of the Ice Bucket Challenge as Satanic ritual, and the imagined Frazzledrip video, suggest the degree to which conspiracists continue to rely on a fear of ritual to drive paranoia, and why places like the Skull and Bones Tomb and the Bohemian Grove make such prime targets. Certainly, such places have embraced various kinds of rituals through the years. It also continues to obscure reliable public knowledge about actual child abuse and sex trafficking.

These rumors have continued to lead to acts of terrible violence. On December 4, 2016, a man named Edgar Maddison Welch drove from his home in Salisbury, North Carolina, to a pizza restaurant called Comet Ping Pong in the DC suburbs with three guns. For months, numerous online websites and posters on various social media sites had been spreading a disturbing rumor that the pizzeria was a front for a ring of child predators, and that terrible things were happening in the restaurant's basement. Welch was convinced "something nefarious was happening" at the pizzeria; he would later tell the *New York Times* that he felt his "heart breaking over the thought of innocent people suffering."

When he arrived at Comet, heavily armed, he fired a single shot, sending patrons and employees fleeing from the restaurant, and then thankfully surrendered quickly. He was arrested, and ultimately sentenced to four years in prison, with an additional fine of several thousand dollars in restitution to the pizzeria. "I just wanted to do some good and went about it the wrong way," he said, admitting that the "intel on this wasn't 100 percent."

If it's tempting to see this incident as that of a lone, deranged individual, it's worth noting that six months after Welch's attack, 45 percent of registered Republicans were willing to agree to the statement that "leaked email from some of Hillary Clinton's campaign staffers contained code words for pedophilia, human trafficking and satanic ritual abuse." Four years later, 15 percent of Americans still agreed with the statement that "the government, media, and financial worlds in the U.S. are controlled by a group of Satan-worshipping pedophiles who run a global child sex trafficking operation." Among those whose primary source of news were the far-right outlets One America News Network and Newsmax, that figure was 40 percent.

Child sexual abuse remains a horrifying, all-too-prevalent problem, both in the United States and worldwide. But it's precisely that deep-seated anxiety about children's well-being that is so easily manipulated. It is impossible to read some of these posts, buried deep in social media, and not feel that the poster is genuinely anguished. And certainly, child sexual abuse is one of those stories where we have ample evidence of actual conspiracies. Most notably in the Catholic Church, when the Boston Archdiocese was exposed as not just harboring sexual predators but shifting them between parishes and jurisdictions to avoid scrutiny, and with Jeffrey Epstein, who had been charged with numerous counts of sex trafficking before his death in a Manhattan holding cell.

With the case of Pizzagate, of course, the accusations were utterly baseless: there were no actual victims who have come forward to claim they were abused at the pizzeria, and the online accusers got basic facts about the establishment wrong—Comet Ping Pong does not have a basement. But the accusations went far beyond abuse into regions more bizarre: this was a den not of artisan pizza and craft brews but of ritual abuse, murder, and cannibalism. Four days before the 2016 election, InfoWars was accusing Hillary Clinton, John Podesta, and other figures in the Democratic establishment of participating in an "occult ritual founded by Satanist Aleister Crowley" known as Spirit Cooking.

The term "Spirit Cooking" comes not from Crowley, but from performance artist Marina Abramović, whose work has quickly become intertwined with these odd conspiracy theories. Podesta's brother Tony, a longtime art collector and patron of Abramović's work, had paid $10,000 during a Kickstarter fundraiser for one of Abramović's projects, which included the reward for a "Spirit Cooking" dinner. The "Spirit Cooking" part was a reference to one of Abramović's works in the 1990s, in which she had used pig's blood to scrawl odd, fantastical recipes on walls, which included descriptions such as "with a sharp knife cut deeply into the middle finger of your left hand eat the pain." Alt-right personality Cassandra Fairbanks reported how Abramović appears in videos "painting the recipe for these 'spirit dinners,' using what appears to be thickly congealed blood. The recipe read, at one point, 'mix fresh breast milk with fresh sperm, drink on earthquake nights.'"

This perhaps seems a bit bizarre to the casual observer, but Abramović's work was part of a long tradition of contemporary and avant-garde art that had been using blood and other bodily fluids to make bold and controversial works that pushed against middle-class sensibilities—including work by feminist artists like Carolee Schneemann and Karen Finley, and Catholic artist Andres Serrano, whose *Piss Christ* led to a sensational controversy when the National Endowment for the Arts was targeted by Republican senators aghast at what they perceived as sacrilege. Hermann Nitsch, a member of the Viennese Actionism school that gained notoriety in the 1960s, is well known for his performance pieces that involve extremely bloody and gory rituals (many have been protested). Nitsch uses animal carcasses and blood (more recently, acrylic paint that mimics blood) to stage rituals in which performers undergo purification and catharsis, in scenes that are both meant as criticisms of mainline religion while also being authentic attempts at sui generis religious experiences.

Within the art world, then, Abramović's *Spirit Cooking* series was not only a small part of a longer tradition, but outside the art world, it immediately gained traction as something sinister and depraved. Such misreadings, then, may be nothing other than a function of "context collapse," a term danah boyd coined to describe the way that certain information—fully legible and understandable in one context—becomes strange, alien, or unsettling when viewed by different audiences who lack that context. As boyd and others have argued, social media, which flattens out the possibility of distinct audiences with shared assumptions and backgrounds, tends to heighten this effect. And certainly the ability of the Internet to fuel context collapse and render things like Abramović's work into uncanny pronouncements of ritual sacrifice is a prime driver of how we experience conspiracy theories in the twenty-first century.

The creation of a shadow elite outstrips the need to understand the actual elite before us. After all, powerful politicians and billionaires are working to shape world events in *plain sight.* They do it every day. Usually, the means to power of the wealthy is both transparent and banal. For the Bush family it was oil, and George Soros's life is that of an unremarkable, almost clichéd immigrant's story. And yet, the conspiracist's job is to mystify these plainly obvious workings of American capitalism into something mysterious and byzantine.

Add to this the myriad of conspiracy theories that tend to collect around large corporations. Once again, the root distrust here has its basis in fact: American tobacco companies, to cite only the most obvious example, *did* conspire to hide nicotine's dangerous side effects from the American public. This, then, has fed any number of conspiracy theories about large-scale hidden malfeasance. Some conspiracy theories attached to corporations have some basis in fact (a 2019 study of a pesticide found in the product Roundup, made by Monsanto—a regular target of conspiracy theories—demonstrated it to be carcinogenic); some of it is outlandish (the theory that circulated in 2016 that food-borne illness outbreaks at Chipotle restaurants were deliberate bioterror attacks in retaliation for the chain's removal of genetically modified foods from its ingredients), and some of it veers into the mystical (the belief that certain brands of fried chicken somehow have a sterilizing agent that renders Black men impotent).

It ought to be easy enough to see such people and corporations as ordinary: powerful, corrupt maybe, benefiting from nepotism and other inequalities, but overall an expression of the way the world works, and the fact that in this country the playing field is unequal. The conspiracist, however, rejects this idea. It is not the case that the playing field is unequal because that's the normal working of capitalism. It's unequal because of an alien, malevolent force who's infected and deranged the normal working order of things. The solution, then, becomes not a question of passing legislation or regulations to make the laws more equitable. The solution is instead to root out the virus and destroy it; once the conspirators have been defeated, the system will simply right itself.

In the process, the attempt to turn the ultra-rich and powerful into actual child-sacrificing Satanists becomes a means of preserving attitudes toward capitalism itself. Rather than accept that men like George W. Bush and Mark Zuckerberg are rather predictable examples of the ultra-rich's hoarding of resources, they are treated as exceptional, aberrant, and abnormal. And it explains why many conspiracists can be filled with spite and vitriol toward some elites (Soros, Gates, Clinton, etc.) while simultaneously championing other, equally powerful elites (Trump).

The morass of global politics is difficult to understand and unpredictable even to experts, but conspiracy theories offer a straightforward explanation that cuts through all that. They suture all available facts together and do the work of organizing the chaos of history into an explainable, overarching theory. They reduce the messy reality of the Bush Era, of competing motives, of surprises and unexpected consequences, and subsume everything under the perfectly executed plans of malicious actors. They replace uncertainty and coincidence with motive and agency.

It is fairly undeniable by now that the US invasion of Iraq in 2003 was driven by a conspiracy: a group of powerful individuals made a decision to invade Iraq and then set about concocting reasons—almost entirely based on flimsy or nonexistent evidence—to justify it. By misrepresenting facts and fabricating excuses, the Bush administration and its allies were able to manipulate public opinion to build support for a military project whose actual aims (the financial exploitation of the country's oil reserves) was markedly different from its stated aims (the search for weapons of mass destruction).

But the Iraq War also demonstrates the wide gulf between actual conspiracies and the world envisioned by conspiracy *theories*. Because the conspiracy theorist not only presumes a hidden hand behind world events but also presumes that this hidden hand is all knowing and all powerful, and that anything that happens is part of this secret, grand design. The Iraq War, on the other hand, is a stunning example of how even the most powerful cabals cannot foresee and account for all unintended consequences of their actions. The neo-Conservatives in the Bush administration wanted a quick military operation followed by the instillation of a government friendly to US business interests; what they got instead was a long, costly, unpopular, and ultimately unwinnable war. (This is not to say, however, that there weren't plenty of people, including those connected to the architects of the Iraq War, who didn't benefit financially from the debacle.) Conspiracy theories, then, are ultimately not about conspiracies; they are about our fear of chaos. Their focus often overlaps with actual conspiracies, but their function is not about understanding the mechanisms of actual conspiracies, but instead working as explanatory narratives for the unpredictable nature of modern life.

Meanwhile, Richard McCaslin's journey finally ended in 2018, in front of the Scottish Rite Masonic Temple in Washington, D.C., where he fatally shot himself in his pickup truck. He was only four miles from Comet Ping Pong.

TWENTY-FOUR

Nothing Is True, Everything Is Permitted

In August 2021, I met a longtime friend in Oakland, California, to talk about QAnon. Sitting in his backyard just after sunset, his dog, Amber, on the bench beside me, resting her head in my lap, I listened to my friend Eric tell me the story of how his ex-wife, Miranda, fell down the rabbit hole.

In spring of 2020, she sent him a video one morning via text, with the comment: "There's a lot in here that really made me think, and I think you should watch it too." It was, Eric told me, "one of those Auto-voice generated, long, rambling, everything-is-connected conspiracy videos." I knew exactly what he meant by this; I've watched a countless number of these videos, all of which follow a similar production pattern: a voice-over set to a cascade of stock or manipulated images, like a half-assed PowerPoint. Their effect can be, depending on your perspective, either riveting or soporific.

For Eric it was the latter; he knew right away something was off. As he remembered it, the video opened with a few tidbits that were actually true, a few legitimate quotes from scientists, but in a matter of moments it had connected the superficially true to accusations that Hillary Clinton was a member of the Deep State, involved in the harvesting of adrenochrome from murdered children.

He responded by poking fun at it before realizing Miranda was serious. "Some of this is ridiculous," she agreed, "but I think there's some truth here." But he simply couldn't buy it. "When it comes to a conspiracy theory this big, the sheer amount of people—you're talking underground bases and wars with mole people—if things of this scale are happening, the amount of people involved is staggering," he reasoned to me. "And for all these people to unanimously agree to keep it a secret—even when they're on opposing sides—there's just no logic to that."

Convincing the mother of his child of this, though, proved increasingly impossible. And his primary concern was not in winning an argument, but in protecting their son; the two of them had worked hard to co-parent since their divorce, supporting each other and sharing decision-making. Now fourteen, Eric's son had never seen or heard them disagree publicly. So Eric was obliged to bury much of his outward disgust. Meanwhile, every month Miranda went a little bit deeper, sending him more and more links, pushing the boundaries of what she thought she could get away with, trying to convince him of a Deep State conspiracy theory against Donald Trump.

When they had been together, Miranda had been a classic liberal, voting for Obama in 2008 and 2012. Nor had she ever, in Eric's memory, espoused any kind of overt racist or homophobic attitudes. Now, though, she was aligning herself increasingly with the cult of Donald Trump, one typically defined by a grievance politics that sees white and straight people increasingly under attack from marginalized communities. Never much of a fan of sports, she had become suddenly concerned about trans women competing in sports, which mystified and depressed Eric, who found her concern inauthentic and disproportionate.

When I asked Eric why Miranda had swung hard to the right, given a lack of a lot of the bigotry that seems to define Trump's supporters, he told me that while she wasn't a stupid person, he described her as "someone who's always had trouble finding a place in life, in terms of career and goals, and what her wants are and what her drives are. And as a result, she's always been—as smart as she is—easily pulled into various groups and things." QAnon was only the latest strange community she'd grabbed hold of: "She's been in pyramid schemes, she's tried to be an independent merchandiser—I don't know how many different Etsy shops or reselling things she's tried to do. She did Herbalife, for example, and a lot of community-driven entrepreneurial things—always to try to find her voice, to try to find her people." The Deep State narrative, Eric felt, was attractive to her because it explained things to her "on some sort of abstract level as somebody who's just sort of struggled to find their place in the world."

As Miranda lost some of her friends, they were replaced by another community, one online that not only provided support and reassurance, but welcomed her as a soldier in a tremendous battle. "Take up this cause, because it's the right cause—here's all these people who know this is the right cause and will back you up and believe the same things that you do. And it's got the extra bonus of 'You're special,' on top of it, because most of the world doesn't even know that this is happening."

Miranda's story is far from unusual. She's one of thousands who got sucked into the morass known as Q, which began in the darkest corners of the Internet in 2017 and gradually mushroomed into a massive movement, taking in, blob-like, nearly every other conspiracy theory that had come before it, growing to a sprawling mass of paranoia and apocalyptic belief, the latest (and perhaps greatest) attempt to allege the existence of a massive secret cabal pulling the strings behind it all.

When QAnon seemed to explode from nowhere on to the scene in 2017, originating in the online cesspool 4chan before migrating to Reddit, YouTube, Facebook, and Twitter, critics and researchers were quick to lay the blame on social media. "Pizzagate, QAnon, and the Seth Rich assassination theory didn't spread solely because people believed—or at least promoted—those particular theories," Whitney Phillips and Ryan M. Milner write in their 2021 handbook to online disinformation, *You Are Here: A Field Guide for Navigating Polarized Speech, Conspiracy Theories, and Our Polluted Media Landscape.* "They spread because social media monetized, incentivized, and surfaced harmful content. They spread because journalists reported incessantly on far-right narratives during and after the 2016 election. They spread because audiences read and responded to what journalists published. They spread because these things, to so many others, influenced and were influenced by everything else."

This attitude—that on some level we are being manipulated by deceitful journalists, and our emotions are being tweaked by social media algorithms, creating a landscape where conspiracy theories are allowed to flourish as they never have before—is a common one. But it creates a picture where conspiracy believers are themselves oddly passive: they are blank slates, onto which Fox and Facebook project harmful content, and, like children, they are powerless to resist. In the same way that Christian moralists argued that listening to heavy metal would lead impressionable teenagers to become Satanists, we have come to believe that social media companies like Facebook are so powerful that merely logging on can transform someone from a rational, thinking human being into a conspiracy obsessed paranoiac.

This argument has the benefit of offering a reassuring narrative to those of us not in journalism or on the board of Facebook: *it's not my fault I was exposed to this disinformation, I'm a passive consumer.* Focusing on algorithms, on social media giants, and on journalists all has the soothing effect of encouraging us to see ourselves as powerless, passive receivers of information, rather than people who actively are shaping our reality.

As Twitter's cofounder Evan Williams put it in 2017, there is a problem with the Internet, in that it rewards extremes. "Say you're driving down the road and see a car crash. Of course you look. Everyone looks. The Internet interprets behavior like this to mean everyone is asking for car crashes, so it tries to supply them." Which is to say, of course the Internet enables our worst behavior. But the behavior is ours to begin with. We believe things not just because Facebook feeds them to us; we believe them because we want to.

This emphasis on social media and the Internet also opens up space for the belief that a movement like QAnon is somehow *new*, something that has appeared from nowhere, a spontaneous upswelling of paranoia and ignorance. As should also be evident by now, conspiracy theories have been a hallmark of American democracy from its inception. Conspiracy theories—particularly those surrounding politics, which inevitably includes fears of secret groups—have been used time and time again to ameliorate unreconcilable contradictions that spur cognitive dissonance. A vital fact about QAnon necessary to understanding its allure is that it is neither sui generis—it is not some unique and abnormal thing unlike anything in America's history—nor is it ex nihilo—it didn't spring from nothing. Conspiracy belief has repeatedly caused riots and murders, ruined lives and careers, and reshaped America time and time again since its inception—as horrible as the past few years have been, they are part of a repeating pattern.

By asking what is new this time, we must be careful not to ignore our own history. But by the same token, paying attention to the past doesn't mean downplaying or minimizing the threats we face now.

QAnon, after all, is not simply a retread of earlier moral panics. Among its stranger features is its origin story: a well-placed government intelligence official, aware of a secret plan that, this insider felt, had to be made public. That insider chose not to go to the *New York Times* or the *Washington Post* or WikiLeaks (or, for that matter, any number of right-wing publications that would have been friendlier to Donald Trump)—but instead came to 4chan, a message board notorious for hardcore pornography and racism. On October 28, 2017, an anonymous user going by the name of "Q Clearance Patriot" posted a thread on 4chan, quoting Donald Trump's cryptic references to a gathering of military leaders as the "calm before the storm." Through a series of posts that appeared at random intervals, Q prophesized the imminent arrest of dozens of enemies of the Trump administration, including Hillary Clinton. Users began to form communities to decode and analyze these posts; the conversation soon moved to YouTube and Reddit, allowing for a far wider spread.

Why did the savior of the Republic choose to offer revelations in the Internet's most vile of cesspools? It's a question that's ultimately only interesting if you believe that there's any ring of truth to the story. Accepting that the entire thing is a fiction allows you to reframe the question: Why was the need to believe this narrative so strong among QAnon adherents that they were willing to buy a story with such a laughably improbable origin?

QAnon did offer one seemingly new aspect: an interactive component. As Mike Rothschild explains in his book *The Storm Is Upon Us: How QAnon Became a Movement, Cult, and Conspiracy Theory of Everything*, "Q talks directly to the people, and the people talk back to Q. It's not monologing, it's dialogue. Q encourages collaboration, and rewards anons who go above and beyond in their theorizing and interpretation." QAnon mirrored the structure of true crime Reddit forums and other online communities, where amateur sleuths could build their own epistemic capital by connecting the dots and sharing their findings with others.

At the same time that QAnon mimicked the structure of a game where anyone could participate, it also encouraged, in a real sense, doing nothing. Repeatedly, Q urged their followers to "trust the plan," a constant catchphrase that recurs through "Q drops" and acts to encourage passivity and inaction. The narrative unfolding on 4- and 8Chan was entertainment, a spectator sport, where, as Rothschild notes, it was "remarkably easy to do nothing while believing you're doing a lot."

This exhortation to "trust the plan" carries with it echoes of another long-standing American tradition: prophecy behavior. "Watching, waiting, and working for the millennium," Leonard Sweet wrote in 1979, "has become, even more than baseball, America's favorite pastime," and QAnon, which urged believers to sit around and wait for the Deliverance of Donald Trump and the Smiting of His Enemies, is only the latest millennium narrative.

But if this makes it sound remotely benign, it's not. Q regularly made space for the usual anti-Semitic canards, often employing dog whistles about "bankers" or the Jewish liberal George Soros. While anti-Semitism isn't necessarily integral to the QAnon ethos, there's a great deal of overlap: a Morning Consult survey from April 2021 found that 49 percent of Americans who believe in QAnon's central premise that "the world is run by Satan-worshipping pedophiles, including left-wing politicians, Hollywood celebrities and religious figures," also believe *The Protocols of the Elders of Zion* is true and accurately describes how a secret cabal of Jews is using liberalism to gain control of the world. (Eric's ex-wife Miranda told him she wasn't anti-Semitic, but then went on to say that those who hold such views "got them for a reason," a kind of meaningless hair splitting that Eric found repugnant.)

Q drops have also indulged adherents' fantasies of hostility toward immigrants, non-white Americans, and those on the political left. None of this is acceptable; QAnon believers have regularly engaged in horrific acts of violence. In June 2018, Matthew Wright occupied the Hoover Dam, upset that Trump was not carrying out the mass arrests that Q had promised. A QAnon supporter smashed up the Chapel of the Holy Cross, a Catholic sanctuary in Sedona, Arizona, claiming to be on a mission to stop human trafficking. In January 2019, a QAnon supporter in Seattle, Buckey Wolfe, murdered his brother with a sword, telling authorities that he thought his brother was a lizard. Perhaps the strangest act of violence was the murder of Francesco Cali in Staten Island on March 13, 2019. While Cali was a member of the Gambino crime family, his assassination had nothing at all to do with organized crime or a mafia vendetta; he was murdered by QAnon adherent Anthony Comello, who believed he would be immune from prosecution due to intervention from Trump himself. Finally, of course, was the Capitol insurrection on January 6, 2021, when a mob of Trump supporters, many of whom were QAnon believers, stormed the United States Capitol in an attempt to violently change the results of the 2020 election, an event that would leave five dead.

And then there are the grifters. The long-running Iraqi dinar scam, for example, which involves selling the nearly worthless currency to underinformed investors, promising untold riches in short order, was given a boost by QAnon. After a press conference in which Trump nebulously stated that all currencies would soon "be on a level playing field," dinar scammers flocked to QAnon pages, encouraging would-be dupes to buy, buy, buy many sunk thousands of dollars into the useless currency, allowing scammers to pocket hefty brokers' fees. Meanwhile, YouTube personalities have built rabid followings they can regularly fleece for donations and subscriber fees as they continue to spew out nonsense and drivel.

QAnon, then, emerges as some sort of bastard child between a MMORPG (Massively Multiplayer Online Role-Playing Game), an End Times prophecy, a violent white nationalist terrorist organization, and a multilevel marketing scheme. This hodgepodge of impulses and impetuses makes it difficult at times to say exactly *what* QAnon is—but then, this is the point.

QAnon has succeeded not by being clearly defined and laser-focused on an articulated set of goals, but by being broad, diffuse, and vague. It welcomes in new recruits by simultaneously offering a menu of beliefs—some extreme and violent, some deceptively anodyne—without requiring anyone to subscribe to one specific credo. It encourages you to laugh at the parts you find ridiculous even as you embrace others. Like the "Mystic Red," QAnon is mostly a name that gives a shape to all these disparate grifts and scams, gathering them all under one banner that adds a level of mythology and makes them strangely transcendent. Like the Know Nothings or the second Klan, its spread is dependent on its vagueness and its malleability, so it can be many things to as many people, continually gathering strength at the expense of focus. This has allowed the movement to spread and to make it seem farther reaching and more ubiquitous than it might otherwise be. At the same time, this structure also allows the more hardcore, conspiratorial, racist, and violent elements a cover of plausibility by the proportion of Q believers looking for confirmation and reassurance rather than a race war.

The only requirement is a belief in one of the main buzzwords, the syntactically awkward rallying cry. "Where We Go One, We Go All," QAnoners all proclaim, knowing fully well that, having said that, they are free to go off in whatever directions they want. Like all secret societies, its strength is in its contradictions. It is at once the sideshow—a parade of clowns and attention-seeking grifters, a spectacle and joke—and also the main event.

After the January 6 insurrection, Los Angeles–based artist Lisa Anne Auerbach began researching QAnon on the social media app Telegraph. Up until that point, she told me, she'd been mostly relying on mainstream media reports that depicted believers as "crazy people," but in Telegraph, she found a "safe space" for people to discuss their true reasonings. "The first-person narratives," she said, "really struck me—I hadn't seen anything like that before." In a zine she subsequently assembled, *The Great Awakening*, she gathered together the origin stories of hundreds of "red-pilled" users of Telegraph. "I wanted to do this because the people in my world have no idea how deep this is going and how serious this is. We don't see the other side at all, except as a carica-ture." Together, the stories represent a wide variety of conspiracy beliefs, all of which have somehow been woven into the same paranoid tapestry.

"Woke up in spring of 2020- found out about the satanic cabal and their pedophilia," Christy Miller wrote of her journey, "had a medical and emotional crisis for a few months while I went farther down the rab-bit hole and then came out an even bigger supporter of Trump than I already was. I will never give up on him- never loved a president before, but sure do now! I thank God for him every day." Another described her "gut feelings in early 2000s with big farm and the commercials and side effects," which led to her "swallowing the red pill" in 2010 with docu-mentaries like *Food, Inc.*, Robert Kenner's 2008 film on the problems with factory farming. "[T]hen the minute this sham virus was brought out—I instantly knew it had to do with the election." A nail salon worker described a conversation with a client, whose LA-based daughter was warned "never to go to any Hollywood parties with elites," due to ram-pant "baby eating." Adrenochrome comes up a lot in these posts.

Kevin was not sure "about the lizard people yet," but suggested he was open to the idea. "Keeping an open mind after all I have had to be-lieve so far with the pedafilia [*sic*] and spirit cooking." For LaDonna, "It was the run on toilet paper—was researching how the media could pos-sibly be using subliminal messaging to cause the unreasonable panic." Janet started with Q in 2017 but only recently had begun researching "the deception of the Catholic Church elites" along with various anti-Semitic conspiracies. (The anti-Semitism, Auerbach remarked, "is so thoroughly part of the movement that it's not even remarked upon." Often, she added, it was so internalized within the movement that it didn't even need to be explicitly referenced: code words about bankers or drinking children's blood was more than enough.) Travis, meanwhile, posted simply that "Conspiracy theorist is a term made up by the CIA to discredit those who want to seek truth."

Repeatedly, people identified a film by Janet Ossebaard, *The Fall of the Cabal*, as their entry point to Q and related conspiracy beliefs. Released in ten parts and totaling over three hours, *The Fall of the Cabal* is done in the same style as the video Miranda first sent to Eric: a cascade of images of war, urban slums, shock medical images, and so on, with a voice-over narration asking rhetorical questions, stoking paranoia with lies and non sequiturs, and attempting to drive the viewer toward an inescapable conclusion.

In the first episode of the series, Ossebaard lists off a number of things that made her go "hmmmmm": these include 9/11 conspiracies, misinformation surrounding abortion ("Did you know it's legal to abort a full-term baby?"), images from Disney cartoons supposedly featuring subliminal advertising, crisis actors (the erroneous belief that mass shootings and terrorist events are staged and that the same actors have played victims in the media), xenophobic musings about migrant caravans from Central and South American (which Ossebaard claims were "timed" to arrive in the United States just in time for the 2018 midterms), random questions about recent California forest fires, false information about the quantity of mercury in vaccines, chemtrail conspiracy theories, misinformation about organ donation, anti-Catholic conspiracies about the pope, supposed reptilian symbolism in the Vatican's art collection, Hollywood celebrities using cosmetics derived from the foreskins of humans ("What's next, drinking baby blood?"), a false claim that diseases like HIV and Ebola are "patented," the ubiquity of spyware on your computer and phone, fears about Monsanto and genetically modified foods, suspicions about why Barack Obama was *really* awarded the Nobel Peace Prize, and Hillary Clinton's emails.

"What do all these things have in common?" Ossebaard asks. "They were completely ignored by the mainstream media." Some of them were not, of course (Hillary Clinton's emails were obsessively covered by the *New York Times*, the *Washington Post*, CNN, and dozens of other mainstream outlets), and many have not been covered because they are bunk. But the point in connecting these seemingly disparate threads into one overarching conspiracy (one that ultimately involves a war pitting Q and Donald Trump against the cabal of Illuminati) is to give as many points of access for the initiate. It's not necessary to believe all of these conspiracy theories; being interested in a single one is more than enough. The work of something like *The Fall of the Cabal* is to provide a big tent for paranoia, such that anyone can find something in the litany that connects. Some of this is even factually correct—there *is* spyware on a lot of our computers, though the question of "who" is watching you all the time is probably far more quotidian than Ossebaard wants you to admit (scammers installing spyware on your computer to skim your credit card info is probably not evidence of a massive conspiracy). And one can certainly critique—as Ossebaard does—the Swedish Academy's decision to award Barack Obama the Nobel Peace Prize, in light of the US's continued presence in Afghanistan and Iraq during his presidency.

The QAnon movement's success depends on its ability to synthesize these disparate conspiracies into a single monolithic narrative, one that takes the believer's individual concerns and yokes them to a larger apocalyptic story. Ossebaard tethers standard disinformation about abortion to conspiracy theories involving Satanic Hollywood elites drinking baby's blood, and reasonable concerns about spyware to paranoia surrounding the Illuminati and a New World Order.

Q, in other words, is ultimately a clearinghouse rather than a definitive conspiracy theory. Like Amazon, its corporate growth strategy is to forever expand into new markets—sopping up new theories and seemingly unrelated anxieties and folding them into its endlessly expanding distributed network of paranoia. And as with the Klan of the 1920s, QAnon works like a pyramid scheme: it can only survive so long as it's constantly growing. Because its narrative is apocalyptic, there must be a constant narrative propulsion—as long as there are some new developments, positive or negative, the cinematic story can unfold further, always leading to its dramatic climax.

Rather than feed this strategy, we may be better off trying instead to demystify this structure, to break apart the constituent elements of QAnon, to stop treating it as a massive, networked organization overtaking the country, and instead break it up into its constituent parts: the racists, the insurrectionists, the puzzle solvers, the End Times believers, the suckers duped into a multilevel marketing scam, the bored online gamers. Of course there's overlap in these categories, but treating QAnon as "one thing" inflates its power. The believers in the child sex abuse ring, for example, draw strength from being lumped together under the giant banner of Q alongside so many others. As do the racists, who are more than happy to count the less extreme Q believers in their numbers (even if some of those believers' views on race may be more moderate).

There's a strange allure, after all, in the idea of a foe as implacable as QAnon. It's easy to become obsessed with this new, strange movement, which seems to represent an inverted America, alienating us from our neighbors. After all, even those of us derisive of Q's supposed revelations are also, in our own way, seeking to know and to understand the thing beneath the surface. We want the hidden, the subterranean, the something that lurks beneath our everyday quotidian lives. It is our own fascination with such things that gives strength to a thing like QAnon, which depends on our lurid fascination to elevate it from a sporadic group of violent dead-enders into a national networked cabal filled with esoteric mystery.

In calling out conspiracists who cling to anti-Semitic narratives because an all-powerful network of Jewish-Illuminati-Catholic-Lizard People explains chaos and randomness, we have to be careful not make a similar move with QAnon itself, turning it into an explanatory mechanism for various cognitive dissonances we, too, are experiencing. To look at a mass of Americans who do not think like you do is terrifying and confusing, after all, and to realize that there is a wide variety and dynamism in them is exhausting. To lump them all together under the heading "Q" is helpful; it shapes them into a specific force you can react to. What secret societies like QAnon do is give shape to a chaotic world—both for their believers and for their detractors.

Q Anon fascinates so many—and manages to get a lot of mainstream press—in part because it's so strange. But the incident at Comet Ping Pong notwithstanding, it remains a far less dangerous peril than the older, pro-forma anti-immigrant conspiracy theories that continue to persist—currently grouped, by both proponents and detractors alike, under the heading "the Great Replacement." It is a theory that argues that white Americans are being phased out through low birth rates and lax immigration, replacing "real" Americans. It is a mainstay of the right-wing media ecosystem, and it has contributed to devastating consequences.

The attack on the Tree of Life Congregation synagogue in Pittsburgh on October 27, 2018, that killed eleven people was motivated, the shooter claimed in a manifesto posted to 4chan, by his belief that the Jewish community was bringing "invaders in that kill our people." The man who killed another twenty-three people at an El Paso Walmart on August 3, 2019, had likewise written of a so-called Hispanic invasion of Texas. And on May 14, 2022, another killer shot thirteen people (eleven of whom were Black) at a Tops supermarket in Buffalo, New York, killing ten. That individual would also claim that the United States belonged only to white people and that anyone else was a "replacer."

This racism is fed by numerous voices in the media, most notably Fox News's Tucker Carlson, who has repeatedly pushed the Great Replacement theory on his nightly prime-time show. "In order to win and maintain power," he told his audience on April 12, 2021, "Democrats plan to change the population of this country." Nor was this the only time; according to a *New York Times* review of over a thousand broadcasts, Carlson warned of some version of this narrative over 400 times.

Its proponents also include prominent political figures. New York

Republican Elise Stefanik ran a series of ads in the run up to the Buffalo shooting that openly and explicitly used Great Replacement rhetoric. "Radical Democrats are planning their most aggressive move yet: a PERMANENT ELECTION INSURRECTION," read one Facebook ad used by her campaign. "Their plan to grant amnesty to 11 MILLION illegal immigrants will overthrow our current electorate and create a permanent liberal majority in Washington." This rhetoric has worked; an April 2022 survey of registered Republicans found that two-thirds of them agreed with the statement that "liberal leaders [are] actively trying to leverage political power by replacing more conservative white voters."

There's little here to distinguish this newest crop of xenophobia from the Know Nothings, the American Protective Association, or the second Ku Klux Klan. If there is a difference, it's in how seamlessly the "ruling elites" trope of long-standing anti-Catholic and anti-Semitic rhetoric has been wedded to the Democratic Party itself. Previous nativist sentiments were, by and large, content to portray immigrants as a foreign, invading horde separate from American democracy itself—individual politicians here and there might have been complicit in this invasion, but by effectively using "Democrats" as a stand-in for the Jews, mainstream figures are able to push violently racist dog whistles while attempting to stay disconnected from the actions of their listeners.

This shift, subtle as it may be, also helps explain the 2020 election results. Usually, conspiracy theories are designed to depress political engagement. If you think the game is rigged, why participate? Conspiracy theories instead encourage either apathy (your vote won't count, so don't bother), or they encourage extralegal violence (take matters into your own hands). But in 2020, Donald Trump got more votes than anyone in history (74 million), except, of course for his opponent, Joe Biden (81 million). This massive electoral turnout by a demographic who is increasingly convinced that the game is rigged reflects the success of this innovation: by shifting the focus of the conspiracy onto the Democratic Party itself, the far right has finally figured out an effective way to use paranoia to drive electoral politics.

Meanwhile, in the wake of these horrific shootings, there is a constant clamor for gun control legislation—one that, among liberals, often coalesces around the National Rifle Association (NRA). Sirius XM host Dean Obeidallah lamented on Twitter shortly after the Buffalo shooting (and another that followed in Uvalde, Texas): "How is [it] that the NRA can advocate for policies that they know lead to deaths of Americans yet they are allowed to operate on US soil?! The NRA is responsible for more American deaths than ISIS." Due to overwhelming public support for gun control legislation, combined with the absolute lack of any kind actual legislative movement, there is a persistent belief that the problem is something external: a force outside of the political system that has corrupted it through money and connections, despoiling the natural political process through conspiracy.

But the NRA is not nearly as strong as it once was; a series of lawsuits, infighting, and corruption have largely hobbled its ability to effect policy. In the wake of the Uvalde shooting, a lobbyist for a rival gun rights organization, the National Association for Gun Rights, quipped "The NRA is not doing anything around the country anywhere; all their staff lawyered up and are fighting amongst each other." It is not toothless, but it is an oversimplification to say that the NRA alone is driving the resistance to gun control. The problem is the lopsided balance in the Senate and the power the Senate gives to rural senators, who represent a minority of Americans who are committed to complete and unfettered access to firearms no matter the cost of human lives. But the NRA stands in as a useful cabal, a specter of an all-powerful, shadowy organization that is hamstringing democracy; structurally, it is akin to the Slave Power conspiracy pushed by Lincoln's Republicans: an exaggeration of a real, structural problem, but one rhetorically used to convince people that democracy itself is being perverted. For if we can convince ourselves that the problem is an external organization conspiring to frustrate democracy, we can convince ourselves that the system itself isn't broken.

So we are, effectively, not too far off from where we were in the 1850s: the question is not whether or not wide swaths of Americans subscribe to a conspiracy theory about some secret group, but *which* conspiracy theory about a secret group. As with the election of 1860, it may be that political power will increasingly accrue to those who are most successful in packaging paranoia into an appealing narrative.

What to make of all this? The point, to paraphrase Karl Marx, is not just to describe the world, but to change it. It's one thing to diagnose the problem, and another to attempt to offer some kind of solution to it. What, if anything, can be done about any of this?

It's important to state that the work of understanding conspiracists and defusing their delusional and often bigoted beliefs does not need to belong to everyone. There is a danger in demanding that the targets of such bigots and racists be asked to offer compassion, or to demand that victims of such violence offer empathy and understanding. The only obligation those who are targeted by conspiracists have is to take care of themselves and their loved ones.

But for those who are in a position to combat these delusions and conspiracy beliefs, it's important to note that it involves more than simply fact-checking. While factual debunking is vital, it remains less important than first understanding the psychological need that drives the conspiracist to seek out alternative stories.

Often, as Miranda's story suggests, believers are looking for purpose, and conspiracy theorists—like cult leaders—don't look for unintelligent people so much as they look for directionless people, people lacking meaning and purpose, who've lost family ties (at one point, Eric said of

Miranda that she disliked the fact that she lived so far from her family in Florida, even though she came to California in part because she never quite fit in with them in the first place). As tempting as socially isolating these people may be, it's the kind of behavior that becomes a vicious circle, driving them further into the arms of a community that welcomes them and nurtures feelings of victimhood and persecution. Whatever ability we have to try to reintegrate these people into other arenas of social life helps break that cycle.

In addition to community, conspiracy groups offer adherents a simplified narrative to dispel chaos in one's life. They may also provide a cover story to justify racist, homophobic, and transphobic beliefs, ideas that a person may believe but feel they can't publicly display. Such theories liberate believers and encourage a kind of free play for forbidden thoughts. The historian Philip Deloria once described Americanness as "a particular working out of a desire to preserve stability and truth while enjoying absolute, anarchic freedom." It is this impulse for anarchic, irresponsible freedom—embedded within the framework of a stable, functional social-service net—that conspiracists crave. Giving into base bigotry and giving up on the social fabric that binds us, while refusing to admit there are consequences for such decisions, is an attitude that has increasingly come to define large segments of the American population. They see themselves free to make racist or transphobic jokes but cry foul when they're fired for such jokes. They assert the right not to wear masks or get vaccinated knowing fully well they can count on the same medical treatment should they get sick. They want to raise hell in their private lives and still keep their day jobs.

This hypocrisy takes work to sustain. If a primary way conspiracy theories work is by resolving cognitive dissonance—projecting the source of an internal conflict onto some exterior, often imaginary, foe—then the increasing virulence of QAnon and right-wing conspiracy theories in the run up to the 2020 election can also be seen in this light. For decades, the Right has pushed a mantra of individual liberty and personal freedom, one that is often at odds with the successful function-ing of democracy, which implies a community where we all generally work toward common goals. There has always been a low-key tension in this formulation, but it has never been starker in recent memory than in the global Covid-19 pandemic, in which it became increasingly clear that one's own personal actions could endanger others. Conspiracy be-liefs have allowed many in this country to stay and play in a realm where their actions don't have consequences, that any cognitive disso-nance they feel is the fault of the government or the Democrats, where they can cling to their irresponsibility and still claim victimhood when they face consequences.

The problem of conspiracy belief and paranoia has taken on a re-newed urgency in the past few years, but these eruptions are never new; rather, they are part of a long-standing continuum. But for such moral panics surrounding secret groups to be successful, each one must be treated as singular and unlike anything that's come before it, which is why they are allowed to be quickly forgotten as soon as the moment has passed. The history of American democracy involves a kind of deliberate historical amnesia, such that each generation can be free to imagine that the moral panic that grips them in their time is a new singularity.

What becomes increasingly clear is that such beliefs are omnipresent, kept in the margins, until such time as there is a new cultural or polit-ical realignment. Then they emerge, as though brand-new yet fully formed, an urgent intrusion onto public consciousness. Their purpose, as always, is to moderate or prohibit social change, to resolve tensions inherent in the democratic process in the most regressive way possible. They need to be attacked not in terms of technical fixes by the media or Facebook, but in a wholesale awareness of how we approach the ques-tion of democracy.

It's comforting, perhaps, to think of the sudden eruption of con-spiratorial thinking as aberrant, something that belongs outside of the "sensible middle," something that is not part of the fabric of "true

America." Believing this can allow us to then believe that it can be dealt with easily: that it is just a matter of ridding ourselves of this troubling tumor and going back to "the way things were." But we cannot. This is America. The panic changes names every generation but remains a durable and persistent reaction to democracy. (While this book focuses specifically on American democracy, looking at other democracies will unearth similar patterns.) Ritual abuse paranoia and anti-Semitism in particular (to cite only two of the most pernicious threads in the current fever swamp) have truly never diminished or abated. In fact, they merely lingered in the fringe communities, waiting for a slight shift in presentation to reemerge.

Depending on your vantage point, the argument that QAnon is only the latest version of a type of reaction that has always been with us is either a hopeful thought or a depressing one. Hopeful in that it's a reminder that we've faced at least versions of this before, in other guises. And for better or worse, the republic has survived. Depressing, though, in the realization that we've been here before, that these problems—which seem utterly solvable—stubbornly persist.

But a good part of the reason why such problems never get solved is due to the way they're allowed to fade into obscurity almost as soon as the heat of the moment has passed. The prevalence of such moments depends on the destruction of a communal memory of these past outrages, a constant culture of forgetting, an almost state-sponsored amnesia designed to treat each emerging moral panic as entirely new.

The French philosopher Michel de Certeau, writing about moral panics in his own country, argues that the "languages of social anxiety seem to reject both the limits of a present and the real conditions of its future." To be in a moment of moral panic, to search in fear for secret groups hiding behind suburban homes or in the elite halls of power, is to suspend the operation of history in favor of a kind of hysterical present. In the process, the possibility of a future is likewise obscured.

The question about what to do about QAnon involves remembering that, if history is any guide, the movement will soon enough exhaust itself (and indeed, is already exhausting itself). In the short term, there is the concern about lone wolf acts of terrorism and violence, grifters profiting off people's gullibility, and the possibility of even more extreme acts.

But the longer term question of what to do about QAnon is the recognition that no sooner will it fade then will our memory of it. It will be treated—as with the Satanic Panic before it—as a strange artifact relegated to the excesses of a previous moment, with no real bearing on whatever new present we may find ourselves in. And in that historical amnesia we will run the great risk of damning ourselves once again, condemned to the eternal return of some future outburst. Some new secret group, or even just some new recombination of existing elements, tailored slightly to a new media environment, and unleashed on the world once more.

Citizens' Commissions

September 1, 2021: the day that the Supreme Court lets a Texas law overturning *Roe v. Wade* go into effect. The law works by empowering ordinary citizens to sue anyone performing or assisting an abortion in civil court, where they can collect bounties of $10,000 and up. It takes an individual woman's body and abstracts it into a shadowy network of abortion providers and activists, of friends and loved ones who donate money, even Lyft and Uber drivers (all of whom become potentially liable under the law's purposefully ambiguous language)—targeting this network in a malevolent attempt at collective punishment. The law, among its many effects, is meant to ennoble a kind of widespread and diffused paranoia, where individuals can circumvent established constitutional law and engage in vigilante witch hunts against their neighbors. It is a law designed to enshrine the mechanisms of moral panics into everyday life, suspending the normal workings of justice into a state of emergency without end, with the goal of targeting women and restricting their freedom.

It is a disastrous day for the rule of law, and I spend much of the day having a hard time thinking or concentrating. In addition, Hurricane Ida, having already made landfall in Louisiana, is sweeping up the East

Coast. By the end of the day, this latest harbinger of climate change will have killed over two dozen people in my home of New York City, another disturbing reminder of the dangers that lay ahead of us and the work required of us all. But for now I'm in Media, Pennsylvania, for a public ceremony that's already been delayed once due to Covid-19 and which is going ahead despite these new unfolding disasters.

At the intersection of North Olive Street and West Second Street stands a small, two-story office building facing the Delaware County courthouse. Fifty years ago, the FBI had been using this building for a small, two-person field office. And fifty years 'ago, on the night of the "Fight of the Century" between Muhammad Ali and Joe Frazier, eight anonymous people changed history.

The plot had originated with a young physics professor at Haverford College in Pennsylvania, who first floated to some confidants the idea of breaking into an FBI office. Eventually eight individuals calling themselves the Citizens' Commission to Investigate the FBI planned and carried out a break-in to unearth confidential documents about the FBI's domestic activities. They chose a remote field office in the hope that it would have lower security, and picked March 8, 1971—the night of the Ali–Frazier fight—in the hopes that any possible security would likely be distracted.

At the time of the break-in, they weren't exactly sure what they expected to find. Despite rumors and whispers of FBI activity, the entirety of COINTELPRO was a secret, and there was at least some fear that they wouldn't turn up anything at all. But that night, the Citizens' Commission found over 1,000 pages of classified material that they made off with, and which they began to selectively leak to news organizations over the next few weeks.

Everything Americans came to know about how their government spies on them began with the COINTELPRO break-in. And we're here now for the unveiling of a plaque commemorating the event and the place where it happened. By the time I arrive at the dedication ceremony, there's a group of maybe forty to fifty people, many with umbrellas, and a light rain.

Despite the audacity of their action, the eight burglars were never caught. Nor were they identified, not until early 2014, with the publication of Betty Medsger's book, *The Burglary*. Medsger had been one of the original *Washington Post* journalists who had reported on the COINTELPRO leaks, and it was to Medsger that seven of the eight collaborators revealed themselves when they decided to go public (two chose to be identified under pseudonyms; the eighth, Judi Feingold, came forward after Medsger's book was published). The main organizer, William C. Davidon, had done work in the 1960s disrupting the Vietnam draft by breaking into government offices and destroying draft records. Together, he and seven cohorts decided to take their efforts to an entirely new and unprecedented level—and because they remained anonymous and free, their work has been allowed to largely be forgotten.

Now, belatedly, there are some attempts to change that. The man responsible for submitting the petition to the Pennsylvania Historical and Museum Commission, is Kevin Tustin, who became interested in the story in college after seeing a short documentary on the event. "Growing up in the area," Tustin had told me a few weeks earlier, "you don't learn anything about the burglary. It's not anything you've ever heard about. It's not taught in schools. It's a hidden secret." It's his hope that, "with this marker, people are always going to see that something historic happened here." Tustin seems nothing short of jubilant as he mingles in the crowd, passing out flyers and welcoming friends and strangers. When I asked him why a historical marker, he told me: "I hope it shows how important even the smallest little bedroom communities can be to history. Literally, if you walked around Media, you would never realize what kind of historic event happened here in the early '70s. You look at it, and it's just the cute little town, nice shops, the people are nice, it's the seat of government for the county, but it had so much more that people don't even realize, so that every time they walk past this marker, they'll see what a profound impact this small little town, having a small FBI office, could change the nation."

Before the work of the Citizens' Commission, the FBI had a nearly stellar reputation among mainstream Americans, who had no idea that they were capable of such things—even as they strove to drive wedges between the public. Like the Texas law, the work of the FBI's COINTELPRO was to turn Americans against one another, to foment paranoia and distrust, to stifle change and progress by erecting barriers to liberty and solidarity. Medsger has said of the COINTELPRO files that the most important thing they revealed were "the depths of Hoover's racist practices, and their Stasi-like collection of files on people, particularly Black people." And while the break-in may not have ended all of that behavior, it was a crucial step toward a better democracy.

Among the first speakers is the mayor of Media, Bob McMahon. He talks about the importance of standing up for what's right, despite the consequences, and at some point it hits me that I am listening to an elected official, sworn to uphold the Constitution, celebrating the good work of some lawbreakers. The rain begins to fall harder as Betty Medsger comes to the podium. There's no microphone today, so we all have to move a little closer to hear her over the rain; even so, many of her words get lost as the drizzle begins to become a downpour. Will Davidon died in 2013, shortly before Medsger's book was published, but his daughter is here, and though her speech is also largely drowned out by the growing rain, I do catch this: "Because in addition to being an activist and a scientist, he was also a dad. And he wanted to do everything he could to create the kind of country that he wanted his children to grow up in."

Two of the original burglars are here today: Bonnie Raines and Keith Forsyth. Forsyth had taken lock-picking classes at night in the 1960s so he could more effectively break into draft board offices. Sometime between the initial casing and the night of the burglary, a new lock had been installed, one that Forsyth couldn't pick. They contemplated calling it off, but Raines pointed out that there was a second door, albeit one blocked by a large file cabinet. So Forsyth returned and forced open this door, pushing back a file cabinet that weighed more than he did.

Posters of Raines's FBI sketch have been posted all over town in anticipation of the event: with a shawl covering her head and sunglasses, she looks like the *Mad Men*-era version of the Unabomber. Her job was to case the joint; posing as an undergraduate journalism student from Swarthmore, she got a tour of the office, looking for cameras and other security while asking anodyne questions about the FBI's heroism.

That kind of courage and tenacity seems to me superhuman, but there is nothing out of the ordinary about Raines and Forsyth. They are—in the best possible way—the most ordinary people you could possibly imagine. These are not members of some secret, all-powerful cabal who changed history by pulling the strings from behind the curtains. These are not the children of privilege, and they did not rely on nefarious networks or subterranean organizations to accomplish their goals. They were everyday individuals who saw an injustice and decided to take action. Conspiring together, they worked with secrecy and purpose and changed America.

Perhaps because of their anonymity for over forty years, and the fact that they were never caught, never stood trial, and were never made into symbols, the eight members of the Citizens' Commission to Investigate the FBI remain among the country's great unsung heroes. They are not household names, even though every American who values their civil liberties owes them a debt.

But despite the good feelings here, the Texas law is never far from my mind. It is difficult to know what lays ahead. And it is easy to give in to the despair, to give in to the frustration and anger as so much is taken away from us. It's hard not to focus on the doom and hardship that lays ahead, especially as a harder rain begins to fall. But as I look out on the crowd, I notice a mix of not just older folks—longtime activists who remember Vietnam and have carried the torch of civil disobedience and resistance for decades—but also younger people like Kevin Tustin, who learned of these stories secondhand and took inspiration from them, as well as more than a handful of younger kids, some maybe ten or eleven years old, who listen with a look that suggests they recognize the importance of these moments even if they don't understand the history just yet. At least three generations, then, of people gathered together to honor the most ordinary of secret societies, a hidden cabal of the most normal, everyday citizens one could imagine—people just like you and me, who had the tenacity to imagine a better country and to take action.

Despair is the easy choice. It is much harder to hold on to hope—the kind of difficult, radical hope which is the only thing that has ever changed anything in this country. As the skies give way to the hurricane's deluge, it starts to feel to me further away than ever. But then I remember that this hope—and this possibility—is there, has always been and will always be there—in the voices of these ordinary conspirators, and in the faces of those willing to brave the rain to hear them.

ACKNOWLEDGMENTS

Thank you first to Brendan Byrne, for the initial conversation that ultimately became this book. Thanks also to Evan Kindley, who provided invaluable advice as this book took shape and throughout the entire process, and to Michelle Legro, for the constant feedback, friendship, and tacos.

Every day I'm grateful to be able to work with Anna Sproul-Latimer, an indefatigable advocate and the best agent a writer could ask for. Everyone at Neon Literary, including Kent Wolf and Gabe Pettegrew, are truly the best people on earth. Thank you also to my fabulous editor, Emily Wunderlich, who saw this manuscript through, and to Paloma Ruiz and everyone else at Viking for making this book a real thing.

Thank you to the staff of the Prelinger Library, and to the folks at the *Los Angeles Review of Books*, *Gen Magazine*, Politico (particularly Katie Fossett), *The Atlantic* (particularly Brendan Vaughn), and the wonderful team at Real Life: Nathan Jurgenson, Soraya King, Rob Horning—and, most especially, Alex Molotkow, who has not just been a wonderful friend with a keen editorial eye, but also literally helped keep me alive during the difficult months when I was first beginning this project.

Thanks, as always, to everyone at Betalevel—particularly Jason Brown, Amina Cain, Amar Ravva, and Heather Parlato—and to the Sucks Magazine Editorial Collective: Benjamin Armintor, Rob Fellman, Karen Gregory, Matthew Harrison, Joe Howley, Vim Pasupathi, and Karl Steel.

ACKNOWLEDGMENTS

One could not ask for a better writing group than Rahawa Haile, Manjula Martin, and Sarah McCarry, who've kept me sane and kept me going.

Thank you to the various people who accompanied me on road trips and research excursions, or who met me for a drink when I was traveling in strange cities: Aaron Bady and Lili Loofbourow (and Pequod and Pepita), Kira Brunner Don (and Nemo), Karl Erickson and Gretchen Larsen (and Mavis), Liz Hansen (and Olive and Gordo), Malcolm Harris, Charlie Loyd, Sarah Michelson, Manny Shah, Lauren Walsh, and Sarah Werner. Thanks also to everyone who talked to me for this book, providing insight, expertise, and their own stories, including Wanda Addison, Dan Fox, Melanie Gallagher, Julie Holland, Kenny Johnson, Jennifer Krasinski, Franz Potter, Patricia Turner, Kevin Tustin, Cypress Williams, and Lenora Williams. Any error of fact or judgment remains mine.

Much of this book was written at Big Mouth Coffee in Beacon, New York, and at Lark in Brooklyn, which are both great places to write a book.

Thank you also to Nicole Antebi, Laura Bellizzi, Alex Dickey and Andee Ziegler, Shane Dickey and Carol Rouzpay, Caitlin Doughty, Charlotte Douglas, Robby Herbst, John Kilbane, Cari Luna, Jennie Matz, Allison Meier, Amy Shearn, Seth Sherwood, Leila Taylor, and Mark Trecka. Special thanks once again to Tricia Matthew.

Thank you, finally, to Elizabeth Harper (whom readers may remember from *Ghostland*), for reasons said and unsaid, and for making it all worthwhile.

NOTES

Introduction: The Paranoid Republic

1 **"any People under the Sun"**: Cotton Mather, *Wonders of the Invisible World* (London: John Russell Smith, 1862), 4, 13.

1 **"over Engld &c &c &c"**: Ezra Stiles, *The Literary Diary of Ezra Stiles* (New York: Charles Scribner and Sons, 1901), 590.

2 **"so particularly characterized them"**: Roger Lamb, *An Original and Authentic Journal of Occurrences During the Late American War, from Its Commencement to the Year 1783* (Dublin, Ireland: Wilkinson & Courtney, 1809), 8.

2 **"often covertly and insidiously"**: George Washington, *Washington's Farewell Address to the People of the United States MDCCXCVI* (Boston, MA: Houghton Mifflin Company, 1913), 7.

2 **"not going the way they like"**: Quoted in Rick Perlstein, *Before the Storm: Barry Goldwater and the Unmaking of the American Consensus* (New York: Public Affairs, 2009), 350.

3 **"would become impossible"**: Richard Hofstadter, *The Paranoid Style in American Politics and Other Essays* (New York: Vintage, 2008), 65.

4 **"expected a year ago"**: Paul Musgrave, "Donald Trump Is Normalizing Paranoia and Conspiracy Thinking in U.S. Politics," *Washington Post*, January 12, 2017.

4 **"Trump has changed the office"**: Maureen Dowd, "Trump's Enablers Feed His Conspiracy Theories," *Seattle Times*, March 20, 2017.

4 **"Jews are all over the government"**: George Lardner Jr. and Michael Dobbs, "New Tapes Reveal Depth of Nixon's Anti-Semitism," *Washington Post*, October 6, 1999.

4 **"global child sex trafficking operation"**: PRRI Staff, "Understanding QAnon's Connection to American Politics, Religion, and Media Consumption," Public Religion Research Institute, May 27, 2021.

5 **loved ones dying**: Chapman University, "Survey of American Fears: The Complete List of Fears, 2020/2021," https://www.chapman.edu/wilkinson/research-centers /babbie-center/_files/Babbie%20center%20fear2021/the-complete-percentage -list-of-fears-2020-highest-to-lowest.pdf.

Chapter One: The Arch and the Cenotaph

20 **"the ones that need to be killed"**: Catherine E. Shoichet, "FBI: Milwaukee Man Planned Mass Shooting at Masonic Temple," CNN.com, January 27, 2016.

20 **"dark souls and evil"**: Jeremy Hainsworth, "B.C. Masonic Lodge Arsonist Who Believed in Illuminati Mind Control Sentenced," *North Shore News*, November 8, 2021.

20 **the Covid-19 pandemic on such beliefs**: Robyn Rapoport, Kyle Berta, and Christian Kline, *Methodology Report: American Fears Survey* (January 2021), 83; Robyn Rapoport and Kyle Berta, *Methodology Report: American Fears Survey* (July 2018), 71.

Chapter Two: The Craft

25 **"everywhere the Illuminati has been"**: Fritz Springmeier, *Bloodlines of the Illuminati* (Ambassador House, 1998), accessed at https://citeseerx.ist.psu.edu/viewdoc/down load?doi=10.1.1.475.3562&rep=rep1&type=pdf.

25 **"is an unfinished work"**: William Cooper, *Behold a Pale Horse* (Flagstaff, AZ: Light Technology Publishing, 1991), 88.

26 **"the conduct of the craft in general"**: Thomas Smith Webb, *The Freemason's Monitor; Or, Illustrations of Masonry: in Two Parts* (Salem, MA: Cushing & Appleton, 1808), 80, 211.

27 **"began as an organized institution"**: Frances A. Yates, *The Rosicrucian Enlightenment* (London: Routledge, 2001), 209.

29 **"free-born"**: The standard language for initiation into Freemasonry can be found in multiple places, including Richard Carlile, *Manual of Freemasonry: In Three Parts, with an Explanatory Introduction to the Science and a Free Translations of Some of the Sacred Scripture Names* (London: Andrew Vickers, 1855), 5.

31 **"a hatred of the light"**: Pope Clement XII, "Papal Bull Dealing with the Condemnation of Freemasonry," 1738.

31 **"to enter into this Society"**: Quoted in John Dickie, *The Craft: How the Freemasons Made the Modern World* (New York: Public Affairs, 2020), 6.

31 *"they have no Secret at all":* Quoted in J. A. Leo Lamay, *The Life of Benjamin Franklin, Volume 2: Printer and Publisher, 1730–1747* (Philadelphia, PA: University of Pennsylvania Press, 2006), 84.

32 **"cabals within cabals":** Gordon S. Wood, "Conspiracy and the Paranoid Style: Causality and Deceit in the Eighteenth Century," *William and Mary Quarterly* 39, no. 3 (July 1982): 407.

32 **"Murders of New born Babes":** Quoted in Thomas More Brown, "The Image of the Beast: Anti-Papal Rhetoric in Colonial America," in Richard O. Curry and Thomas M. Brown (ed.), *Conspiracy: The Fear of Subversion in American History* (New York: Holt, Rinehart, and Winston, Inc., 1972), 11.

32 **"give an Enemy . . . good Encouragement?":** Quoted in Ibid., 14–15.

33 **"reducing us to slavery":** Quoted in Wood, "Conspiracy and the Paranoid Style," 421.

33 **"regular, systematic plan":** George Washington, letter to Bryan Fairfax, July 4, 1774.

33 **"such arbitrary sway":** Quoted in Robert Middlekauff, *Washington's Revolution: The Making of America's First Leader* (New York: Alfred A. Knopf, 2016), 207.

33 **"least grievous to people":** Quoted in Bernard Bailyn, "The Logic of Rebellion: Conspiracy Fears and the American Revolution," in Curry and Brown, *Conspiracy*, 25.

34 **"indeed the nation too":** Ebenezer Baldwin, "The Heavy Grievances the Colonies Labor Under," in David Brion Davis (ed.), *The Fear of Conspiracy* (Ithaca, NY: Cornell University Press, 1971), 32.

34 **"contriving against us":** Samuel A. M. Sherwood, "The Church's Flight Into the Wilderness: An Address on the Times, Containing Some Very Interesting and Important Observations on Scripture Prophecies," (New York: S. Loudon, 1776), 22.

35 **"the cause of any event":** Samuel Stanhope Smith, *Lectures on Moral and Political Philosophy, Volume II* (1812), 24.

35 **"recesses of his own heart":** Quoted in Wood, "Conspiracy and the Paranoid Style," 414.

35 **"operation of contrary causes":** David Hume, *The Philosophical Works of David Hume, Volume 1* (Frankfurt, Germany: Outlook Verlag GmbH, 2020), 177.

36 **"perfect humiliation and slavery":** John Jay, "To the People of Great-Britain," in Donald T. Critchlow, John Korasick, and Matthew C. Sherman (ed.), *Political Conspiracies in America* (Bloomington, IN: Indiana University Press, 2008), 8.

37 **"immensely large and very minute":** Alexis de Tocqueville, *Democracy in America* (Garden City, NY: Anchor, 1969), 513.

37 **"naked, sometimes clumsy ambition":** Ron Chernow, *Washington: A Life* (New York: Penguin Press, 2010), 69.

37 **"any power upon Earth":** George Washington, letter to Elkanah Watson, August 10, 1782.

38 racist attitudes of American Masons: For more on the Prince Hall Masons, see Peter P. Hinks and Stephen David Kantrowitz (ed.), *All Men Free and Brethren: Essays on the History of African American Freemasonry* (Ithaca, NY: Cornell University Press, 2013).

39 "that was ever seen in America": Daniel Fisher, quoted in Steven C. Bullock, *Revolutionary Brotherhood: Freemasonry and the Transformation of the American Social Order, 1730–1840* (Chapel Hill, NC: University of North Carolina Press, 1996), 53.

Chapter Three: The Dreadful Fire

40 "doctrines of the Illuminati": George Washington, letter to G. W. Snyder, September 25, 1798.

40 "of this fact than I am": George Washington, letter to G. W. Snyder, October 24, 1798.

41 "aided by these vile slanders": Quoted in Vernon Stauffer, *New England and the Bavarian Illuminati* (New York, 1918), 232.

42 "spread for this purpose": Jedidiah Morse, *A Sermon Delivered at the New North Church in Boston, in the Morning And in the Afternoon at Charlestown, May 9th, 1798, Being the Day recommended by John Adams, President of the United States of America, For Solemn Humiliation, Fasting and Prayer.* (Boston: Samuel Hall, 1798).

42 "these great purposes": Timothy Dwight, "The Duty of Americans at the Present Crisis," in Critchlow Korasick, and Sherman, *Political Conspiracies in America*, 12.

45 "the Illuminization of Freemasonry": Augustin Barruel, *Memoirs Illustrating the History of Jacobinism, Vol. IV* (London; T. Burton, 1798), 87.

45 "your History of Jacobinism": Barbara Lowe, P. J. Marshall, and John A. Woods (ed.), *The Correspondence of Edmund Burke, Volume X* (Chicago, IL: Cambridge University Press, 1978), 38.

46 "the place of its first explosion": John Robison, *Proofs of a Conspiracy against All the Religions and Governments of Europe, Carried on in the Secret Meetings of Free Masons, Illuminati, and Reading Societies* (Philadelphia, PA: T. Dobson, 1798), 304.

47 "idle and profligate poor": Ibid., 158.

48 "the enemy of his country": Quoted in Stauffer, *New England and the Bavarian Illuminati*, 283.

48 "the respectability of his testimonies": Quoted in ibid., 254.

48 "of a political fulmination": Quoted in ibid., 304.

49 "of a Society of Illuminati": Quoted in ibid., 292.

50 **conspiracy he had uncovered**: Ogden's saga is discussed in Alan V. Briceland, *"The Philadelphia Aurora*, the New England Illuminati, and the Election of 1800," *Pennsylvania Magazine of History and Biography* 100, no. 1 (January 1976).

50 **"Hydra of clerical despotism"**: Quoted in ibid., p. 14.

50 **"The Illuminati"**: Quoted in ibid., p. 21.

50 **"four hundred parochial bishops"**: Quoted in ibid, 27.

Chapter Four: "There Is Something Earnest in All This, but the Object Is Concealed"

55 **"the verge of destruction"**: Samuel D. Green, *The Broken Seal; or, Personal Reminiscences of the Morgan Abduction and Murder* (Boston, MA: n.d.), 29.

56 **law into their own hands**: Hiram B. Hopkins, *Renunciation of Freemasonry* (Boston, MA: John Marsh & Co., 1830).

56 **"such stuff as that"**: Green, *The Broken Seal*, 34.

57 **"small towns of up-state New York"**: Jasper Ridley, *The Freemasons: A History of the World's Most Powerful Secret Society* (New York: Arcade, 2001), 176–77.

57 **"all honest Masons would see . . . executed"**: Green, *The Broken Seal*, 36.

58 **"so vile a wretch as he"**: Ibid., 36–37.

59 **"highest authorities in the masonic councils"**: Ibid., 74–75.

61 **the era's Watergate**: William Preston Vaughn, *The Anti-Masonic Party in the United States, 1826–1843* (Lexington, KY: University of Kentucky Press, 1983), 2.

61 **"the Prince of Darkness himself"**: Quoted in Gerald J. Baldasty, "The New York State Political Press and Antimasonry," *New York History* 64, no. 3 (July 1983), 265.

62 **"but the object is concealed"**: Henry Dana Ward, *The Anti-masonic Review and Magazine* (New York: Vanderpool & Cole, 1828), 6.

Chapter Five: Mysteries of Iniquity

70 **"than it was an accident"**: Quoted in Jill Lepore, *New York Burning: Liberty, Slavery, and Conspiracy in Eighteenth-Century Manhattan* (New York: Knopf, 2007), 47.

71 **"latent Enemies amongst us"**: Serena R. Zabin (ed.), *The New York Conspiracy Trials of 1741: Daniel Horsmanden's Journal of the Proceedings* (Boston, MA: Bedford/St. Martin's, 2004), 60.

71 **"Monsters in Iniquity: "**Quoted in Lepore, *New York Burning*, 96.

71 **"at the Bottom of it"**: Quoted in ibid., 176.

72 "a prank that grew out of proportion": Lepore, *New York Burning*, 143.

74 "attendant upon human bondage": Lewis Tappan, "Circular Letter Urging Opposition to the Expansion of Slavery" (New York: 1850).

74 "the subjugation of freemen": William Goodell, *Slavery and Anti-Slavery; A History of the Great Struggle in Both Hemispheres; with a View of the Slavery Question in the United States* (New York: William Harned, 1852), 584.

Chapter Six: "Do Not Open Your Lips"

77 "all the way to Boston": Eber M. Pettit, *Sketches in the History of the Underground Railroad* (Fredonia, NY: W. McKinstry & Son, 1879), 35.

78 "into one of the cars": Quoted in Eric Foner, *Gateway to Freedom: The Hidden History of the Underground Railroad* (New York: W. W. Norton, 2015), 107–8.

78 likely been in the basement: James Baron, "Storied Brooklyn Church to Lose Its Keeper of History," *New York Times*, November 22, 2015.

80 "cruelty and bloodshed": Lyon G. Tyler (ed.), *The Letters and Times of the Tylers* (Richmond, VA: Whittet and Shepperson, 1884), 576.

80 "exhibited in the nursery": Ibid., 578.

81 "behind the curtain": W. W. Sleigh, *Abolitionism Exposed! Proving that the Principles of Abolitionism Are Injurious to the Slaves Themselves, Destructive to this Nation, and Contrary to the Express Commands of God* (Philadelphia, PA: D. Schneck, 1838), 20–21.

81 "deep-laid scheme": Pettit, *Sketches in the History of the Underground Railroad*, 35.

83 "Yankees have not penetrated": Edward Ruffin, "Consequences of Abolition Agitation," in J. D. B. De Bow (ed.), *De Bow's Review*, vol. XXIII (New Orleans, 1857), 546.

83 "breath of the fanatics": William Drayton, *The South Vindicated from the Treason and Fanaticism of the Northern Abolitionists* (Philadelphia, PA: H. Manly, 1836), 158.

83 "insubordination into their minds": Quoted in John Ashworth, *Slavery, Capitalism, and Politics in the Antebellum Republic* (Cambridge, UK: Cambridge University Press, 1995), 140.

84 "the imps to work the better": Quoted in Donald B. Cole, *A Jackson Man: Amos Kendall and the Rise of American Democracy* (Baton Rouge, LA: Louisiana State University Press, 2004), 201.

85 "who will take yours down": David Robertson, *Denmark Vesey: The Buried Story of America's Largest Slave Rebellion and the Man Who Led It* (New York: Vintage, 1999), 70–71.

86 "for his fellow creatures": Ibid., 8.

86 gatherings by Black Carolinians: Richard C. Wade, "The Vesey Plot: A Reconsideration," *Journal of Southern History* 30, no. 2 (May 1964).

87 the severe lethality of Vesey's plot: Carrie Hyde, "Novelistic Evidence: The Denmark Vesey Conspiracy and Possibilistic History," *American Literary History* 27, no. 1 (2015).

88 "arguments against emancipation": Lenora Warren, *Fire on the Water: Sailors, Slaves, and Insurrection in Early American Literature, 1789–1886* (New Brunswick, NJ: Rutgers University Press, 2019), 41.

88 "being enslaved itself": Interview with the author, February 22, 2021.

88 "collapses these things on themselves": Ibid.

89 "as you shall see me do": Robertson, *Denmark Vesey*, 6.

89 "in many families": Ibid., 112.

Chapter Seven: In the Convent's Crypt

93 "where the Catholic Church predominates": Quoted in Gregg Cantrell, "Sam Houston and the Know-Nothings," *Southwestern Historical Quarterly* 96, no. 3 (January 1993), 332–33.

94 "and religion expires": George Bourne, *Lorette: The History of Louise, Daughter of a Canadian Nun; Exhibiting the Interior of Female Convents* (New York, NY: Wm. A. Mercein, 1833), 124.

94 "hot-beds of lust debauchery": Quoted in Tyler Gregory Anbinder, *Nativism and Slavery: The Northern Know Nothings and the Politics of the 1850s* (Oxford, UK: Oxford University Press, 1992), 115.

95 "the control of public affairs": Scipio de Ricci, *Female Convents: Secrets of Nunneries Disclosed* (New York: D. Appleton & Co., 1834), xxii.

95 denied access to political power: Linda Kerber, "The Republican Mother: Women and the Enlightenment—an American Perspective," *American Quarterly* 28, no. 2 (Summer 1976).

96 "I ever heard talk": Quoted in James J. Kenneally, "The Burning of the Ursuline Convent: A Different View," *Records of the American Catholic Historical Society of Philadelphia* 90, no. 1/4 (March–December 1979), 15.

97 "excited in consequence": *An Account of the Conflagration of the Ursuline Convent* (Boston, MA: 1834), 5.

97 "garb of Holy Religion": Quoted in Georgianne McVay, "Yankee Fanatics Unmasked: Cartoons on the Burning of a Convent," *Records of the American Catholic Historical Society of Philadelphia* 83, no. 3/4 (September–December 1972), 159.

97 **the entire nunnery would come down**: Daniel A. Cohen, "Alvah Kelley's Cow: Household Feuds, Proprietary Rights, and the Charlestown Convent Riot," *New England Quarterly* 74, no. 4 (December 2001), 558.

98 **"whip you all into the sea"**: *Some Events of Boston and Its Neighbors* (Boston, MA: State Street Trust Company, 1917), 49.

98 **"kindling of a great bonfire"**: McVay, "Yankee Fanatics Unmasked," 162.

98 **"we ought to be grateful to them"**: Quoted in Theodore M. Hammett, "Two Mobs of Jacksonian Boston: Ideology and Interest," *Journal of American History* 62, no. 4 (March 1976), 848.

99 **"and must be awaked"**: Samuel Morse, *Foreign Conspiracy Against the Liberties of the United States* (New York: Leavitt, Lord & Co., 1835), 96; Lyman Beecher, *A Plea for the West* (Cincinnati, OH: Truman and Smith, 1835), 72.

Chapter Eight: Fresh from the Loins of the People

102 **"enthralled, ignorant, and debased"**: Quoted in Anbinder, *Nativism and Slavery*, 114.

102 **"to the nod of the Pope"**: Quoted in ibid., 115.

103 **"dangers of foreign influence"**: "Constitution of the Order of United Americans," *The Republic: A Monthly Magazine of American Literature, Politics, and Art*, Vol. 4, No. 2, 108.

103 **"in such a hurry"**: Quoted in Anbinder, *Nativism and Slavery*, 12.

104 **"absorbs all other considerations"**: Quoted in ibid., 32.

104 **"without regard to party"**: Quoted in ibid., 24.

105 **"to any office in this city"**: Quoted in ibid., 54.

106 **over $100,000 a year**: Nicholas Carnes and Noam Lupu, "It's Time to Bust the Myth: Most Trump Voters Were Not Working Class," *The Washington Post*, June 5, 2017.

106 ***"anti-Catholic triumph"***: Quoted in Eugene H. Roseboom, "Salmon P. Chase and the Know Nothings," *Mississippi Valley Historical Review* 25, no. 3 (December 1938), 335.

107 **"fears of the Pope"**: Quoted in Anbinder, *Nativism and Slavery*, 96.

107 **"religious hierarchy of Rome"**: Quoted in Michael F. Holt, "The Politics of Impatience: The Origins of Know Nothingism," *Journal of American History* 60, no. 2 (September 1973), 322.

107 **"reprehensible coalitions" ever assembled**: Quoted in Anbinder, *Nativism and Slavery*, 96.

108 "fraud, corruption and treachery": Quoted in John R. Mulkern, *The Know-Nothing Party in Massachusetts: The Rise and Fall of a People's Movement* (Boston, MA: Northeastern University Press, 1990), 63.

108 "no one can tell": Quoted in Anbinder, *Nativism and Slavery*, 53.

109 "bottom of all our troubles": Quoted in ibid., 219.

110 "single field officer": Quoted in ibid., 276.

111 "all government but theirs": Quoted in ibid., 278.

Chapter Nine: A Piece of Machinery, So to Speak

113 "by the slave power": Salmon P. Chase, "Appeal of the Independent Democrats in Congress," January 19, 1854.

113 "decline to be its tool": Charles Sumner, *The Crime Against Kansas* (Boston, MA: John P. Jewett & Company, 1856), 7.

113 "They rule in the House of Representatives": Quoted in Andrew L. Slap, *The Doom of Reconstruction: The Liberal Republicans in the Civil War Era* (New York: Fordham University Press, 2006), 53.

113 "arbitrary governments of Europe": Quoted in ibid.

114 "tool of the slave power": John Smith Dye, *The Adder's Den; Or Secrets of the Great Conspiracy to Overthrow Liberty in America* (New York: 1864), 94.

114 "the ruling interest of the republic": Foner, *Gateway to Freedom*, 47.

114 "at home and abroad": John Niven, *Salmon P. Chase: A Biography* (Oxford, UK: Oxford University Press, 1995), 148.

115 "mandates of the Slaveocracy": Quoted in Joanne B. Freeman, *The Field of Blood: Violence in Congress and the Road to Civil War* (New York: Farrar, Straus and Giroux, 2018), 199.

115 from the beginning: Abraham Lincoln, *Speeches and Writings, 1832–1858* (New York: The Library of America, 1989), 426.

116 "no other hypothesis": Abraham Lincoln, *Complete Works of Abraham Lincoln, Volume IV* (New York, NY: Francis D. Tandy Company, 1905), 214.

117 "conscience in the dust": William Lloyd Garrison, *Selections from the Writing and Speeches of William Lloyd Garrison* (Boston, MA: R. F. Walcutt, 1852), 137.

117 "for the last sixty years": William Goodell, "The Role of the Slave Power in American History," in David Brion Davis (ed.), *The Fear of Conspiracy: Images of Un-American Subversion from the Revolution to the Present* (Ithaca, NY: Cornell University Press, 1971), 113.

118 **"promise of American life"**: David Brion Davis, *The Slave Power Conspiracy and the Paranoid Style* (Baton Rouge, LA: Louisiana State University Press, 1970), 85.

118 **a feeling shared by both sides:** This distinction between positions is explored by Michael Pfau, *The Political Style of Conspiracy: Chase, Sumner, and Lincoln* (East Lansing, MI: Michigan State University Press, 2005).

118 **"Garrison wants it at the other":** Quoted in Henry Mayer, *All on Fire: William Lloyd Garrison and the Abolition of Slavery* (New York: W. W. Norton, 2008), 363.

121 **"the spirit of slaveholding":** Quoted in Roseboom, "Salmon P. Chase and the Know Nothings," 337.

Chapter Ten: The Mystic Red

122 **"light that shines on this land":** Henry David Thoreau, "The Last Days of John Brown," quoted in David S. Reynolds, *John Brown, Abolitionist: The Man Who Killed Slavery, Sparked the Civil War, and Seeded Civil Rights* (New York: Vintage, 2005), 433.

123 **"the work of an incendiary":** Quoted in Donald E. Reynolds, *Texas Terror: The Slave Insurrection Panic of 1860 and the Secession of the Lower South* (Baton Rouge, LA: Louisiana State University Press, 2007), 34.

124 **"white men of the North in our midst":** Quoted in ibid., 102.

124 **"the country is terribly excited":** Quoted in Donald E. Reynolds, *Editors Make War: Southern Newspapers in the Secession Crisis* (Carbondale, IL: Southern Illinois University Press, 2006), 100.

124 **"the foulest fiends in human shape":** Quoted in Reynolds, *Texas Terror*, 43.

125 **"let one guilty one pass":** Quoted in ibid., 55.

125 **"established for our own protection":** Quoted in ibid., 65

125 **"great danger of breaking":** Quoted in ibid., 66.

127 **"soon sting itself to death":** "The Texas Excitement: Some Insight into the Cause of It—A Curious Document—An Evident Forgery," *New York Times*, September 6, 1860.

127 **"Its bogus character is sufficiently apparent":** Ibid.

128 **"you buy and sell":** Quoted in Steven A. Channing, *Crisis of Fear: Secession in South Carolina* (New York: Norton, 1974), 270.

128 **"how can we stand it":** Quoted in ibid., 269.

129 **"to burn other towns":** Quoted in Reynolds, *Texas Terror*, 114.

129 **"of the traitorous Brown":** Quoted in ibid., 113.

129 **"in a predetermined fashion":** Channing, *Crisis of Fear*, 236.

130 **"a framework of irrational perception":** Ibid., 286.

Chapter Eleven: Abraham Lincoln's Secret Confidant

134 **"metaphorically framed as a body"**: Mark. J. Landau, Daniel Sullivan, and Jeff Greenberg, "Evidence that Self-Relevant Motives and Metaphoric Framing Interact to Influence Political and Social Attitudes, *Psychological Science* 20, no. 11 (2009).

134 **"indigestible mass"**: Quoted in Kitty Calavita, "Collisions at the Intersection of Gender, Race, and Class: Enforcing the Chinese Exclusion Laws," *Law and Society Review* 40, no. 2 (June 2006), 256.

134 **"undigested, undigestible"**: Quoted in Anbinder, *Nativism and Slavery*, 7.

134 **"the old papal machine"**: Quoted in John Corrigan and Lynn S. Neal, *Religious Intolerance in America: A Documentary History* (Chapel Hill, NC: University of North Carolina Press, 2010), 166.

134 **"designed to digest"**: Jane Coaston, "Watch: Tucker Carlson Rails Against America's Demographic Changes," *Vox*, March 21, 2018.

135 **"a waste of time and money"**: Washington Gladden, "The Anti-Catholic Crusade," *Century Illustrated Monthly Magazine*, vol. XLVII, 790.

136 **"who are now employed"**: Ibid.

136 ***"the jurisdiction of the United States"***: "The A. P. A. Conspirators," *Catholic World* 57, no. 341 (August 1893), 692.

137 **"could not do it shrewdly"**: Quoted in Gustavus Myers, *History of Bigotry in the United States* (New York: Capricorn Books, 1968), 178.

138 **"actual Catholic teachings"**: Humphrey J. Desmond, *The A. P. A. Movement: A Sketch* (Washington: The New Century Press, 1912), 19.

139 **Lincoln could "speak freely"**: Charles Paschal Telesphore Chiniquy, *Fifty Years in the Church of Rome* (Chicago, IL: Craig & Barlow, 1885), 662.

140 **"liberties, and our lives"**: Ibid., 705.

140 **"base alloy of hypocrisy"**: Abraham Lincoln, letter to Joshua F. Speed, August 24, 1855.

141 **"the freed blacks"**: Michael J. Sobiech, "Chiniquy's Lincoln: Aiming Booth's Bullet at the Roman Catholic Church," *American Catholic Studies* 127, no. 4 (Winter 2016), 39–40.

Chapter Twelve: The Man Who Threw the Bomb

145 **"using for political purposes"**: Quoted in Kevin Kenny, *Making Sense of the Molly Maguires* (Oxford, UK: Oxford University Press, 1998), 79.

146 **"the workmen of other countries"**: "The Pennsylvania Coal Mines," *New York Times*, November 7, 1863.

147 "suffer the consequences": Kenny, *Making Sense of the Molly Maguires*, 308.

147 "All should be securely masked": Quoted in ibid., 206.

148 "the courtroom and the hangman": Harold W. Aurand, *From the Molly Maguires to the United Mine Workers: The Social Ecology of an Industrial Union, 1869–1897* (Philadelphia, PA: Temple University Press, 1971), 71.

151 below the surface order: See Luc Boltanski, *Mysteries and Conspiracies: Detective Stories, Spy Novels, and the Making of Modern Societies* (Cambridge, UK: Polity Press, 2014).

152 "defeating the eight-hour movement": Quoted in James Green, *Death in the Haymarket: A Story of Chicago, the First Labor Movement, and the Bombing that Divided Gilded Age America* (New York: Anchor Books, 2007), 171.

153 "All right, we will go": Quoted in ibid., 186.

153 "peaceful citizen and Nihilist assassin": Quoted in ibid., 189.

154 consideration than "wild beasts": Quoted in Paul Avrich, *The Haymarket Tragedy* (Princeton, NJ: Princeton University Press, 2020), 220.

154 "been able to understand": Quoted in Green, *Death in the Haymarket*, 141.

154 "this is the stuff": Quoted in ibid., 25.

155 "who threw the bomb": Howard Zinn, *A People's History of the United States, 1492–Present* (London: Routledge, 2003), 272.

155 "conspiracy extended in every direction": Michael J. Schaack, *Anarchy and Anarchists: A History of the Red Terror and the Social Revolution in America and Europe* (Chicago, IL: F. J. Schulte & Company, 1889), 124.

156 "period of police terrorism": Richard T. Ely, *Under Our Feet: An Autobiography* (New York: Macmillan, 1938), 70.

156 "and what of Chicago": Quoted in Green, *Death in the Haymarket*, 200.

156 "need not even be indicted": Quoted in ibid., 214.

157 "a duly constituted agent": Schaack, *Anarchy and Anarchists*, 156.

157 "for years and years": Quoted in ibid., 526.

Chapter Thirteen: A Matter of Trusts

163 "to serve their own ends": Quoted in Roger Lowenstein, *America's Bank: The Epic Struggle to Create the Federal Reserve* (New York: Penguin, 2005), 72.

165 "but patriotic conspirators": Ibid., 119.

166 "an added enslavement": Ibid., 117.

166 **"in the history of American finance"**: B. C. Forbes, "Men Who Are Making America," *Leslie's Weekly* 123, no. 3189, October 19, 1916.

167 **"to deceive the people of the United States"**: See Charles Lindbergh, *Banking and Currency and the Money Trust* (Washington, DC: National Capital Press, 1918), 303.

167 **"so useful and profitable"**: Quoted in Lowenstein, *America's Bank*, 150–51.

168 **"benefiting well-connected financiers"**: Ibid., 53.

169 **"small group of dominant men"**: Medea Sulamanidze, "A Fake Facebook Account Posts a Spurious Woodrow Wilson Quote," mythdetector.ge, February 9, 2021.

Chapter Fourteen: The World's Enigma

171 **"Russia worse than hell"**: John Buchan, *The 39 Steps* (Boston, MA: Houghton Mifflin Company, 1915), 5.

172 **"one-horse location on the Volga"**: Ibid.

173 **"and in the whole world"**: Quoted in Victoria Sake Woeste, *Henry Ford's War on Jews and the Legal Battle Against Hate Speech* (Stanford, CA: Stanford University Press, 2012), 31.

173 **"I'll have them soon"**: Quoted in ibid.

174 **"contained in the gospel"**: William H. McGuffey, *McGuffey's Newly Revised Eclectic Fourth Reader* (New York: Clark, Austin & Smith, 1849), 191.

174 **"tortured to death on the cross"**: Quoted in Maurice Samuel, *Blood Accusation: The Strange History of the Beiliss Case* (London: Weidenfeld & Nicolson, 1967), 17.

175 **"true enemies of the government"**: Quoted in Steven G. Marks, *How Russia Shaped the Modern World: From Art to Anti-Semitism, Ballet to Bolshevism* (Princeton, NJ: Princeton University Press, 2003), 144.

176 **"interpretations of commentators"**: Quoted in Corrigan and Neal (eds.), *Religious Intolerance in America* (Chapel Hill, NC: University of North Carolina Press, 2019), 153.

176 **"plotting, plotting, plotting"**: Telemachus Thomas Timayenis, *The Original Mr. Jacobs: A Startling Exposé* (New York: The Minerva Publishing Co., 1888), 2.

177 **"power behind many a throne"**: *The International Jew: The World's Foremost Problem* (Dearborn, MI: The Dearborn Publishing Co., 1920), 10.

178 **"a smile on his lips"**: See Norman Cohn, *Warrant for Genocide: The Myth of the Jewish World-Conspiracy and the Protocols of the Elders of Zion* (London: Eyre & Spottiswoode, 1967), 78.

180 **"the way in which they use that power"**: William Pierce, "The New Protocols," *American Dissident Voices*, October 30, 1999.

180 **"dominant forces of modernity"**: Stephen Eric Bronner, *A Rumor About the Jews: Reflections on Antisemitism and "The Protocols of the Elders of Zion"* (New York: St. Martins Press, 2014), 2.

181 **"proof we have of their authenticity"**: Leonard William Dobb (ed.), *Ezra Pound Speaking: Radio Speeches of World War II* (Westport, CT: Greenwood Press, 1978), 283.

181 **"other ground from the beginning"**: Jean-Paul Sartre, *Anti-Semite and Jew: An Exploration of the Etiology of Hate,* trans. George J. Becker (New York: Schocken Books, 1978), 19.

186 **"that of a Bolshevik orator"**: Quoted in Neil Baldwin, *Henry Ford and the Jews* (New York: Public Affairs, 2001), 120.

186 **"every Jew is a Bolshevist"**: Louis Marshall, *Champion of Liberty: Selected Papers and Addresses, Volume 1* (Ann Arbor, MI: University of Michigan Press, 1957), 343.

Chapter Fifteen: The (In)Visible Empire

188 **"registered in the Stock Exchange"**: "Klan Assailed in House Hearing," *New York Times*, October 12, 1921.

189 **"Fraternal, Beneficiary Order"**: Quoted in David J. Chalmers, *Hooded Americanism: The History of the Ku Klux Klan* (Durham, NC: Duke University Press, 2013), 30.

191 **"colored man in the United States"**: Quoted in Felix Harcourt, *Ku Klux Kulture: America and the Klan in the 1920s* (Chicago, IL: University of Chicago Press, 2019), 105.

191 **"here and hereafter"**: Quoted in Wyn Craig Ward, *The Fiery Cross: The Ku Klux Klan in America* (Oxford, UK: Oxford University Press), 143.

192 **"to make sure success"**: Quoted in ibid., 159.

193 **"no apologies to anybody"**: Quoted in ibid., 195.

194 **"in defiance of the law"**: "Klan Assailed in House Hearing."

195 **"from start to finish"**: "Wizard in Vigorous Defense of Ku Klux," *New York Times*, October 13, 1921.

196 **"Congress *made* us"**: Quoted in Ward, *The Fiery Cross*, 166.

196 **"very fundamentals of the Nation"**: Quoted in Linda Gordon, *The Second Coming of the Klan* (New York: Liveright, 2017), 12.

197 **"Promotion of Pure Americanism"**: Quoted in Ward, *The Fiery Cross*, 150.

199 **"and conduct his business"**: Randolph Bedford, "The World Menace: Grafters and Gunmen Masquerade," *New Zealand Truth*, September 22, 1923.

201 **"far from being exhausted"**: "Another 'Invisible' Order," *Evening Star*, September 19, 1922.

201 **"methods of the Klan itself"**: Bedford, "The World Menace: Grafters and Gunmen Masquerade."

202 **"I *am* the law in Indiana"**: M. William Lutholtz, *Grand Dragon: D.C. Stephenson and the Ku Klux Klan* (West Lafayette. IN: Purdue University Press, 199), 233.

203 **"today a crumbling shell"**: Quoted in Ward, *The Fiery Cross*, 253.

203 **"nor figs of thistles"**: John Moffatt Mecklin, *The Ku Klux Klan: A Study of the American Mind* (New York: Harcourt, Brace and Company, 1924), 240.

Chapter Sixteen: Subliminals

208 **"something you did not consciously desire"**: Herbert Brean, "'Hidden Sell' Technique Is Almost Here," *Life*, March 31, 1958.

209 **"without seeing them"**: Vance Packard, *The Hidden Persuaders* (New York: Ig Publishing, 2007), 67.

Chapter Seventeen: Truth Drugs

212 **"you'd probably electrocute yourself"**: Quoted in Stephen Kinzer, *Poisoner in Chief: Sidney Gottlieb and the CIA Search for Mind Control* (New York: Henry Holt and Company, 2019), 142.

212 **"were very adept at these practices"**: Quoted in ibid., 145.

212 **"we sent it to San Francisco"**: Quoted in Gary Kamiya, "When the CIA Ran a LSD Sex-House in San Francisco," *San Francisco Chronicle*, April 1, 2016.

213 **"carried away with playing spook"**: John Jacobs, "The Diaries of a CIA Operative," *Washington Post*, September 5, 1977.

213 **"blessing of the All-Highest"**: Quoted in Martin A. Lee and Bruch Shlain, *Acid Dreams: The Complete Social History of LSD: The CIA, the Sixties, and Beyond* (New York: Grove Press, 2007), 35.

214 **"prepared by hypnosis"**: Quoted in Dominic Streatfeild, *Brainwash: The Secret History of Mind Control* (New York: Picador, 2008), 143.

215 **"something we can't otherwise explain"**: Lorraine Boissoneault, "The True Story of Brainwashing and How It Shaped America," *Smithsonian*, May 22, 2017.

215 **"our own defeats"**: Louis Francis Budenz, *The Techniques of Communism* (Chicago, IL: H. Regnery Company, 1954), 232.

217 **"other forms of mental control"**: *Project MKUltra, the CIA's Program of Research in Behavioral Modification: Joint Hearing Before the Select Committee on Intelligence and the Subcommittee on Health and Scientific Research of the Committee on Human Resources, United States Senate* (Washington, D.C.: U.S. Government Printing Office, 1977), 79.

219 **"I've made a terrible mistake"**: Kinzer, *Poisoner in Chief*, 114.

219 **"answers to disturbing questions"**: Paul Vidich, "Did the CIA's Dr. Frank Olson Jump to His Death or Was He Pushed?," *Daily Beast*, February 17, 2020.

219 **"onto a hard surface"**: Kinzer, *Poisoner in Chief*, 252.

220 **"resulted from a homicide"**: "Autopsy of Researcher Given LSD by CIA Proves Inconclusive," *Los Angeles Times*, November 29, 1994.

220 **"that these drugs existed"**: Interview with the author, August 13, 2021.

220 **"such as self-preservation"**: Jan Goldman (ed.), *The Central Intelligence Agency: An Encyclopedia of Covert Ops, Intelligence Gathering, and Spies* (Santa Barbara, CA: ABC-CLIO, 2015), 26.

221 **"their secret wars"**: Rupert Cornwell, "Obituary: Sidney Gottlieb," *Independent*, March 16, 1999.

221 **"foreign intelligence services"**: *Project MKUltra, the CIA's Program of Research in Behavioral Modification*, 70.

222 **"military and intelligence operations"**: Jonathan Vankin and John Whalen, *The 80 Greatest Conspiracies of All Time: History's Biggest Mysteries, Coverups, and Cabals* (New York: Citadel Press, 2004), 7.

222 **turn ordinary Americans into assassins**: Tom O'Neill with Dan Piepenbring, *Chaos: Charles Manson, the CIA, and the Secret History of the Sixties* (New York: Little, Brown and Company, 2019).

223 **"from the wildest conspiracy theories"**: Malcolm Harries, "Did you know the CIA _____?" *N+1*, March 7, 2018.

Chapter Eighteen: Purity of Essence

224 **"prepare it for them"**: E. H. Bronner, "Letter to the Editor," *Catholic Mirror*, January 1952.

225 **"whenever a Communist desires"**: Gretchen Ann Reilly, "Not a So-Called Democracy: Anti-Fluoridationists and the Fight Over Drinking Water," in Robert D. Johnston (ed.), *The Politics of Healing: Histories of Alternative Medicine in Twentieth-Century North America* (New York: Routledge, 2004), 130.

225 **"advertisers beating the drums"**: Gladys Caldwell and Philip E. Zanfagna, *Fluoridation and Truth Decay* (Resada, CA: Top-Ecol Press, 1974), 19.

227 **"all kinds of fronts"**: Robert Welch, *The Blue Book of the John Birch Society* (Boston, MA: Western Islands, 1961), 64.

228 **source of red tape**: Lisa McGirr, *Suburban Warriors: The Origins of the New Right* (Princeton, NJ: Princeton University Press, 2002).

229 "their energies and loyalty": Jack Mabley, "Bares Secrets of 'Red-Haters': They Think Ike is a Communist," *Chicago Daily News*, July 25, 1960.

229 "good, patriotic Negroes today": Tom Buckley, "When Good Birchers Get Together," *New York Times*, June 5, 1966.

230 in a word, "pathetic": Stanley Mosk and Howard H. Jewel, "The Birch Phenomenon Analyzed; A Report by the California Attorney General's Office Examines the Methods and Speculates on the Motives of the Controversial John Birch Society," *New York Times*, August 20, 1961.

231 "I have ever had on an investigation": Bill Becker, "Rightists Stirred by Youth's Death," *New York Times*, July 15, 1962.

231 "very core of their strategy": Quoted in D. J. Mulloy, *The World of the John Birch Society: Conspiracy, Conservatism, and the Cold War* (Nashville, TN: Vanderbilt University Press, 2014), 133.

232 "Ku Kluxers out of nightshirts": Quoted in ibid., 109.

232 "I won't even have it around": Quoted in ibid., 79.

233 "almost pathetically optimistic": Quoted in John B. Judis, *William F. Buckley, Jr.: Patron Saint of the Conservatives* (New York: Simon and Schuster, 2001), 194.

233 "barring a miracle": Quoted in Mulloy, *The World of the John Birch Society*, 79.

234 "to influence public policy": Alvin Felzenberg, *A Man and His Presidents: The Political Odyssey of William F. Buckley* (New Haven, CT: Yale University Press, 2017), 136.

234 "consequences of his acts": Quoted Judis, *William F. Buckley, Jr.*, 195–96.

235 "let's call this ruling clique simply the INSIDERS": Quoted in Mulloy, *The World of the John Birch Society*, 183.

236 "power-lusters at the top": Quoted in ibid., 196.

236 "that I have in mind": Hofstadter, *The Paranoid Style in American Politics and Other Essays*, 3.

Chapter Nineteen: Beware of the Siberian Beetle

243 "illegitimacy of black protest": Richard Gid Powers, *Secrecy and Power: The Life of J. Edgar Hoover* (New York: The Free Press, 1987), 324.

244 "the viewpoints of the Communist Party": Quoted in David Cunningham, *There's Something Happening Here: The New Left, the Klan, and FBI Counterintelligence* (Berkeley, CA: University of California Press, 2004), 88.

244 "defeat of the United States in Vietnam": Quoted in ibid., 33.

245 "drive us off the college campuses": Quoted in ibid., 50.

245 *"the SDS in your territory"*: Quoted in ibid., 102.

246 "during the coming academic year": Quoted in ibid., 103.

247 "with a mystical connotation": Ward Churchill and Jim Vander Wall, *The COIN-TELPRO Papers: Documents from the FBI's Secret Wars Against Dissent in the United States* (Boston, MA: South End Press, 1990), 205.

247 "a reasonable chance for success": Quoted in ibid., 206.

247 "currently going on in the New Left": Ibid., 207.

248 "these two black extremist organizations": Quoted in ibid., 138.

248 "directly attributable to this program": John Kifner, "F.B.I. Sought Doom of Panther Party," *New York Times*, May 9, 1976.

250 "of course they're watching us—so what": Quoted in Cunningham, *There's Something Happening Here*, 173.

250 "swallow his pride and obey orders": Quoted in ibid., 163.

252 "intelligence agencies and even the military": Jim Marrs, *Crossfire: The Plot That Killed Kennedy* (New York: Basic Books, 2013), 53.

Chapter Twenty: Networks

257 "out of your skull": Thomas Pynchon, *The Crying of Lot 49* (New York: Penguin, 2012), 140–41.

258 *"the unwanted by-products of such actions"*: Karl Popper, *The Open Society and Its Enemies* (Princeton, NJ: Princeton University Press, 2020), 305.

259 "evils from which we suffer": Ibid., 306.

259 "or the imperialists": Ibid.

261 governmental mind control program: J. Eric Oliver and Thomas J. Wood, "Conspiracy Theories and the Paranoid Style(s) of Mass Opinion, *American Journal of Political Science*, Vol. 58, no. 4 (October 2014).

262 "in order to cope with difficult emotions": John Sides, "Fifty Percent of Americans Believe in Some Conspiracy Theory. Here's Why," *Washington Post*, February 19, 2015.

263 "like some crazy Illuminati Freemason Nazi Airport of Doom": u/Hooopes, "A freaky mural from the Denver International Airport I spotted today on my way into the baggage claim area," reddit.com, January 3, 2012, https://www.reddit.com/r/WTF/comments/o22nb/a_freaky_mural_from_the_denver_international.

263 "I got really intrigued": Jared Jacang Maher, "DIA Conspiracies Take Off," *Westword*, August 30, 2007.

264 "under the control of the reptilians": David Icke, *The Biggest Secret* (Wildwood, MO: Bridge of Love Publications, 1999), 37.

264 "a cathedral to the world that they're making": Quoted in Maher, "DIA Conspiracies Take Off."

Chapter Twenty-One: The Suburban Uncanny

265 "private rites of an aesthetic nature": Erin Sweeny, "Welcome to the Funhouse: Mike Kelley's 'Mobile Homestead,'" *Art21*, May 23, 2013.

266 "experienced in some dream-states": Sigmund Freud, *The Uncanny*, trans. David McLintock (New York: Penguin, 2003), 143–44.

268 "I'll keep you in this room all day": Eric Malnic, "Bakersfield Torn by Horror Stories of Child Molesting," *Los Angeles Times*, August 4, 1985.

269 "throwing knives that they had": Ibid.

270 "told the sheriff's department": Quoted in Richard Beck, *We Believe the Children: A Moral Panic in the 1980s* (New York: Public Affairs, 2015), 170.

270 "as part of a large conspiracy": Kenneth V. Lanning, *Investigator's Guide to Allegations of "Ritual" Child Abuse* (Quantico, VA: National Center for the Analysis of Violent Crime, 1992), 1.

270 that no parent could match: Ibid., 20.

271 "that peaceful, comfortable way of life": Beck, *We Believe the Children*, 96.

272 "no more than shared oppression": Shulamith Firestone, *The Dialectic of Sex: The Case for Feminist Revolution* (New York: Farrar, Straus and Giroux, 2003), 73.

272 "symbols, victims, or dependents": Cynthia Enloe, "Womenandchildren: Propaganda Tools of Patriarchy," in Greg Bates (ed.), *Mobilizing Democracy: Changing the U.S. Role in the Middle East* (Monroe, ME: Common Courage Press, 1991).

274 "that's what they're going to do to me next": Michelle Smith and Lawrence Pazder, *Michelle Remembers* (New York: Congdon & Lattès, 1980), 177.

Chapter Twenty-Two: Attack of the Lizard People!

279 "make you a hybrid of Satan": Anna Merlan, "COVID Conspiracy Theorists Wreak Havoc with a Story About Snake Venom," *Vice*, April 18, 2022.

279 Green Party politician, David Icke: David Gilbert, "QAnon Surfer Who Killed His Kids Was Radicalized by Lizard People Conspiracies," *Vice*, April 5, 2022.

280 "their real faces—metaphorically speaking": Kristen Baldwin, "'V' for Television Victory," *Entertainment Weekly*, April 30, 1999.

280 "love with limitless potential": David Icke, *The Robot's Rebellion: The Story of the Spiritual Renaissance* (Bath, UK: Gateway Books, 1994), xvii.

281 "symbols of the Brotherhood societies": Ibid., 40.

281 "part of or what the final goal will be": David Icke, *. . . And the Truth Shall Set You Free* (Wildwood, MO: Bridge of Love Publications, 1995), 36.

282 "what the game plan was": Ibid., 269.

282 "with the word 'cattle'": Milton William Cooper, *Behold a Pale Horse* (Flagstaff, AZ: Light Technology Press, 1991), 267.

284 vests them with epistemic capital: David Robertson, *UFOs, Conspiracy Theories and the New Age: Millennial Conspiracism* (London: Bloomsbury, 2016).

285 "run by the U.S. Central Intelligence Agency": Gary Webb, "Dark Alliance: America's 'Crack' Plague Has Roots in Nicaragua War," *San Jose Mercury News*, August 18, 1996.

286 "where I got my degree from": Quoted in Seth Mnookin, *The Panic Virus: The True Story Behind the Vaccine-Autism Controversy* (New York: Simon & Schuster, 2012), 254.

286 "once I feel I've done enough research": Nicki Minaj (@nickiminaj), "They want you to get vaccinated for the Met. If I get vaccinated it won't for the Met. It'll be once I feel I've done enough research. I'm working on that now. In the meantime my loves, be safe. Wear the mask with 2 strings that grips your head & face. Not that loose one." September 13, 2021, https://twitter.com/nickiminaj/status/143752 6877808128000?lang=en.

286 "having knowledge just shoved to you": Matt Bonesteel, "Flat-Earther Kyrie Irving Says He Just Wants Everyone 'to Do Their Own Research' (on Instagram)," *Washington Post*, January 12, 2018.

286 "the exact opposite of what D.Y.O.R. is supposed to accomplish": Nathan Ballantyne and David Dunning, "Skeptics Say, 'Do Your Own Research.' It's Not That Simple," *New York Times*, January 3, 2022.

287 "the implications of our beliefs": Gary Alan Fine and Patricia A. Turner, *Whispers on the Color Line: Rumor and Race in America* (Berkeley, CA: University of California Press, 2004), 63.

Chapter Twenty-Three: The Banality of Evil

289 "people who are more privileged than you": Interview with the author, July 11, 2021.

291 "These people are deadly serious": Alex Jones, *Dark Secrets: Inside Bohemian Grove*, 2000.

291 "there's a bunch of gay stuff going on": Interview with the author, September 23, 2021.

291 **looking to prevent crime:** McCaslin's story is told in Tea Krulos, *American Madness: The Story of the Phantom Patriot and How Conspiracy Theories Hijacked American Consciousness* (Port Townsend, WA: Feral House, 2020).

293 **"as they leave the place":** James Pollock, *Notorious Secret Societies: The Illuminati, Bilderberg Group, Freemasons, Scientology, Skull and Bones, Knights Templar and More* (Createspace Independent Publishing Platform, 2017), 63.

293 **"little tiny stairwells everywhere":** Alexandra Robbins, *Secrets of the Tomb: Skull and Bones, the Ivy League, and the Hidden Paths to Power* (New York: Little, Brown, 2002), 88.

293 **"I'm not gonna tell my listeners that":** Quoted in David Lefflcr, "Alex Jones Is Mad as Hell," *Austin Monthly*, October 2020.

294 **still an elite at Yale:** See Robbins, *Secrets of the Tomb*, 38.

295 **"Antichrist Lucifer Satan":** Selena Owens, "The Dark Side of the Ice Bucket Challenge," *WND*, September 2, 2014.

295 **"Stay safe everybody":** Oprah Winfrey (@Oprah), "Just got a phone call that my name is trending. And being trolled for some awful FAKE thing. It's NOT TRUE. Haven't been raided, or arrested. Just sanitizing and self distancing with the rest of the world. Stay safe everybody." March 18, 2020, https://twitter.com/Oprah/status/1240150930840051712.

295 **clogging up social media channels?:** Jane Coaston, "YouTube's Conspiracy Theory Crisis, Explained," *Vox*, December 14, 2018.

296 **"innocent people suffering":** Adam Goldman, "The Comet Ping Pong Gunman Answers Our Reporter's Questions," *New York Times*, December 7, 2016.

296 **"intel on this wasn't 100 percent":** Ibid.

296 **"global child sex trafficking operation":** Public Religion Research Institute, "Understanding QAnon's Connection to American Politics, Religion, and Media Consumption," prri.org, May 27, 2021.

297 **"Satanist Alesiter Crowley":** Paul Joseph Watson, "'Spirit Cooking': Clinton Campaign Chairman Practices Bizarre Occult Ritual," infowars.com, November 4, 2016.

298 **"drink on earthquake nights":** Cassandra Fairbanks, "Spirit Cooking: The Most Disturbing Podesta Email Yet?" wearechange.org, November 4, 2016.

298 **different audiences who lack that context:** danah boyd, "How 'Context Collapse' Was Coined: My Recollection," zephoria.org, December 8, 2013.

Chapter Twenty-Four: Nothing Is True, Everything is Permitted

302 **"everything-is-connected conspiracy videos":** Interview with the author, August 24, 2021.

305 **"influenced by everything else"**: Whitney Phillips and Ryan M. Milner, *You Are Here: A Field Guide for Navigating Polarized Speech, Conspiracy Theories, and Our Polluted Media Landscape* (Cambridge, MA: MIT Press, 2021), 183.

306 **"so it tries to supply them"**: Quoted in David Streitfeld, "'The Internet Is Broken.' @ev Is Trying to Salvage It," *New York Times*, May 20, 2017.

307 **"in their theorizing and interpretation"**: Mike Rothschild, *The Storm Is Upon Us: How QAnon Became a Movement, Cult, and Conspiracy Theory of Everything* (New York: Melville House, 2021), 4.

308 **"believing you're doing a lot"**: Ibid., 10.

308 **"even more than baseball, America's favorite pastime"**: Leonard I. Sweet, "Millennialism in America: Recent Studies," *Rochester Center for Theological Studies* 40, no. 3 (September 1979), 531.

308 **gain control of the world**: Morgan Halvorsen, "Not Every QAnon Believer's an Antisemite. But There's a Lot of Overlap Between Its Adherents and Belief in a Century-Old Antisemitic Hoax," morningconsult.com, June 28, 2021.

311 **"except as a caricature"**: Interview with the author, October 22, 2021.

311 **due to rampant "baby eating"**: Quoted in Lisa Anne Auerbach, *Great Awakenings: Tales from Telegram* (Meow Sings Meow, 2021).

311 **"not even remarked upon"**: Interview with the author, October 22, 2021.

315 **"invaders in that kill our people"**: Jessica Kwong, "Robert Bowers Gab Before Synagogue Shooting: 'Screw Your Optics, I'm Going In," *Newsweek*, October 27, 2018.

315 **Hispanic invasion of Texas**: Alex a Ura, "A Racist Manifesto and a Shooter Terrorizes Hispanics in El Paso and Beyond," *Texas Tribune*, August 5, 2019.

315 **anyone else was a "replacer"**: Khaleda Rahman, "'Great Replacement Theory Has Inspired 4 Mass Shootings in Recent Years," *Newsweek*, May 16, 2022.

315 **this narrative over 400 times**: Karen Yourish, et al., "Inside the Apocalyptic Worldview of 'Tucker Carlson Tonight'," *New York Times*, April 30, 2022.

316 **"permanent liberal majority in Washington"**: John Wagner, "Rep. Stefanik Claims in Ads That Democrats Seek a 'Permanent Election Insurrection' by Providing Pathways to Citizenship," *Washington Post*, September 16, 2021.

316 **"replacing more conservative white voters"**: Will Carless, "Month Before Buffalo, Poll Finds, 7 in 10 Republicans Believed in 'Great Replacement' Ideas," *USA Today*, June 1, 2022.

317 **"more American deaths than ISIS"**: Dean Obeidallah (@deanobeidallah), "How is that the NRA can advocate for policies they know lead to deaths of Americans yet they are allowed to operate on US soil?! The NRA is responsible for more American

deaths than ISIS. #NRAconvention #NRAIsATerroristOrganization," May 27, 2022, https://mobile.twitter.com/DeanObeidallah/status/1530278517191081988.

317 **"fighting amongst each other":** Isaac Arnsdorf and Carol D. Leonig, "The NRA Has Weakened. But Gun Rights Drive the GOP More than Ever." *Washington Post*, May 26, 2022.

319 **"enjoying absolute, anarchic freedom":** Philip J. Deloria, *Playing Indian* (New Haven, CT: Yale University Press, 1998), 186.

321 **"the real conditions of its future":** Michel de Certeau, *The Possession at Loudun*, trans. Michael B. Smith (Chicago, IL: University of Chicago Press, 1996), 1.

Epilogue: Citizens' Commissions

326 **"could change the nation":** Interview with the author, July 30, 2021.

326 **"particularly Black people":** Tom Jackman, "The FBI Break-in That Exposed J. Edgar Hoover's Misdeeds to Be Honored with Historical Marker," *Washington Post*, September 1, 2021.